WILLIE MAYS AIKENS

Safe At Home

Gregory Jordan

TRIUMPH
B O O K S

Library of Congress Cataloging-in-Publication Data

Jordan, Gregory.
  Willie Mays Aikens : safe at home / Gregory Jordan.
     p. cm.
  ISBN 978-1-60078-696-9 (hardback)
  1. Aikens, Willie Mays. 2. Baseball players—United States—Biography.
3. Athletes—Drug use—United States. I. Title.
  GV865.A3J67 2012
  796.357092—dc23
  [B]
                              2011047434

This book is available in quantity at special discounts for your group or organization. For further information, contact:

Triumph Books LLC
542 South Dearborn Street
Suite 750
Chicago, Illinois 60605
(312) 939-3330
Fax (312) 663-3557
www.triumphbooks.com

Printed in U.S.A.
ISBN: 978-1-60078-696-9
Design by Patricia Frey
All photos courtesy of Willie Mays Aikens unless otherwise noted.

"I knew that if I could succeed at being demolished,
I could succeed at anything."
— Tony Hoagland, "Patience"

Contents

Author's Note

This book is based upon hundreds of interviews, archival research, and letters.

Conversations are re-constructed as precisely as possible according to the recollections of the individuals.

The internal thoughts and musings of Willie Mays Aikens result from hours of reconstruction by Mr. Aikens and the author.

Certain names have been changed to protect the identity of accomplices and comrades during the drug years.

Prologue

July 25, 1999

Willie watched with one eye on the door because the television room was the most dangerous place in the prison—except when the inmates watched *Days of Our Lives*.

Tonight he skipped dinner to see Gorgeous George's induction into the Hall of Fame.

The sportscaster led with the Braves, and then sure enough he cut to George Brett in the sun in Cooperstown. The sun was always George's stage light, and there he was on the podium, shining in his suit and tie. The camera panned the crowd, and their eyes followed the light, and all the light was on George.

Willie smiled. He rarely talked about baseball in prison—only with the guards. That was his policy because the guards liked him, and he liked most of them. Once in a while they would sneak him a *Sports Illustrated* or some cake their wives had packed.

But he sort of wished the D.C. boys were here right now to see George, too. The inmates from Washington were always the most dangerous, the quickest to take the slightest offense. They might see him in a highlight next to George; they might understand who he was; they might steer clear of him if they saw him on television.

The clip showed a tearful Brett barely choking out his speech. *For God's sake George, you are stuttering,* Willie thought. *All the times you teased me, and now you are doing it yourself, George.*

He smiled but then felt the tears, too.

Pull it together, George. Man, pull it together, he thought. *Please don't poop your pants like you always used to.*

He laughed to himself. George had famously quirky bowels, and oh how they used to laugh about it in the locker room, George always laughing the most.

He felt close to George, like he had seen him only a few days ago and laughed with him the way they always laughed when they were together. What he didn't know was that George and Hal McRae and others would one day help him cobble his life back together.

Willie said to himself over and over: *I let the man down.*

They had brought him to Kansas City to be the cleanup hitter, but the only real cleaning up he did, he reminded himself yet again, was clearing platefuls of cocaine with his nose. A few big homers, the legendary World Series in 1980, but he was no cleanup hitter. Should have been. Could have been.

"Kansas City Royals, please don't snort the foul line!"

Oh, how the Royals laughed in the dugout when they noticed the guy holding up the poster behind their dugout at Comiskey Park!

They laughed for innings on end. Even George laughed, and George never once got high with them.

After five years in prison, Willie had come to terms with his disgrace. He had thought on many a too-quiet night in his cell: *I am a disgrace.*

But he had resisted fancying himself a baseball version of Job from the Bible. He held a record not Reggie Jackson or even Babe Ruth had matched: two home runs in the same game, twice in the same World Series. He always got tongue twisted saying it, and people usually had to pause and ask him to say it again.

But these days he saw himself as a record setter in all of professional sports— the guy who didn't get off the hook, the guy whom fame couldn't save, the guy who got 20 years and eight months even though many, many guys had done far worse and gotten far less.

He had seen Doc Gooden and Darryl Strawberry turn their adventures and indulgences into fancy memoirs. He would eventually see Michael Vick serve 19 months for strangling dogs.

But he would remain the grand disgrace, the laughingstock.

The D.C. boys straggled in from dinner as a blonde woman was giving the weather. Willie stood up and pretended to not be afraid, but he was. They would kill you over a TV show, these guys. A game show was starting now, and Willie knew the D.C. boys watched that together, too.

He nodded to one of them and walked out the door toward the cafeteria. He could still get a few leftovers from his buddy the cook.

Willie wondered what George was eating for dinner: steak, lobster, or both—surf and turf like they called it at the fancy restaurants where they used to eat together after games on road trips.

But God bless him, Willie thought. *God bless George Brett. I will pray for him tonight. I just wish I had done what I was supposed to do, what I was called to do. I just wish I had cleaned up better for him.*

But I'm going to keep cleaning things up now.

1

Seneca

1954–1973

The sunlight bounced off the shiny field of wet watermelons and smacked Willie in the face. An old man sitting next to him in the pickup was sweating moonshine the whole ride over to the fields. Willie could see the sweat dripping through the holes in the old man's shirt. The stench made Willie's nose pinch; he hid his head in Cille's belly. She smelled, too. The black kids didn't start school until October so they could pick cotton, and Willie held his nose and wished he could start school in September like the white kids did.

As he hopped out of the truck, a tall white man handed Willie his bag. The burlap pricked his fingers, and the bag was bigger than the bag the white man gave his sister Hattie.

"Cille," Willie said as he tugged at his mother's purple dress. "He guh-guh-give me the wruh-wruh-wruh-wrong bag."

Cille did not look down at him. He studied that long single hair growing out of the mole on her chin, and he wanted to reach up and yank it and see if she would come tumbling down.

"You take the bag the man gives you, Willie," Cille said.

Willie and Hattie followed her into the line of red soil between two cotton rows.

He bent down for a chunk of clay and, as he raised it to his mouth, he turned back to look at the hundreds of watermelons behind him, glistening in the field. He pretended the clay tasted like watermelon as it crunched in his mouth.

Hattie was alongside him, and Willie saw her stick her first stone into the bag.

"You guh-guh-gonna get caught this year, Hattie," Willie said.

She shushed him and looked around nervously.

His best friend Cuda was in the next row.

Willie stood and called over to him.

"Hey, Cuda, H-h-h-Hattie doin' it a-a-again!"

Cuda. His smile was as wide as his belly, and his teeth stuck out when he laughed.

Willie suddenly frowned.

"How come they give you that bag, Cuda?"

Willie held up his bag to show Cuda, and Cuda leaned back and belly-laughed—the boys teased him that he was always laughing twice what with his mouth and his belly both moving.

"If you tell on me no one will believe you 'cause you talk so funny, Willie," Hattie said.

Willie felt a clogging in his throat. There were words somewhere that he wanted to fling back at Hattie like dog dirt, but he couldn't get them through his throat. Hattie smiled mean at him and bent back down to the cotton. Willie wanted to say to her, "At least I ain't as black as your papa made you. I'm a nice brown."

I talk the way God wants me to talk, he said to himself.

It was hard to tell if the sun was rising as the morning proceeded because the sun filled the whole sky. But the dew had burned off the watermelons, and Willie wanted one now not because he was hungry but because he was thirsty.

"I ain't doing it this year, Willie," Cuda said as Willie stepped over two rows of cotton and came up alongside him. "I ain't helpin' you, Willie."

"You, yes, yuh-yuh-yes you are," Willie said. He pinched Cuda's backside and Cuda yelped as they walked toward the water buckets on the beds of the pickups.

"You guh-guh-go talk to that man there," Willie said to Cuda. "You ask him about fishing and he'll talk forever."

Cuda obeyed, as he usually did. Willie leaned against the pickup closest to the watermelon fields and watched Cuda measure out the size of catfish while he talked with the foreman.

Willie reached into the back of the pickup and grabbed a burlap bag. He slipped under the rear of the pickup and crawled toward its front. There was no more than a foot from the front bumper to the first row of watermelons.

He shimmied out and pulled in a watermelon with part of its vine still on it. He rolled onto his back and slipped it into the bag. He slid back under the truck and tied the bag in a gap in the chassis.

Then he poked his head out from under the truck, looked at Cuda looking back at him as he kept talking about fishing with the foreman, and wandered to his place beside Cille out in the middle of the cotton field.

THAT NIGHT AFTER SUPPER as the mosquitoes rose from the Seneca soil, Willie walked up to the make-do ballfield the boys had swept and scratched out at the edge of their neighborhood. They were at the highest point in Seneca, a sort of infinity ridge. And when Willie hit a ball, it looked like it might sail over town until it dropped out of sight.

Willie walked up to the boys and stood proudly in front of them as he lifted the bag and rolled the watermelon onto the grass.

The boys stared as Willie threw the bag behind him, lifted up the melon, and punched his fist into it. He passed out chunks of it, and at the end of the feast, they spit seeds at one another, assumed their spots in the field, and played until they couldn't see the ball anymore and their parents started calling them home.

As he ran past the brick ranchers, the neighbors' lights guided him to the one dark spot on the street where his family's shack sat on block and beam. Closer now and his approach muffled by the crickets' racket, he saw Guy Webb stand up and blow out the kerosene lamp.

"Ju-ju-ju-just in time!" he said as he opened the creaky door and dove into the bed beside Hattie.

No one said anything back.

He poked Hattie once. She slapped him on the forehead.

"Hattie, that watermelon wa-wa-was the best I ever tasted," he whispered to her.

She pretended to be asleep and he moved closer to her, holding his hand over her nose.

"Smuh-smuh-smell it, Hattie," he said.

He was proud. He loved how his buddies reacted. As much as the taste of the watermelon, he already loved the taste of the limelight.

COACH SHAVER, A SQUAT white man with a paunch and a hairy neck and ears, walked like he hailed from a long line of tillers. He was carrying armfuls of bats, gloves, and baseballs from the back of his station wagon to home plate on the field where the black kids played on the back side of town. His kneecaps pointed inward toward one another with each step; his head was bent down toward his feet; and he walked the same precise line back and forth with each armful of equipment.

Coach McNeil, a short black man with his own tics, saw him from center field and leaned his head into his left shoulder.

The boys at first never knew if Coach McNeil was talking to them or muttering to himself. But they realized after a time that this was how he held his head when he talked to anybody.

Willie nodded as Coach McNeil walked past him and turned to the second baseman.

"He ta-ta-ta-talks funnier than I do," Willie said.

The second baseman laughed then pounded his glove.

"Nah he don't, Willie," he said. "He just turn his head funny. You talk funny."

The boys put their hands on their knees and waited for another coach to resume hitting line drives.

McNeil and Shaver didn't shake hands; they didn't even make eye contact. They were, in the eyes of many in the South at that time, up to no good—conspiring to have black kids and white kids play baseball together.

Coach McNeil turned and wound his hand in a circle to convene his players.

"Okay, this here you probably know is Coach Shaver," McNeil said. "He is the head of the Department of Parks and Recreation for the town of Seneca. All this equipment he is bringing to you boys comes out of the kindness of his heart. You all thank him now."

The boys shouted and started to jump up and down.

Shaver smiled, holding his head higher for a moment, then suddenly looked back toward town.

"Okay, let's play ball," Coach McNeil shouted. "Oh, and boys. Wait now. You don't say nothin' to nobody about Coach Shaver bringin' all these gifts! This our little secret."

Willie's team batted first, and Willie saw the station wagon still parked alongside the road up the hill. Shaver had moved it, but Willie could see his forehead sticking out the window, watching them in the setting sun. Willie hoped Coach Shaver would stay longer because he wanted to try to hit a ball all the way to his wagon.

WILLIE'S MOTHER HEAVED the big iron pot of hot water off the wood stove. She carried it over to the tub and held her face away from the steam as she tilted it. Some of the hot water splattered in spots on the dirt below the floorboards and bubbled up through the cracks.

She nodded to Willie, and he carried the big pot from the other wood stove and dumped it into the tub. His sister waited in her towel beside the bin, and Willie stood there feeling the steam rise out of the tub and engulf his face. He closed his eyes for a second.

"Get in there," Cille said to his Hattie.

"I ain't getting in nowhere until Willie turns around!" Hattie shouted back.

"Turn around Willie Aikens!" Cille shouted.

Cille went to slap him, but she missed him by an inch as he jumped away.

As he walked outside, he heard his sister step into the water, one leg splashing in and then the second.

His dog Blackie ran up to him and wrapped his front legs around Willie's belly as he jumped up. Willie rubbed Blackie's belly and kissed him back, and as he did he heard Guy Webb snarl.

"That dog's been out here eatin' shit all mornin'," Guy Webb—Cille's current husband, though not Willie's or Hattie's father, though certainly Willie's tormentor—said from his chair in the shade of a big tree. He had a jug of moonshine beside his chair. He arrived home at noon on Saturday—he got paid on Friday nights and never came home with any money left. He had been sitting in an old, rusty chair drinking ever since he arrived.

"You let a dog kiss you on the lips like that you're eatin' shit, too," he slurred.

He speaks worse than me, Willie thought. *His words slide together and get half said. At least I eventually get the whole word out.*

"AIN'T IT FUNNY we use a white bus and they use a yellow bus?" Cuda said to Willie as they pulled into Seneca's recreation center and a few passersby stared at their bus.

"Ya would think they'd drive a white bus since they's white," Cuda said. "And we'd drive a black bus, not a yellow bus."

Willie looked sideways at him.

"A black bus and we-we-we'd be burnin' up in here, Cuda," Willie said. "Black bus only for the puh-puh-penitentiary."

The white boys were already on the field throwing and running around. Willie saw Coach Shaver in the distance. He was walking the same funny way as ever.

As they stepped down from the bus, Coach McNeil waved to Coach Shaver, Shaver waved back, and a few of the white parents looked surprised to see them waving at each other.

In Willie's first at-bat, he hit a fastball farther than anyone on this particular field has ever hit one. There was no fence, and the ball rolled into the woods. The outfielders gathered and wandered along the tree line until a coach from the bench shouted out to them to forget about the ball.

Willie homered again in his next at-bat. The third time he went up, the catcher stood up and waited for the pitcher to throw the first intentional ball.

Willie stood there with his bat resting on his shoulder and stared at the catcher.

"Wha-wha-wha-whatcha doin' that for?" he said.

The catcher looked at him.

"Coach said so," he said through his mask. "I am sorry, Willie. I got to do what Coach says."

Willie watched the second pitch land in the catcher's big mitt, and he stomped his foot. He looked over to Coach McNeil and shouted.

"Kuh-kuh-coach they walkin' me!"

After the third pitch, he started to cry. He took ball four and ran to first, and his teammates noticed he was crying and the white team did, too. Soon all the boys black and white boys were laughing in racial harmony. Coach McNeil shook his head and came out to first.

"Willie, when they walk you that means they fear you," he said into his own shoulder. "That is a good thing."

Willie sniffled and wiped his nose.

"I-I-I wanna hit, Coach," he said. "I-I-I just wanna hit."

Mrs. Brown called him as the bell rang and the other boys and girls ran out the classroom door.

Willie was too wide for the rows, and he bumped into desks as he walked up to her with his head down. He weighed nearly 200 pounds already as an 11-year old. His shoes had holes in them, so as he walked the sweat on the bottom of his feet made him slip and made the shoes squeak.

"Willie Aikens, I am very proud of you," Mrs. Brown said.

Willie blushed. For the first time he looked up.

"You are a very fine speller, young man, very fine," she said.

He wanted to run into the hall and drag Cuda back to hear this.

"And I want you to keep on trying, you understand me?"

She was speaking more tenderly now, tilting her head sideways as if about to give him a kiss on the forehead.

"Does your mama take you to church, Willie?"

"Muh-muh-muh-my mama ain't my mama," Willie said.

She straightened her neck and looked puzzled.

"Tell me what you mean, Willie."

"I-I mean me and Hattie loved my grandma more so we called her mama," he said. "My real mama, I call her by her first name, Cille. I call her Cille, and I called my grandma mama."

Mrs. Brown's forehead wrinkled.

"I see, Willie. Well, you are still blessed to have at least someone to love. Willie, I just wanted to say to you that I see how your speech pains you, but you are a very smart boy. God makes us each the way we are, and he made you the way you are for a reason. You are a wonderful speller, Willie."

He thought to himself that someday he would like to bring Mrs. Brown flowers. He knew just the ones from the edge of the woods by the ballfield that he wanted to pick for her.

Two summers later the youth league of Seneca was completely integrated by executive decree. Coach Shaver said so, all the townspeople said to each other. That was it. Coach Shaver said so. It was 1968, and Willie was 13 years old.

A couple of parents asked who the hell was Coach Shaver to decide that.

Some said it was bound to happen anyway; best if Coach Shaver started with the sports before we bring them into the schools.

A few, Coach Shaver and Coach McNeil among them, said, "Seneca is going to win ourselves a state championship one day very soon."

Even more started to say that after Willie started clobbering balls all over the county. He played a decent catcher, too, not just because he was slow afoot and played there by default but because it was the position where he could stay most involved in the game. And the whole county realized how much this kid loved to play the game.

ONE EVENING LATER that summer he walked home with his bat dragging on the hardtop and his glove on his head. After most games, Mr. Cunningham took the boys out for sundaes, and today Willie got two because he asked for it and because Mr. Cunningham agreed two home runs deserve two sundaes.

The lightning bugs were so thick that he could swat them. As he stepped onto their lot he waited for Blackie to run up to him like he always did, but Willie made it all the way to the door and Blackie never came. The smell of fried beans stuck to the air around the house, and after all that ice cream Willie had to stop for a second before opening the door. Standing there, he heard his mother's moans again and the grunts of Guy Webb.

He reached the screen door, and as he gripped it he felt something slick. He wiped his hand on his pants. He bumped into the kitchen table, but they kept on making their noises even as he undressed and slid in bed next to Hattie.

He poked her.

"Hattie," Willie whispered. "Wuh-wuh-where's Blackie at?"

Hattie turned suddenly, and he could tell she was sniffling.

"Blackie's dead!" she whispered.

Willie sat up on his elbows.

He sat up and lit a candle, and across the room he could see Guy Webb sprawled out on top of Cille.

Willie looked at his hand and there was blood. He held up his hand to Hattie.

"Hattie, I got Blackie's blood on my hand!"

He pulled on his baseball pants and went running out the door.

Willie ran around the yard in the moonlight, and he saw a stain on the grass leading toward the brush. He threw himself down into the weeds, and he scrambled all around looking for Blackie until Hattie came out holding a candle and called to him.

"He's dead, Willie," she said. "Guy Webb said some animal dragged Blackie off and he seen the tail end of it."

Willie walked straight past Hattie into the house. He started shaking Guy Webb.

"You kuh-kuh-killed Blackie, Guy Webb!" Willie shouted. "I know you gone and ki-ki-killed my duh-duh-duh-dog!"

Guy Webb looked at him with a drunk's disregard.

"You blow that candle out Hattie Jean and you both get in that bed before I beat you," Cille said. "Guy Webb's been inside here with me all night, and you get what you deserve for leavin' that dog outside alone all the time like you do."

Willie backed up into Hattie, and she pulled him toward their bed. He pulled away and walked outside and lay on the grass looking up at the lightning bugs.

"SPELL THE WORD 'until' for us, please, Willie Mays."

Willie stood up from his folding chair on the stage and walked to the podium in front of the class. He won the spelling contest last week in Mrs. Brown's section to place him here in the school championships. He remembered the calm way she asked him to spell each word and how kindly she looked at him as he said it, then spelled it, then said it again right into her kind, dark eyes. He looked for her now in front of him but could not spot her. He felt something funny in his throat and tried to cough to clear it, but a cough wouldn't clear out something that wasn't there.

The moderator was a woman, too, but Willie had never had her for class.

"Willie Mays, your word is 'until'," she said.

Until, he thought. The first ones are always easy, just warm-ups, but this is a piece of cake.

But he got distracted because she did not call him by the right name. Everyone said Willie Mays but Cille didn't know Willie Mays from Babe Ruth and she named him Willie after her brother. It was Dr. Mays the obstetrician who must have stuck his middle name on there, everyone told him.

He saw the letters in capitals right there in front of him: U-N-T-I-L. But the thing in his throat had grown—clogged his mouth, too, and nothing would come out, not even spit. *I couldn't even spit at those kids right there in front laughing at me right now,* he thought.

He gurgled "U-U-Un" and then stopped and flopped his hands by his sides. He looked at the yellow line at the end of the gym floor down below him at the foot of the stage. And suddenly that yellow line was the shoreline of the Seneca River, and he wanted to jump right in and disappear underwater and come back up somewhere else far away from all the laughing kids in front of him.

He hung his head and walked off the stage and stood next to the dangling ropes that controlled the curtain. He could hear all the kids laughing, and he wished Mrs. Brown were here to hug him. *She likes my stutter,* he thought. *And my father wasn't Aikens,* he thought, *and I don't know what his name was and Aikens wasn't Hattie's father either and maybe I should just climb up these ropes right here and swing out and kick all them in the teeth as they laugh.*

WILLIE COULD HEAR Guy Webb vomiting so much in the backyard that night that he thought bits of his drunken brain would shoot out of his mouth. Then suddenly Guy Webb stormed inside and pushed Cille to the floor. He raised his arm up to hit her, and Willie shot toward him. He pushed Guy Webb backward into the kitchen and looked down at Cille. He did not pity her or kneel down to touch her, but he did know that he had to defend her.

He stood there not changing his expression or his pose and Guy Webb started to smile, and in the moonlight Willie saw the knife in his hand. Guy Webb made a drunken charge, and the knife itself was wobbly but coming at him. But suddenly Cille knocked Guy Webb. He staggered and collapsed on the floor. Cille crumpled to the floor behind him, blood pouring from her neck.

Willie lifted Cille into his arms and turned and kicked open the door. He was running now, and he felt her blood on him warm and soft and sticky. He ran down the street and turned right and ran down the next and ran more than a mile to the hospital where someone misnamed him 15 years before.

A nurse rushed over to him as he kicked in the door and then some men brought a bed over and rushed her away.

I will kill Guy Webb, he thought as he sat there. *I will kill him with my baseball bat, and I will kill him on a day when he is not drunk so he will know I am beating him to death.*

An hour later the nurse came out. Willie lifted his head from his hands and realized that light was slowly filling the room.

"Your mother is gonna be okay," the nurse said.

The nurse motioned for Willie to follow her.

At her bedside, tears started to slip down his cheeks, then he stopped crying almost at will and sat down beside her and fell asleep.

THE STEAM OVER the outfield was so thick that line drives seemed to slow down in it. A few white parents were standing alongside the single tier of metal bleachers on the third-base line. The bench was too hot to touch. The black parents stood up by the cars and were using their hands to block the sun from their eyes.

Coach McNeil was pitching in a home-run-hitting contest to end the workout. The winner could name a reasonable prize, and Willie knew he would ask for supper at Coach McNeil's house because Mrs. McNeil fed him pot roast in thick gravy every time he came by, and that meal lasted him a few days every time he ate it.

Coach McNeil threw the first pitch too high, and Willie passed. He stepped back, pulled down his cap over his forehead, and the sweat tickled him as it dripped down the gaps behind his ears. As he let another ball pass, Willie noticed something that would start happening to him again and again and for years to come: his eyes stopped blinking. Even with the sunlight stabbing his eyes and sweat tickling his forehead, he could lock onto the ball and never let go of it.

He sent a ball slicing through the steam and over the fence; then another, and then a third, and then one so high it seemed to rise up above the steam into cleaner air and accelerate without any humidity sticking to it.

The parents stopped talking; the boys did, too. Willie knew that it was the time to entertain. He hit another over the wall in left field, one to straightaway center, and then one over the chain fence in right field. He did the same thing again—left, center, right. And again.

He stepped out of the box and surveyed the spectators. The black parents had all moved down along the first-base line now except for one, the mother of a freshman. She had patted Willie on the shoulder after his last game and smiled at him. She was sitting on the grassy hillside below the cars and leaning back on her elbows. Her skirt was pulled up into her lap, and her bare legs glistened.

This sight pulled Willie's attention from the ball. It was the first time he had lost sight of it and as he stepped back into the box he felt himself blink. Coach McNeil did his funny windup and dropped his arm down a bit, and Willie noticed the sweat spin off his wrist and forearm as he released the ball. Willie popped up the ball into the steam. It stopped for a few seconds at its summit, and the players and parents alike stared, but Willie looked back at the mother on the hillside and she was looking at him and not at the ball, either.

WALKING HOME HE HAD his shirt hung over his shoulder, and he was kicking stones on the road and thinking about the ball. He imagined he had some superhuman vision that would make him the greatest baseball player of all time because God had given him a sort of eyesight that he had never given to a ballplayer before to make it up to him for the stutter.

As he turned off the main road, he looked up at the canopy of pines. There were buzzards on the tippy-top of the trees. He picked up a stone and threw it through the branches, and they scattered out into the setting sun. He heard a car chopping the rocks and dirt behind him and started to walk again. But the car was taking its time, and he turned and waved for a ride before he even looked. He waved to everyone for a ride.

The car stopped, and Willie smiled at the mother who had been watching him from the grassy slope. He kept walking, then he realized she was talking to him and driving alongside him, so he stopped and leaned into the side window.

"Wuh-whu-whaddya think about them huh-huh-home runs?" Willie asked.

She smiled at him and turned off the car. He looked down at her thick hands on the wheel. She had a ring on every finger and even her thumb, and he wondered why she would wear so many rings.

"Open the door, please," she said.

She nodded to the door handle. He opened it and stepped back, and as she turned her body to get out of the car he saw her legs again. Her skirt was all scrunched up into her lap just like before, and this time he could see clear up to her hips.

She stood and smiled at him and kept looking at him as she walked into the shade of the first line of evergreens and then straight into the woods behind them.

"Whuh-whuh-where you goin'?" he asked.

She stopped about 20 feet deep into the woods and sat down, and he walked slowly toward her.

She motioned to him, and he kept walking toward her, but all he could think was that she was sitting in a mushroom patch because he stopped here many times to pick them and take them home to Cille.

She was squatting, then sat back on her bottom and kicked out her legs in front of her. Then she forcefully threw the top of the skirt up and pulled off her underwear with one tug. He had seen his sister's private parts and had seen his mother get out of bed with Guy Webb, the both of them naked and stumbling drunk. But he had never been this close before, and she lifted her pelvis up in the air for him to see more clearly.

"You take down your pants and come over here," she said. She was staring at her privates, too.

Willie walked up to her, and she sat her bottom back down on the skirt-covered ground. She reached up and unsnapped his baseball trousers. He wobbled, and the back cleat of his left shoe stepped on her calf. She winced but steadied him and pulled him back toward her by his pants. Then she leaned her

head back and laughed deep and loud so that her laughter echoed through the woods. He could see down into her throat she was laughing so hard.

She pulled his pants down with one hard tug, and he was pantless there right in front of her and she looked up at him unblinking.

There were bugs darting around his head, and he felt his sweat drop off his body onto her as she pulled him down.

And the only thing she said when it was over was that she liked the way he talked.

HATTIE THREW THE HOT WATER at him because he had been teasing her all day long. The hot dogs were what burned most as the water landed on his belly. Cille grabbed him by the hand and dragged him for blocks and blocks until they came to a shack even more decrepit than theirs.

A woman answered the door and stared right at Willie's belly. She led him to a table and told him to lie down. She bent over him and put her eyes so close to his belly that it looked like she was going to stick her head into his belly button. Her pink hair curlers stabbed his side.

The woman lightly blew through her pursed lips. She tugged his pants down to his hips and blew in straight lines on his belly over and back.

Then she started to talk about the devil. She talked and blew at the same time, and Willie loved her cool breath on his belly but her voice started to scare him. He opened his eyes and saw his mother sitting on the couch across the room. She was looking at a magazine.

The woman took a bowl of water, rubbed dirt between her hands above it. She dipped her hands into the bowl, closed her eyes, and talked and talked in that tongue like a witch, Willie thought. He had heard of her before, the woman who will talk the fire out of you. He knew one boy whose house burned down, and his parents stole him from the hospital and took him to her.

She started to rub the mud all over the burn up and down and in circles. The mud scratched him but the burning had faded. The mud was red like the clay he ate when he was hungry, and he started to giggle now because it was all starting to tickle when her fingertips grazed his sides.

She stopped talking, closed her eyes, and stood up abruptly.

He saw Cille hand her money before Cille walked over and dragged him back home.

THE NIGHT WAS SO COLD that Cille laid newspapers over the big blanket that covered Willie and Hattie. Willie filled the wood stove just before they blew out the candles, and smoke wisped into the shack.

Hattie was wearing her boots in bed, and Willie wore plastic bags over his socks.

He found it amazing that he was the only one wondering why Guy Webb didn't show up since it was Sunday, and he always came back from his binges on Sundays no matter how drunk he was.

He thought he heard a knock on the door, but he thought again and told himself it was only the wind. But he heard the knock again and decided it was a knock and sat up in bed.

"Cille, thuh-thuh-there's someone knockin' a-a-at the door, Cille," he said.

She did not respond.

"Cille!" he shouted.

She sat up as the knocker knocked even harder.

She got out of bed, cracked the door, and nodded to the man to come inside. In the darkness, Willie could see that the man was white, and then he saw the uniform and realized he was a policeman.

"Ms. Aikens, I am sorry but I need to ask you to come down to the station," he said. "We believe we have Guy Webb there and that he froze to death out along the train tracks, but we need you to come down to the station because we need you to identify the body. I am very sorry to disturb you, but I can almost assure you one good thing is that the police car I will drive you in is warmer than this house."

He heard Cille trudge back over to the bed. He heard her putting on her dress and saw the outline of the man turn toward the door so as not to see what he would not be able to see in the darkness anyway.

Cille walked back to the door and walked out of the shack with the policeman. Hattie slept through the whole visit.

Guy Webb is dead and gone gone gone, Willie thought. He rolled over and buried his head in the feather pillow.

He imagined Guy Webb there stiff as a tree trunk, and then imagined the train coming around the bend. He hoped Guy Webb was spread across the tracks and not alongside them so that the train cut him in half or better yet in thirds to be sure he was dead and gone now and forever.

It was well-known and well-tolerated that Willie struggled with priorities. And pinball and pool started to take priority over baseball and football. He was a standout on the defensive line, too. Not as good as Cuda, but strong and stout. Cuda could get after the quarterback; Willie just stood guys up. But he loved baseball first and pool second and pinball third and didn't love football at all.

This warm fall afternoon he'd had enough of football practice. The game was the ticket out of Seneca, far more than baseball. But he loved the center stage that being a batter offered. One on one, not disappearing under all those pads.

So no practice today. Pool. Or pinball.

Pool tables ran the length of the hall downtown, and pinball machines with all their lights flashing and their balls pinging lined the right wall.

Willie nodded to everyone as he walked in and stopped to watch an old man hit a bank shot. He clapped twice as the ball slowed and trickled into the pocket.

"At-at-at-attaway old-timer!" Willie shouted. He walked right to the last pinball machine.

The only reason the owner let him in was because Willie struck a deal with him—underage pinball when the place wasn't busy in exchange for racking balls every Thursday night.

"Those cops see you playin' a machine with a white woman in a bikini on it they gonna take my license away and shut this place down," the owner said.

A ball dropped down the chute on the left side of the machine. He cocked the flipper and waited another split second and then let it rip. The ball climbed up the blonde woman's right leg, crossed her right hip, crossed over to her belly button, and ran up her rib cage. It was slowing but on target and approached her right breast, and then it seemed to get its gumption up and just dropped in there, sat there on her nipple, and the alarms started to sound as Willie raised his arms in triumph.

Football ain't nothing like this, he thought. *This is skill. This is as hard as hitting a baseball.*

The kids were bouncing around the bus like grasshoppers, and Willie was getting angry. He looked in the rearview mirror and saw a girl doing a handstand in the aisle. The kids were spanking her bottom as she walked on her hands to the back of the bus. A boy was trying to throw a younger boy out the window face first, but the kid kept splitting his legs out like a scissors to keep from falling.

Willie stepped hard on the brake. He was a senior now and had been driving the bus for a year. He earned a dollar a trip, two dollars a day. The bus was a runt—it carried about 20 kids and looked like someone cut a real school bus in half.

It was May, and the last game of the season was that night.

He turned and tried to make eye contact with each kid.

"You-you-you's all actin' like a bunch of farm animals!" he shouted.

Then they all started imitating his stutter and making farm animal sounds.

He got up and started to walk down the aisle. He was 6'3" and weighed north of 250 pounds. He had weighed more or less that much since the eighth grade. The kids had all stopped teasing him about his stutter.

"Thuh-thuh-thank you!" he said.

He looked at his watch and realized all this fooling around was going to make him late for the game. He had been offered a football scholarship to South Carolina State but no baseball scholarship anywhere since no scout ever set foot in his corner of the state. But unending optimism was already his strong suit, and he hoped that on the last night of the season some scout might have heard of his hitting and decided to show up in Seneca.

It was time to take the shortcut—a dirt road between two straw fields. He stopped at the intersection with the main road and waited for two cars to pass. He looked carefully each way and pulled out. Then he turned to the kids and smiled.

He looked into the distance and then into the rearview mirror to make sure no one saw him. Then he slowed down and took a wide turn because the entrance to the shortcut was so narrow.

The wheels kicked up little rocks, and the bus started to bounce up and down so that it launched the kids a couple feet out of their seats each time.

And then it slammed to a stop. The last bounce lifted the whole bus up and over a couple feet and into a trench.

He forgot to factor yesterday's rain into his decision—the bus was stuck.

He rested his chin on his chest and closed his eyes.

But his brain immediately began to ponder solutions. He had started to like to get himself into jams and work his way out of them.

He looked at the young straw all around them.

"Let's go," Willie said as he opened the door. At times like this he rarely stuttered. "Start grabbin' all the straw you can and laying it under the tires."

After they stuffed it under all the tires, he raised his hand and the kids stopped.

"Now get back there and push when I say so," he said.

He turned the key, unlocked the brake, and slowly stepped on the gas pedal. The wheels started to spit mud out and up into the air and all over the kids. They stopped pushing and ran into the field.

He floored it now, and the mud spat higher.

The bus wiggled for a few seconds and then lunged forward.

As he pulled up to the field he was already searching for a strange face in the stands that might be the face of a scout.

The bleachers were full, and Coach McNeil actually seemed nervous for the first time in his life.

Coach told him Cuda's arm hurt, so Willie was pitching today.

By now he knew he stuttered less when he was angry, but he was so pissed at Cuda that he knew he would stutter if he started yelling at him.

He walked around the mound and acted like he was looking at the sky, but he was really surveying the crowd to see if that scout had arrived. But he saw no unfamiliar faces.

Cuda came over from third base.

"You seen any scouts in the stands?" Willie asked, scowling at him.

"Nah, Willie," Cuda said. "Why you so worried about scouts? We gonna play football together at South Carolina State, Willie!"

I never had a problem with white people, Willie thought, *but I can hit the ball way better than most white kids, and they're all going to college for baseball and no scout even looked at me once. Just ain't right.*

He walked around the mound one more time. Then he walked the first batter on five pitches. And he walked several batters after that. He decided to try his curveball, and the next guy popped it into the sky.

"I got it, Cuda," Willie said.

"No, no, no, I got it!" Cuda shouted.

The ball began its slow fall, and Willie already knew they were in the grips of a scene he could not undo.

Why the hell is he insisting on catching it? Why? He knows I can catch better than he can.

Willie kept staring as the ball banged into the heel of Cuda's glove, bounced onto his chest, and then off his knee into foul territory.

Cuda looked up at Willie before he even looked for the ball. The whole time the runners were running, but Willie and Cuda were standing there just looking at each other as the ball came to rest against the fence in front of Utica's bench.

"You stupid son of a bitch," Willie said. He rarely cursed. But Cuda needed to be cursed.

Cuda dropped his head and started to walk off the field.

Willie came up right behind him and pushed into Cuda's back with his chest.

"You stupid stupid son of a bitch, Cuda," he said over and over.

Coach McNeil walked up and pushed them apart. But Willie kept going after Cuda, cursing him with words he had only heard but never used up until now. He felt like all his anger at everyone in his life was about to burst out, and poor Cuda was gonna bear the brunt of it.

2

The Great American Game

1973–1980

In August 1973, he steered his used shiny blue 1961 Chevrolet into Orangeburg. His sister had left for Greenville earlier in the year. *They must have been having a hard time coming up with names for towns in South Carolina back in the day,* he thought. *Just picking colors and adding -villes and -burgs.*

Cuda was grooving to the radio the whole trip.

"Let's Get It On" was on again. Cuda spent the whole trip turning the silver dial to different channels to find the song, and each time he found it he sang and rolled his jelly belly in the passenger's seat.

They drove straight to the dining hall where the football team gathered for the first team meal. Most players were already sitting hunched over with their heads buried in heaps of food. Cuda went through the line first and stacked two plates high with pork chops and spaghetti, and Willie tried to match him.

They sat down at a long table. Donnie Shell, the future star Pittsburgh Steelers safety, was sitting there. Harry Carson, the future star linebacker for the New York Giants, was there, too.

Coach Willie Jeffries, who someday would be inducted into the College Football Hall of Fame, walked in and gave a short speech about being on time and studying hard. He said they were going to have more water on the field this year because the administration told them they had to.

Willie kept turning his eyes to the assistant, Coach Willie Simon, because he knew Coach Simon was also the baseball coach, and his plan was to play football just long enough to play baseball and to play football just hard enough just not to get hurt so he could play baseball, and to play football well enough to keep his scholarship so he could play baseball.

But guile was not his game. He knew he was not as good at football as baseball. And he loved this place already. He felt it: the big, droopy trees; the girls walking on the trimmed lawns; the endless food. *And Coach, I can sure bring a lot more to South Carolina State as a baseball player than a football player,* he imagined himself saying to Coach Simon after the season.

After dinner the players wandered through the dining hall to the student lounge. Folding chairs stood around a few television sets, and to the side by the windows there were chairs squeezed around card tables. Willie's eyes grew big when he saw a pool table.

By the third game they were playing for money.

At 10:00 the clock buzzed, and the security guard was standing behind them watching the game instead of locking up and Willie had nearly $50 in his pocket.

"Puh-puh-puh-pool!" he said.

The guard shook his head.

"You'll be playin' plenty of pool, but now it's time for me to lock up 'fore I lose my job," he said. "Coach is gonna fire me if he hears I let you all stay up this late the night before the first workout."

The players grumbled and slowly walked to the exit. But Willie walked more slowly, and as the guard lured the jangling keys out of his pocket with the chain tied to his belt, Willie winked at Cuda and turned back.

"You sh-sh-sh-shoot?" Willie asked the guard.

"I do not shoot, I lock up," the guard said.

Willie smiled at him and reached into his pocket. He took out the money he had won playing pool and counted it. Then he stuck it in the guard's pocket where the keys were jangling.

"Let's go shoot," Willie said. "Just one game."

Cuda shook his head because as he walked down the steps he saw the lights behind him go off and then go back on. He turned, looked inside, and saw the guard racking the balls at the table in front of the window.

COACH JEFFRIES SEEMED to like push-ups and jumping jacks as well as most football coaches. Willie had arrived late for his first practice, as did two other freshmen. And they had to stay after practice to do more.

"Around here we live and work as a team, and that means everyone doin' the same thing in support of the team," Coach Jeffries began. "Now three of you were late. And bein' late ain't bein' part of the team. Now you three who were late come with me to the end zone. The rest of you, good first practice."

In the end zone the three of them stood in front of Coach Jeffries, and he suddenly dropped to the ground in front of them and started to roll toward the 5-yard line and then the 10. He popped back up and walked straight and fast back to them.

"Now you do it!"

Willie's two teammates plopped down first and rolled, and he kneeled down and followed them.

They stood back up at the 10-yard line, and Willie rolled into them. They helped him up, and the three walked back to the end zone with lowered heads and drooping shoulders as if to convey that the punishment had fit the crime.

"Now, good," Coach said. "Good. You boys got some talent. Now get down there and roll to the other end zone and then roll back!"

One of the players dropped slowly to his knees, looked penitently at the Coach, and then lay down. The other did the same, and they both started to roll.

"Get down there, Willie Mays," Coach Jeffries said with a kind of seriousness in his voice Willie had never heard a Coach use. *This dude's serious*, he thought. *This really ain't no joke.*

He kneeled down. And then he rolled, and he kept rolling. The field seemed like it was on a conveyor belt, always turning up to face him. At the end zone he slammed into one of the guys on his way back, and they scrambled over each other. He stopped and lay with his facemask in the ground and felt his stomach in his lungs and then felt a foot tap his backside.

"Back, back now, Willie Mays."

And then Coach started blowing the whistle *tweet-tweet-tweet,* and Willie rolled back this time holding his helmet with his arms to try to keep from getting so dizzy. He crossed midfield and the 40 and the 30 and then he felt his whole belly move upward into his throat, and he threw up without any warning, without even the fluid running up his throat first to warn him like it usually did when he threw up. He laid there, the vomit filling his helmet and dripping into his hair and then trickling into his left ear.

He opened his eyes and reached into his facemask to clear vomit from his eyes. And all he could think about was taking batting practice for hours on end until his hands hurt and his wrists burned and his calves cramped.

PAULETTE WAS SITTING on the porch of the women's dorm in a rusty metal chair, and Willie could see her out his window again, just like he saw her there yesterday and the day before that. He had found out her name that morning, and it struck him as funny. He wondered if her parents wanted a boy and wanted to name him Paul so badly that they just threw the "-ette" on there when she was born because they couldn't think of anything else. He decided that the first time he teased her he would tease her about this. And he would begin that teasing as soon as he called his sister from the payphone downstairs.

Hattie picked up and said hello and then said nothing else like she always did when she wanted to show Willie something was stewing. But over the past year Hattie had become Jean, for her full name was really Hattie Jean and she had outgrown the Hattie, and Jean struck Willie as a new and improved Hattie. Jean had a husband now and a baby soon. *After all that scrappin' and teasin', I love her like a sister,* Willie thought.

"Cille is a harlot," she said after she cleared her throat like she always did to announce the end of the silence.

Willie tightened his grip on the phone.

"I known it for two years," Willie said.

"Why you didn't say nothin'?"

"She's your mother, Jean. I ain't gonna tell you your mother's a harlot!"

He dropped the phone cord and looked out the window toward Paulette's dorm.

"Hey, Jean. I just wanted to say hello, okay? I miss you, and I'm hah-hah-happy you're my sister, okay?"

"Okay, Willie. Hey, Willie. How's college?"

He smiled.

"I-I'm tryin' to play baseball here, and I think I know how to geh-geh-get on the team."

"Good," Jean said. "Okay, Willie. I talk to you soon."

"I talk to you soon, Jean."

He hung up the phone and imagined the call booming over loudspeakers and everyone on campus hearing it and knowing his mama's a harlot, and Paulette looking across the lawn at him and getting up from her chair and walking inside.

Then he turned to look at her, and she was still sitting there looking at her fingernails and pushing on them like the women did in Church.

I'm goin' to talk to that girl, then I'm goin' to talk to the baseball coach, he said to himself. All in one fell swoop. He knew his charm, with a little help from his stutter, could take him to the places he wanted to go.

"Hey puh-puh-puh-Paulette," he said as he approached her. The girls all stopped and stared at him, and she blinked and turned her eyes away for a second but then came back to him.

"Hey," she said.

The other girls giggled, but she smiled sweetly at him without laughing.

"I wuh-wuh-was wonderin' if you'd like to take a walk."

The girls giggled some more, but Paulette stared them into silence. She leaned forward slightly in her metal chair.

"It might be nice to tell me your name before askin' me if I'd like to take a walk with you," she said.

The other girls leaned forward, too, and looked at her instead of at him.

"I-I-I'm Willie Aikens!"

"Well, Willie, thank you," she said. "I ain't walkin' today cause we're havin' a chat. But if you'd like to come by some other time maybe we can take a walk."

"Yeah, we can do that," Willie said, smiling.

The girls all laughed again, and this time Paulette laughed, too.

"So I guess I-I-I'll see you tomorrow then," Willie said as he turned and walked away.

WILLIE COULD SEE the light under the door to Coach Simon's office. It was getting dark early now, and one game was left in the football season. He had gotten into a few games, showed up on time for each practice after the first one, and apart from a twisted ankle had preserved himself for baseball season.

Suddenly Coach Simon opened the door and said, "Hello, Willie. What can I do for you?"

"Huh-huy-hey, Coach, I just was goin' to knock on your duh-duh-door."

Coach Simon smiled.

"Sit down, Willie. I been meanin' to talk to you," he said.

Willie looked at all the baseball team photographs on his shelves and walls, and he relaxed immediately.

"Willie, I understand you are quite a baseball player," Coach Simon said.

Willie grinned wide and nodded his head.

"I wuh-wuh-was, sir, yessir I muh-muh-mean I am," he said. "But nobody come to suh-suh-Seneca to recruit us for baseball. You ever heard of Coach McNeil? He taught me a whole lot about baseball."

"Never met him, Willie. But he did call me last week out of the blue to talk about you. We have a good team here. No scholarships, but a darn good team, and I'd love you to be a part of it."

Willie looked at the photographs again and decided he was going to go directly to Paulette's dorm and ask her to take that walk with him right now. *Today it's all turnin' up aces for me*, he thought, *and when it plays that way you got to keep doublin' down.*

SHE LET HIM HOLD her hand on that first walk, and on several walks after that, and one Saturday night she bent her neck to let him kiss her on the cheek, and instead of kissing her on the cheek where she intended he kissed her on the lips. And she didn't slap him or push him away like he expected she would.

And for weeks thereafter they walked each evening after dinner, and he kissed her a few more times and told her she was his first kiss. She wouldn't believe him but he swore it and was pleased to be telling the truth because he never kissed that woman by the side of the road and she never even tried to kiss him.

Then Christmas came and she asked if he could drive her home to Estill instead of her taking the bus, and his heart surged like it had never surged before.

She was waiting with a brown suitcase in her hand as he drove up to her dorm, and she did not look into the car once as she walked down the steps. She opened the back door first and put the suitcase in. Then she opened the front door and sat and closed the door and kept sitting without saying a word. He stared at her and started laughing as he let off the brake and slowly pulled out of the campus.

"Puh-puh-Paulette," he said and turned to her as he drove. "I-I was wonderin' if maybe we might stop in that motel on the way out of tuh-tuh-town and maybe go inside for a little while."

She kept looking at the road as if to make up for his inattention to it.

He stopped looking at her and looked back at the road and felt his throat tighten up and knew he wouldn't be able to say another word the whole trip without stuttering if she said no.

She turned her head to look out the side window.

"That would be fine," she said.

He sped up slightly then caught himself and braked. He felt his palms wet on the wheel even though it was chilly outside.

He parked in the motel lot and ran to her side and opened the door for her. As she got out, he saw her knees for the first time and turned away. *I think I am falling in love,* he said to himself. And he took her hand, and they walked to the motel reception with the same matching stride and swung their arms in unison, too.

HE RECKONED THAT more people lived in the single group of row houses at the back of the baseball field at Morgan State in Baltimore than in all of Seneca. He had hit two home runs and two doubles in the blowout and decided he liked the Baltimore humidity. As Willie walked to the South Carolina State team bus, a short, fat man with big sideburns approached him.

"Willie Aikens," the man said. "I asked your coach there, and he said I might speak with you for a moment. I'm Walter Youse. Come on over here in the shade of that tree with me."

Willie followed him and looked back at the bus. Coach Simon was watching him from beside the door and nodded.

"You quite a slugger, young man," Youse said. "See, I run this team here in Baltimore called the Johnnies. A summer amateur team. We're pretty famous. Brooks and Frank Robinson and all the Orioles will tell you. We got tradition. And you, Willie, I think I want you to be a Johnnie. We'll get you a job and housing for the summer. You just get yourself up here, and a bunch of pro scouts'll be watchin' you hit balls like you hit today. Here's my card. You come on up here to Baltimore. You gonna like this town. You ever have a crab cake?"

Youse patted him on the bottom and took a cigar out of a plastic pocket protector on the breast of his short sleeve shirt. He lit it and blew the smoke upward.

Willie walked back over to Coach Simon and shook his hand.

Willie heard a man calling out the names of fruits and turned. There in the middle of the street a donkey pulled a wagon filled with produce.

He hit .472 that season for South Carolina State and won the conference Rookie of the Year award. Paulette didn't know what to make of him going so far away to Baltimore, but he told her he was going to be a star for her, become a big leaguer for her, and hit home runs for her. She still didn't seem impressed.

By July 1974, he officially became a supernova. The Johnnies were playing in Cumberland, Maryland, in the westernmost part of the state. It was cooler here near the mountains and less humid than in the Baltimore hothouse, and the ball lifted more quickly. He cut back on his effort and raised his bat slightly during his swing, and it felt like he was patty-caking the ball, but it just sailed and sailed.

He hit a home run in his first at-bat, then another in the second, and as he came to the plate in the sixth inning his teammates were chanting, "Reg-gie! Reg-gie!"

Some of the fans joined in, and Willie smiled. He nodded at the new pitcher. And as he dug in he decided he would swing with all his might at the first good pitch. The good pitch did not come. The pitcher walked him on four straight balls, and the fans booed and his teammates did, too. He walked in his final at-bat, too.

And as the game ended, a few kids approach him with copies of *Sports Illustrated*. Walter had the coaches hand out a copy to each player on the bus ride from Baltimore, and Willie read the piece about 50 times.

> The name of The Team may have changed, but Jackson is still being used as a measuring stick. "That's the way Reggie used to hit them," Jimmy Foit, one of The Team's coaches, said admiringly as he watched a youngster named Willie Aikens slam one batting-practice pitch after another toward Swann Park's distant softball fields.

He memorized that part.

He gave his first autograph ever, and as the boy walked away a teammate came up behind him chanting, "Reggie! Reggie!" again.

Willie laughed and turned to him.

"I juh-juh-just love hittin' the baseball, man," Willie said. "I just love it."

Johnny Wilbanks, the team owner and namesake, hopped to the door of his used car dealership as Walter escorted Willie in.

The car salesmen looked up from their coffees and cigarettes, and then looked back down at their newspapers.

Johnny fell into Willie, and Willie did not know whether he was hugging him or holding onto him to stay up. He had heard of Johnny's two amputated legs, so he expected him to be on crutches, not jumping around like the girls in Seneca used to do on pogo sticks.

"Willie Mays Aikens," Johnny said as he steadied himself.

Willie looked at Walter, and Walter laughed and nodded for him to follow Johnny into his office.

The fluorescent light kept blinking on dozens of gold trophies, and it felt to Willie like he was walking into a mini Baseball Hall of Fame.

"Al Kaline, too," Johnny said. He pointed to a photograph of Al Kaline wearing a Johnnies uniform. As Willie looked at it he noticed that the whole wall to the right side of Johnny's desk held photographs of him with Reggie Jackson.

"And Walter tells me you can hit the ball farther than any of them, Reggie included. What kind of car do you drive?"

Willie looked at Walter, and Walter nodded again.

"A 1961 Chevrolet."

"How much you pay for it?"

"One hundred fif-fif-fifty dollars," Willie said.

Johnny looked at Walter.

"Boy's got a bad stutter," he said.

Willie's body stiffened. He had come to realize that women often liked the stutter, and most men ridiculed it.

"But that don't matter a thing in baseball," Johnny said. "What matters is what you do with the bat, not your mouth, son. Now I'm going to get you a good deal on a car before the summer's over, but in the meantime I want to make you a very special deal. You keep playing like you do, and next Monday you are going to take batting practice with the Baltimore Orioles. Brooks, Frank, Boog!"

As they walked out, a man with a camera raised his hands and motioned for Willie to stand still. Walter came up alongside Willie, and Johnny stood slightly in front of them both as the flash went off. Then Walter moved away, and Johnny grabbed Willie's hand and held it. He kept holding it. Johnny's face changed expressions for each of a dozen more photographs to the point where Willie thought he must stand in front of the mirror in the morning and practice like a professional clown.

THE RUSTY RADIATOR that the landlord installed and said was good as new shot packets of steam mixed with dust into the shack. Cille sat in a high chair with frayed red upholstery while Willie sat on a stool, and they both kept looking at the phone. Somewhere in New York City the supplementary draft started at 10:00 AM on this January 5.

The phone had rung 12 times in the past hour, but it was always someone calling to see if a team had called.

It rang again at noon, and Cille looked at Willie as he let it ring and ring.

"Why didn't you pick it up?" she asked.

"I know who it was," Willie said.

"How you know who it was?"

He looked at her and smiled.

"The sound of the ring."

"You can't tell who it was by the sound of the ring!"

"I can," Willie said.

He stood and picked up a caulk gun and shot the caulk into a hole in the sideboards.

"First thing I'm guh-guh-gonna do is get you a fine house, Cille," he said. "But you got to do somethin' to get it, too."

The phone rang again, and this time Willie nodded his head.

"This is it, major league baseball, Cille," he said.

He put down the caulk gun and stepped to the phone. Cille kept looking at the floor.

"Willie," she heard a voice say as he lifted the phone to his ear.

Willie's face tightened with surprise.

"Walter?" he said. "Walter, why you callin' me?"

"Willie, I got you!"

Cille had never met Walter but she cringed a bit as his high voice shouted over and over: "I got you!"

Willie held the phone away from his ear momentarily and looked at Cille.

"He says he got me," he said to her.

He held the phone back up and waited for Walter to pause.

"Walter, how'd you get me? You told me the Orioles were picking far down, and I was gonna go high up. There ain't no money that far down the draft!"

They then heard Walter cackle.

Willie took the phone from his ear again and held it up so Cille could hear.

"Willie, I got you, I got you!" Walter said again, and Cille shook her head up and down as if to say, *Okay, be done with it.* "But I got you with the Angels! California, Willie! You going to be hittin' home runs in California! I left the Orioles two weeks ago for the Angels! I told them all about you, and the whole organization is ready for the next Reggie Jackson, Frank Robinson, Boog Powell— the next great American slugger, Willie Mays Aikens from sleepy Seneca, South Carolina! Now I'll be down there next week and we'll get this all signed up and you'll make $12,000 your first year, Willie. I'll be down there next week!"

The phone clicked on the other end, and Willie stood there. He did not smile but pursed his lips and blinked a couple times.

"He-he-he got a pool of money for all his players, Cille," Willie said. "And he muh-muh-makes his money by keeping what he don't spend. So he's sayin' he's gonna pay me $12,000, but I know he can pay me more than that. I ain't signin' for less than $14,000. I ain't cause Walter knows how good I am. Nobody else does and he thinks he can use that to sign me for less, but he knows what I can do for his ruh-ruh-reputation."

"Cille, they are building new apartments out at the edge of town," Willie said. "I looked at them yesterday, and I'm gonna put down a deposit on one for you today. They got nice toilets. I'm movin' you over there, Cille, but you gonna stop sleepin' around." He sat back on the stool and looked her straight in the eye.

Cille folded her hands in her lap and looked up at the caulking sticking out of the wall.

Willie looked at his feet.

"You got to start luh-luh-livin' clean now, Cille," he said. "People gonna start talkin' now that I'm a pruh-pruh-pro ballplayer. I'll take care of you if you start livin' clean."

"Wuh-wuh-wuh-why you talk like that, big fella?"

The players laughed and looked at Willie sitting on his white stool in front of the locker he shared at the California Angels training camp with a Latin player who might be called Julio. *Or Jose,* he thought.

At South Carolina State they waited to tease him. And they usually did it in a fun way.

One Latin player stood up and walked in front of Willie and leaned his face forward. "*Guh-guh-guh-gordito!*" Fat man!

Everyone laughed but Willie. The only man who ever made him angry was Guy Webb, and here in the tiny mildewed locker room full of Angels minor leaguers, he remembered Guy Webb the night he came at him with the knife.

They will see, he thought. *They will see.*

During practice, Bobby Knoop began to work with him on his fielding at first base, and Willie knew this was a good sign because Bobby Knoop used to be a hell of a ballplayer, and they wouldn't have him work with Willie if they didn't think he had something.

But at the end of the drills Moose Stubing stood behind them, and Bobby nodded to him.

"Okay, Willie, now it's my turn," Moose said.

All the other players, even the ones who stayed behind for special drills, were gone by now, and Moose beckoned for Willie to follow him to the outfield.

He stopped in center field and turned to face Willie.

"You weighed in at 252 pounds, young man," Moose said.

Willie looked down at the outfield grass. *That's what this is all about*, he realized. He hadn't set foot on a scale for a year, never thought to.

"And I bet a hundred bucks with the other coaches that says you'll be down to 220 by the end of the month."

Willie looked up at him.

"Yep. One hundred bucks. Every coach here is betting against you except Bobby and me. And you got a stake in the bet, too."

"How much I got in it?" Willie said.

"Your job," Moose said.

Willie looked at him.

"Yep, you heard me, son," Moose said. "They're gonna cut you if you don't weigh in at 220 on April 2. So I lose a hundred bucks, which I won't be happy about, and you'll be going home to wherever it is that you eat so good. Maybe I'll come visit you in the off-season, and your mother can cook for both of us."

And so the post-practice Moose regimen began. After one week: 237. Week 2: 229. During week three the rains came, and Moose stood under an umbrella the whole time: 225.

The curveballs and change-ups gave him fits the whole of spring training. He struck out four times in one game twice.

"The way you're hitting they might cut you anyway," Moose said. "Walter Youse's big signing and you show up fat and you can't hit a curveball."

The final pounds resisted their shedding. He didn't eat the night before or breakfast that morning, and his belly ached.

He wore a sweatshirt under his uniform and two t-shirts below that and refused water throughout the whole practice. By the time they did their final infield drills, he had to catch the ball with two hands because he was so wobbly.

The scale stood in the entrance to the locker room, and cardboard boxes with labels reading Davenport and El Paso jutted out into the walkway. Moose walked beside him, and all the players were busy packing.

The trainer stood at the scale, and Moose patted Willie on the back as he stepped on it.

"You watch," Moose said. "This boy's going to Iowa to eat as much steak as he wants tonight!"

Willie peeled off his shirt and pants, thought about prizefighters at weigh-in, and wiggled out of his wet sweatshirt and T-shirts and shorts, and Moose slid the scales to 219.

"Your jock strap weighs an eighth of a pound, so that goes too if my hundred bucks are in jeopardy," Moose said.

The scale read 218. The other coaches laughed and started handing Moose money. Willie kept staring at the numbers on the scale and didn't hear or see anything until he felt Moose lift up his hand and stick a bunch of bills between his fingers.

Willie stood there and looked at Moose, but Bobby Knoop was looking back at him, and Bobby's eyes were demanding something of him.

"We're on the same flight this afternoon, Willie," Knoop said.

"Thuh-thuh-thuh-thank the Lord," Willie said back. He stepped off the scale and hung his head and exhaled with gusto. He lifted his head and walked back to his locker without looking left or right, the last naked man in a roomful of newly, proudly dapper dressers waiting to commence their dream-chasing.

HE HAD NEVER HEARD music like this, and in his slumber on the Davenport team bus it sounded like torment. This was the sound of torment like Moose Haas' pitches are the sight of torment. Willie went 0-for-4 that night against this pitcher called Moose who was the star of the Burlington Bees and the star of the whole Midwest League.

Grumpy. Not one hittable fastball from this Moose. *Nobody giving me fastballs anymore*, he thought.

Iowa at 4:00 AM looked to him like Iowa at 4:00 PM. A long flat plain in the moonlight.

Coach Knoop's extra work with him on the curveball wasn't paying off. Step back, wait, lock, wait, wait, now. You ain't gonna hit a home run off a good curve, so just work with it, shoot for the gap, and be happy they know you can hit it 'cause they'll start throwing you fastballs again. Knoop kept saying the same thing, day after day.

He knew what the music reminded him of now—pinball machines in the pool hall in Seneca. But this was pinball music on fast forward.

This is not right, he thought. He lifted himself up to look over the seat and in the mirror saw Coach with his chin in his chest and everyone else sleeping, too.

How the hell can they all sleep through this, he thought. *How the hell?*

He got up and walked to the row in the Latin section. *They all sat together and stretched together and showered together and never tried to learn a drop of English,* he thought.

Snoring in unison, Alex Guerrero and Rafael Kellys were each hugging the boom box with one arm and, as Willie stood over them, he could see the bass sound make the flaps on their shirts move as if it were blowing in a breeze.

He tapped Guerrero on the shoulder, and as he stirred, Kellys stirred, too. They both rubbed their eyes and looked at him.

"Please turn down the music," Willie said.

They frowned.

"*La musica,* puh-puh-please tuh-tuh-turn it down," he said again.

Kellys made a hissing sound, and Willie reached over between them and turned the boom box off and suddenly half the bus woke up. *Insane,* he thought. *They wake up now.*

The two Latin players, each still with one arm wrapped around the box, looked shocked as they pushed themselves up from their slouching.

"Sleep, I can't sleep," Willie said.

Suddenly Guerrero jumped up and started ranting at Willie in Spanish.

"Be cool, Alex," Willie said. "I cuh-cuh-cuh-can't sleep."

Guerrero hissed at him then sat back down and turned the boom box back on, lowering the volume slightly.

This guy is too much, Willie thought. *How the hell do you do that to your teammate?*

He reached back over and grabbed the music box and flipped it off again.

Guerrero reached out for it. Willie pulled it further out of his reach. Then Guerrero and Kellys both jumped up and stood in his face, and the two of them were not even as wide as Willie put together.

They started pointing their fingers right at his eyes and grabbing the boom box and shouting words in Spanish faster than the singer they were listening to sang them.

Then Bobby Knoop walked up. He didn't say a word but took the boom box from Willie and looked at Willie the whole time as he escorted him back to his seat with his eyes. Then he turned, pushed Guerrero and Kellys back into their seats with his eyes, too. And then he turned and carried the boom box with him back to the front and put it in the empty seat beside him.

The next day was a day off, but Willie showed up at the park in Davenport to work with Bobby Knoop on hitting the curve. On his walk to the park from the Clayton Hotel he envisioned curveballs coming at him down the street.

A few players were seated at their lockers. As he changed, he felt someone walk closely to him and say something in Spanish. He didn't look back but pondered the sound of the words and realized it was Rafael Kellys and that he had said, "*Besa mi culo.*"

This one he knew, and he knew, too, that the boom-box saga would continue. Guerrero was standing at the end of the locker room looking at him and winking.

I'm here to learn to hit the curveball and become a big leaguer, Willie said to himself. *I'm not here to fool around with these guys.*

On the field Knoop started hitting grounders to Willie at first base. While he fielded them, Willie could see Kellys and Guerrero watching from the third-base line, and he heard Spanish chatter as some of the other Latin players gathered around them.

Next Willie went into the cage and Knoop threw him nothing but change-ups and curveballs for 20 minutes. Stand. Wait. Wait. Now. Over and over he stood and waited, and by the end he realized that his problem wasn't with the curveball itself but with the patience required by the standing and waiting.

He drove the last one to the right-field wall, and Knoop raised his fist.

Willie smiled at his mentor as he walked toward the locker room.

The clubhouse guy had laid sandwiches on the table, and a few players were munching on them. Willie walked up to the table and grabbed a chicken sandwich and a bag of potato chips, but then the image of Moose Stubing came into his head, and he put the chips back. He set the plate on his stool, undressed, and walked to the shower feeling like suddenly he had a shot at hitting this damn curveball once and for all.

The shower never got hot, and that was fine because ever since he arrived at South Carolina State he considered any shower a lovely thing, and he read that cold showers help you lose weight anyway.

He stood there with the water smashing into his face and heard other showers start to hiss behind him. The soap felt pasty on his feet as he turned, and directly across from him stood Guerrero and Kellys smiling wide and buck-naked. They just stood there smiling and staring into his eyes.

"*Que pasa?*" Willie said. He already had a knack for Spanish.

And that must have been the password because they both lunged for him at the same time. Willie raised his fist, but Kellys hit him in the gut and kept pounding him in his belly while Guerrero kept slugging him in the back of his head. Willie took a big swing at Kellys, and as he did Guerrero grabbed his arm on the back swing and held it behind him. Kellys kept pounding away until Guerrero slipped off and fell on his back. Willie heard his head smack the tile, and he swung hard at Kelly's face and knocked him clear across the shower.

Willie turned, and in his mind he was already imagining beating Guerrero's head into the tile, but other players came rushing in. Then Bobby Knoop, unaware, walked in with his towel over his shoulder and walked right up between the naked combatants exactly as he did on the bus at 2:00 AM the night before.

"I need to see the three of you in my office right now," he said.

Bobby Knoop turned and headed straight out of the shower with his towel still on his shoulder and walked that way all the way back to his closet-sized office in the corner of the cinder-block locker room.

Julio Cruz escorted them, Willie on one side and Guerrero and Kellys on the other, and didn't leave them until all three stood side-by-side in Bobby's office.

Bobby Knoop had wrapped his towel around himself by now, and he stood right in front of Willie and looked at him.

"Do you know what you can do to your career, Willie?" he shouted.

"Coach, I didn't start this, same as last night. I dih-dih-didn't start nuh-nuh-nuthin!"

Then Bobby turned to Guerrero and said, "*Que paso?*"

"He hit us in the shower, Coach! He attack us!"

Bobby shook his head and sighed.

"So, Willie, you know I'm supposed to report every incident to the front office, and now we have two incidents. You know that? You realize that, Willie?"

"Bobby," Willie said. "I promise you…."

And suddenly both Guerrero and Kellys were saying "I promise, I promise Señor Knoop," over and over and Willie thought, *You two have no idea what the hell you are promising, you kiss-ass troublemakers.*

Bobby held up his hand.

"Stop it!" he said. "Shake hands, now!"

Guerrero and Kellys raised their hands instantly. *How is it that these guys can understand English when they have to?* Willie thought.

They scurried out before Willie could even turn.

As he raised his head to look at Bobby Knoop one more time, he noticed Bobby Knoop's towel was hanging over his shoulder again.

"Willie, quit doing this to me," Bobby Knoop said. *His face looks sad, actually sad,* Willie thought.

"Ack Ack!" the public address announcer with a knack for nicknames shouted that night as Willie walked to the plate in his second month playing for the El Paso Diablos after his promotion the next season to Double A.

Mona the elephant swung her trunk over a bale of hay in the rear of her cage beyond the outfield wall.

Fans shouted: "*Muévete Mona! Muévete mas cerca!*" Move closer, Mona!

Then the PA announcer called to her: "Mona! Mona! Move closer, Mona! Catch Ack Ack's home run! Catch it!"

Mona slowly lifted her head, and her ears perked up at the ruckus. Willie looked at the pitcher, who turned and looked back at the elephant. But everyone knew that Willie had hit balls close to Mona before, and anyone who played the El Paso Diablos had to grow accustomed to lions and monkeys mocking them from the zoo behind the stadium.

From the ballpark, the sunset looked vicious. He had seen dry earth before in California and Utah but never desert like this. The moon sat halfway up on one side of the mountain splitting El Paso, and the sun still shone on the other.

And the air felt sharp and smooth, and when he swung it felt ever-so-slightly faster. Balls came in sleeker and cleaner from the pitcher. He began to get it: wait, wait, wait, pop. He started to want them to throw curves. *Throw them. Throw them to me.*

Even his grip felt different—he would still sweat but sometimes as night fell and coolness came, he would take off his batting glove and just hold the bat in his bare hands like when he was a schoolboy playing pickup ball.

But he knew he couldn't hit Mona if the pitcher threw a curveball. Jimy Williams was his manager now, and Jimy kept repeating every BP the whole Angels organization's mantra with him—put the curveballs in play; don't try to drive them.

But tonight was the night. He had put enough balls in play—going with them, connecting with their arc, and sending them to pockets in the outfield in the direction that their curve allowed—that he knew now he could both place them and drive them.

Last night he drove one to the warning track for a double, and as he scored later Jimy Williams stood in line to shake his hand but frowned at him as he did it. *Jimy knows I'm getting it,* Willie thought. *Jimy knows I am gonna hit home runs off curveballs, too. He wants to slow me down. That's what a coach is for.*

Mona moved closer, sort of pranced closer, as Willie watched and the whole stadium cheered and shouted in Spanish. *This poor pitcher,* Willie thought. *This poor Mexican dude in front of this crowd of Mexicans thinks he can get me with curveballs.*

He took the first one for a ball, and the second one he jacked barely right of the foul pole. Then he took a third curveball for a strike, and then another curve for a ball, and he thought, *At least vary it, man. At least mix it up a bit.*

And as the pitcher entered his windup for the third pitch, Willie could tell it was going to be his first fastball. In the bottom of his eye he could see Mona, and then the ball lined up with her and he tightened his wrists, waited, waited, and then catapulted his bat into line with the ball and then into line with Mona and the whole place stood up silent and entranced.

Mona lifted her head, too, and the ball seemed to slow as it approached her, seemed to slow even more as it started downward toward her, and then it plopped right there in her cage and she immediately nudged it with her trunk.

Eruption. As he jogged the bases the Mexicans went crazy, and the announcer kept shouting: "Ack Ack Ack Ack Ack Ack! Ack Ack Ack Ack Ack Ack!"

As his teammates slapped him, he looked out toward the zoo and Mona looking at the ball. *All those Angels coaches should be here now,* he thought. *All those fellas who thought I was a big, fat, stuttering elephant should know that I'm coming. I'm coming soon. I'm coming, and I'm going to be bigger than Reggie Jackson.*

HE HEADED TO JUÁREZ one night toward the end of the season to celebrate. He had not gone there to party the entire season, even though lots of guys from the team went a few nights each week.

But The Diablos had made the Double A league championship, and Willie thought the Angels might even call him up at the end of the season, so he might as well pre-celebrate just in case they did. His teammates went to Juarez all the time, and this time he agreed to join.

The customs agents knew them, and one portly lady with a badge shouted, "Ack Ack!" as he passed, and he raised his hand to salute her. As they crossed the bridge over the gulley separating the two cities, he looked down at all the trash below and thought of the Seneca River flowing so sweetly near town. He remembered his first swim there, how Cuda just pushed him in, and he had never swum before but floating came to him right away and he floated half the day.

They walked past a bunch of trinket shops and turned right, and the few neon signs and dozens of soldiers from Fort Bliss told him they had arrived at the famous Calle and Willie felt funny already. He felt like Paulette was always watching him. He felt her face over his shoulder, watching his heart stay true.

They entered a bar with a picture of a donkey hanging above the door. Soldiers from Fort Bliss sat at tiny round tables, and Mexican girls sat on most of their laps. On the stage, three chubby Mexican girls swayed half-heartedly but fully unclothed. He had told Paulette that he had smoked marijuana a few times, and even though the smell of it in the air here called to him, he resisted because Paulette hung up the phone on him and wouldn't take his calls for a week.

The bartender poured tequila into their shot glasses, and everyone shot it except Willie. He looked at the blank faces on all the whores, and he wanted to run to the phone and call Paulette and tell her he was going home tomorrow to marry her then and there.

He pushed away his shot glass and walked out. He hailed a taxi, and as they drove, he started seeing red lights everywhere—on houses, on top of buildings, halfway up the mountain. People used red lights here instead of white lights.

At home, his roommate's pot pipe sat stuffed full on the table in front of the television. So many ballplayers talked about how it relaxed them, and tonight Willie needed that so he sat down and lit it up. He coughed on the first inhalation and on the second, and it felt like he was breathing in little pieces of dry, scratchy hay. And then he sneezed over and over. He got up and could still smell the place, smell those poor girls, and he showered and didn't even towel off as he staggered into bed.

The mean sun woke him early. He thought about Paulette as he lay there, and after he had a glass of water he half ran to the pay phone to call her. She did this to him—she made him run for her letters and run to the phone to call her and drive fast to see her.

She answered the phone on the second ring, and he heard himself stuttering before he even started to talk.

"Puh-puh-Paulette," he said.

"Hello, Willie," she said softly. And her softness made his cheeks relax and his throat ease, and suddenly he felt the stutter cease its hold on him as it usually did once he heard her voice.

"Paulette, I'm comin' back to see you in two weeks," he said. "We finish the season next week, then I'm gonna meet with the Angels' staff and then fly on back to see you."

"Willie," she said, "something has changed. You've changed. And I was gonna wait to tell you face to face, but I don't want you to lose time. I joined the army."

He looked out of the glass phone booth at two guys jacking hubcaps off the cars parked along the street in front of him. He wanted to say things, but his tongue felt like it was getting twisted deep in his throat.

"You crazy, Paulette," he said. "Why the hell you go and do somethin' crazy like that for?"

He heard her breathe and thought he heard her crying but couldn't be quite sure.

"I think you're changin', Willie," she said. "I think you're gonna be a big ballplayer, and you're changin'. Those stories you told me about trying marijuana. I know you didn't like it. But you left me Willie, and you're gonna keep leavin' me with that baseball life. I got to build my own life. I can't count on you."

"You sayin' cuh-cuh-crazy things, Paulette," he said. He had told her a few weeks ago that he had tried pot, but he told her because he hated it and missed her and never thought she would judge him for it. *But she did,* he thought. *She judged me.*

"You're bein' a fuh-fuh-fool, Paulette," he said. And suddenly he felt his stutter welling up, rising in his throat and confounding his tongue, and he instantly decided he wasn't going to talk more so she wouldn't hear it.

"I'm sending your ring back to you, Willie," she said. "I'm sending it back today. I don't want to hurt you, but this is the best thing for both of us. And I hope you become Reggie Jackson. I know you will."

And five seconds became 30 seconds, and he thought he heard her sniffle.

And then she said it again just before she hung up: "I know you will."

I know I will, too, he thought. *I will.*

HE DIDN'T GET CALLED UP to the big leagues, though, so he flew to Charlotte because he wanted to go home. He felt right at home as soon as Cuda and their friend Raymond Brown picked him up in Raymond's new Pontiac Grand Prix T-Top. Cuda was drinking a beer and driving and talking about the car's pickup as he brought it up to 95 mph.

Willie sat in the back seat and felt higher than they were, like the car was elevated in the rear so that as they drove into Seneca he was like a king coming home in his carriage.

"Take me straight to my mother's," Willie said. "I'll just let her know I'm here, and then we'll shoot some pool!"

Workers were planting bushes around the sign at the entrance as they drove in. *This is a fine place*, Willie thought as he noticed the lawn trimmed right up to the curb and the sharp white paint on the buildings.

Cille opened the brown door and stood in front of the metal screen door looking at Willie.

"Hi, Cille," he said.

"Just a minute and I'll figure out this lock," she said back.

She jiggled the lock, and Willie studied her there in a big purple sweater as the air conditioning rushed out even on this mild October day.

She pulled open the door and looked at him for a second but then looked down as he walked through the door.

A gold frame with a blonde, praying Jesus sat on a table looking straight at the door, and little prayer booklets lay on the table in front of it.

Willie turned back and watched her as she closed the door and walked back across her room to the chair beside the air conditioner.

"How you doin', Cille?" he asked.

"Fine, Willie, just fine."

He walked to the gold-colored couch beside her and sat. He sunk down, and his knees were level with his head.

"Jean told me you're a Jehovah's Witness now, Cille," he said.

"Yes I am, Willie. I have found the way, and I have no need for nothing in this world except the Lord."

"That is good, thuh-thuh-that is good, Cille," he said.

They sat there together without speaking for several minutes, and he got up and looked around the room at all the religious magazines and Bibles and Bible story books.

"I am pruh-pruh-proud of you, Cille," he said.

She nodded without smiling and reached for the television guide.

"I'm going to Greenville to buy a Pontiac Grand Prix, and I'll be around here for a few weeks. We'll go out to dinner, Cille."

She reached for her glasses, slowly put them on, and looked up at him.

"That would be a nice thing to do," she said.

He smiled.

"Okay, Cille. I'll stop back in a couple days. Nice seein' you here."

"Yes," she said.

He let himself out, and as he walked to the car he saw Cuda holding a pocketbook mirror to his nose and Raymond sneezing and laughing.

HE WORKED OUT every day in Seneca and arrived at spring training in the best shape of his life. But there was a logjam at first base in Anaheim, so the Angels sent him to their Triple A club in Salt Lake. When the announcer there called him to the plate, the crowd would clap in unison and chant *Wil-lie! Wil-lie!* just like *Reg-gie! Reg-gie!* And he would oblige. And when he would walk off after home runs, men, women, and children would shout, "Big Willie! Big Willie!"

Jimy Williams gave him the last piece in the curveball puzzle. He called Willie the ballerina because Willie would arch his front leg right up on the big toe and hold it there like a dancer holds a position.

"All you need is a tutu," Jimy said.

But Willie felt the power from that high toe—it pushed his center of gravity up into his hips and belly by holding his leg that high.

"You can keep doing that," Jimy said. "Hell, I've seen flat feet and angled feet, and guys try to wait with their toes up in the air. But the key is to get that foot back on the ground before the pitcher releases the ball, Willie. You want to do your pump and get it planted almost instantaneously with the release of the pitch. That's how your real power is gonna come. And that's gonna allow you to adjust to the curveball. You can't adjust if you still have your foot up in the air!"

He listened. And he adjusted. And he kept hitting like a star. He pretended in each at-bat that he was hitting for the Milwaukee Brewers or Baltimore Orioles or whoever wanted him.

But he grew more solitary.

He pulled up beside a park one night and sat there with his windows down and sunroof back, and he felt lonelier than he had ever felt. *They never prepare you for all this moving around*, he thought.

He realized he felt less lonely when his car was moving, so he started the car.

At the next light a kid in the car beside him honked. Willie looked over, and the guy motioned to him then motioned down the road. There was a line of lights but otherwise an empty street.

"Let's go!" the kid shouted.

Willie realized what he meant after a few seconds and looked at the kid's car. *You've got to be kidding me*, he thought. *A black Trans-Am. You've got to be kidding me.*

He nodded to the kid. Willie caught up to him after about 500 feet and then pulled even, and the road was so straight that he could look at the kid while he drove. He had a big nose and crazy eyes and a crew cut. He shook his fist at Willie not as a challenge but with glee. And that is when Willie hit the brakes. *I'm giving a punk the night of his life but Bobby Knoop told me once to never fuck up again and I ain't going to fool with some punk kid at midnight in Salt Lake.*

And then the flashing red lights came up from behind them. Willie pulled over so the cop zeroed in on the kid, and he pulled over, too. The cop motioned to Willie to pull forward, and he sat there while the cop talked to the kid. And then the kid pulled away. And the cop walked back to Willie.

"You having a good time tonight?" the cop said as he walked slightly past the window and bent over.

Willie could see his hand on his gun in the rearview mirror.

"Lost my head fuh-fuh-for a minute, officer. That kuh-kuh-kid challenged me, and I just luh-luh-lost my head," Willie said.

"Get out of the car, please."

Willie counted the beers he'd had as he got out and knew he would be fine. *Five beers and I'm fine.*

But the cop suddenly pushed Willie up against the hood of the car and handcuffed him. He pushed his face so hard against the hood that his teeth cut into his cheek, and then the cop jerked him backward and pushed him to the squad car and pushed him into the backseat. And all Willie could do was wonder where Bobby Knoop was. *Probably still in Iowa teaching rookies and telling them not to fuck up, and here I am fucking up just like I promised him I wouldn't.*

They allowed him his phone call, and Jimy Williams had been through far worse at 3:00 AM, so when Willie stuttered out what had happened Jimy didn't miss a beat. He had learned to do this in his sleep. He arrived at the jail within half an hour, signed the paperwork, posted bail in 15 minutes, and drove Willie to the pound to pick up his car.

He was silent the whole time, but not angry silent. *Sleepy silent,* Willie realized from the beginning, and that was good.

As Willie got out of the car he walked around to the driver's side and pinched Jimy on the elbow.

"No more drag racing," Jimy said.

Willie smiled.

"I never drag raced in my life," he said. "I play pool and cards, Jimy. Duh-duh-don't worry about that. Just somethin' got into me."

"Well, I hope this got it out of ya. Ballpark at 2:30."

And Willie started to realize it was true—a ballplayer, a good one, can get away with just about anything. *You keep hittin', you keep gettin' away with it.*

WILLIE ARRIVED AT 2:15, and the owner of the Gulls was standing in front of the locker room with his arms folded. But Willie noticed his face was not an angry face.

As Willie drew closer in the narrow dim hallway, the owner dropped his arms and started walking toward him.

"Willie, you don't worry about a thing," he said. "No police officer is going to treat one of my players like they treated you last night."

Willie stopped and looked down at the owner. He expected a reprimand, a fatherly warning in keeping with the pattern that was starting to evolve. But as the owner spoke, he started moving his arms all around and his voice rose and squeaked and he talked so fast that it took Willie a minute to understand that the owner was listing all his players who'd had incidents with the police.

"I-I-I never had no problem with the puh-puh-police before, sir," Willie said, feeling deep down that he still needed to explain himself.

The owner stopped talking and suddenly looked enraged.

"You don't have to explain anything, you just keep hitting that ball like you have been. That's all you need to do, and I will take care of the rest. You're selling out this stadium every night for me, young man. You don't worry about anything but those home runs."

A few mornings later the phone rang in his apartment at 7:00 AM, and it took him a moment to realize it was Jimy saying, "Good morning, Willie," as if he had been up for hours already. Willie sat in the chair beside the phone and readied himself for some news on the police and punishment by the Angels.

"Pack your bags, Willie," he said. "You're headed up, son. You're on a flight at 12:30, and they want you there for tonight's game."

He felt the phone shake in his hand, and his toes curled up.

"Jimy, uh uh I, ah, what am I gonna do with my car then?"

Jimy laughed so hard that Willie grew perturbed. He felt like he felt sometimes with Raymond and Cuda when they laughed and he didn't understand why.

"By the way, Willie, you've got to wear a suit and tie. You call me if you have any questions."

He walked to his closet and took out his white suit and black tie and decided not to even shower. He put them on with a white shirt and white shoes, too, and stood at the mirror.

He used to visit his aunt and she would give him candies and bake him pies, and whenever he finished she sat there with him at the kitchen table and said "You handsome devil!"

He looked at himself and chuckled.

You handsome devil, he said to himself in the mirror. *You handsome major league devil.*

HE GOT ON BASE in his second plate appearance against Ferguson Jenkins and the Red Sox that night. It was a sharp shot to the shortstop that the scorekeeper ruled an error at first but then later changed to a single. He had 91 at-bats in 42 games as a first baseman, pinch-hitter, and occasional DH and hit .198 with no homers and six RBIs. And the day he was sent back down to the minor leagues, an assistant coach walked by his locker and handed him an airplane ticket and said, "See you in September, kid."

The flight back to Salt Lake was the first time he had experienced turbulence, and a woman in the seat next to him grabbed his hand and closed her eyes and started praying. He started praying with her.

As the taxi dropped him off at his apartment complex, he saw the Mormon babysitter that many of his teammates used walking on the sidewalk. He had heard stories about her, too, but didn't want to believe them. He noticed her turn to walk his way as the taxi pulled up to the curb. He gave the driver what he had and realized he didn't have enough cash.

"Cuh-cuh-can you wait here a minute? I'll run up and get you the rest."

The driver nodded and smiled and as he got out of the car the girl was right there in front of him. She had long brown hair and wore a baseball undershirt with blue arms and a gray body and the blue word "Gulls" on the front. Her jeans were bell-bottoms all the more belled because she was barefoot.

"Huh-huh-hi, I'm Willie," he said.

"I know your name is Willie," she said.

"Cuh-cuh-can you wait here with my bags a minute? I got to run upstairs and get some more dough to pay the tuh-tuh-taxi driver."

She smiled and stuck her hand in her pocket.

"I got $5, you can pay me back," she said.

He looked at her hand holding the $5 bill and her fingernail polish was pink.

"Uh, I can't do that," he said. "I can't borrow money from a young girl like you."

She laughed.

"I'll come up with you right now. You can pay me right back and a dollar more in interest!"

His eyebrows tightened as he looked at her, and she pushed the bill into his hand before he could even lift it.

"Thank you," he said.

He paid the driver, who smiled again and asked him how to get out of the complex. The girl stepped in front of Willie and explained.

Willie lifted his bag and she led him down the sidewalk and up the two flights of stairs to his apartment. They didn't speak the whole time, and she didn't look at him the whole time, but walked right in as he opened the door and sat on the couch.

He set his bags in the bedroom, took $7 out of the drawer, and walked out and handed them to her.

She looked at him and slowly raised her hand to take the money then lifted her bottom off the couch and stuffed it in her back jeans pocket.

"Yuh-yuh-yuh-you Mormon ain't ya?" he said.

"Yes. We're Mormon," she said with a smile that unsettled him.

"Okay, then, it was nice seeing you," he said.

"You haven't seen me," she said. "Don't you want to see me like your teammates have seen me?"

He squeezed his cheeks into his teeth and looked at the floor.

"Yuh-yuh-yes, I guess I do," he said.

"You don't have kids so I can't babysit for you, but I thought you should still see what they've seen."

And she showed him, and when they finished, she leaned over the bed and reached into her jeans and took out a piece of gum and started blowing bubbles in bed.

"Where you been dressed in a suit like that?" she asked in between bubbles.

He looked out the window that faced her family's apartment.

"I been in the big leagues. And nuh-nuh-now I'm back here for a while."

She turned and blew one so close to his face that the air blew out onto him as it popped.

"Well then, maybe I'll come back tomorrow."

She got up and dressed, bending over and twisting and tying and snapping right there in front of him, and she didn't say another word as she walked out, and he heard her footsteps down the stairwell.

He lay there looking at the ceiling. His wrists felt sore, and he thought back to the plane ride and grabbing the armrest and holding the lady's hand with the wings bouncing up and down, and he wondered if you become a big leaguer and fly all over the country how many times that happens if you fly that much.

He played 77 games for the Gulls that season and hit .336 with 14 home runs and 73 RBIs. And when the day for September call-ups came, he picked up his white suit at the dry cleaners.

He packed his bags at the apartment and filled boxes with newspaper clippings. He left them in the hallway—he paid a clubhouse attendant to come get them and ship them for him—and drove to the ballpark. Along the way he bought a chocolate milkshake and burger with extra bacon and ate it while he drove.

He walked into the clubhouse with his shake gurgling as he sucked at the straw. The list was posted on the wall just inside the door—Rance Mulliniks was at the top, then Tom Donohue, and three pitchers. He walked into Jimy's office, and Jimy was sitting there in the chair waiting for him, and before Willie could say anything Jimy just said, "I don't know, Willie. I just don't know."

"Ain't right, Jimy," Willie said. "I didn't get no rhythm up there playing as little as they played me. No man could hit well like that. Then I come back down here, and I'm the best hitter in the league, Jimy. You know that. Everybody know that."

"Now you go home for a while and then I'm suggesting to them you play winter ball in Mexico, in Obregon."

Willie dropped his head and felt tears push at his eyelids, but his eyelids pushed them back and he looked back up at Jimy.

"Okay, thanks Jimy," he said. "I thuh-thuh-thank you for all you done for me."

Jimy nodded and smiled slightly as Willie turned, fully unaware that Willie walked right out of the locker room and drove his Grand Prix straight to Anaheim and parked right in front of the Angels front office and asked to see the general manager. He sat there waiting for 20 minutes and knew he looked angry because the receptionist at the Angels office spilled a cup of soda and finally got up and disappeared for 10 minutes with the soda slowly dripping off her desk onto the floor. Finally she reappeared and still looked frightened but nodded up and down. Willie stood and followed her into a conference room where the baseball brain trust sat.

"So wuh-wuh-wuh-what's up?" he said. He knew he would stutter, but he didn't care. *That way they'll know I'm angry*, he thought. *Stutter away.*

"Willie, you have great future, and we want to see that future...."

He cut the man short.

"My fuh-fuh-future is now," he said. "You all should've called me up. I'm a ballplayer since I was a little child, and you're makin' a mistake here and you know it."

Willie finally realized that Tom Sommers, the director of the Angels' minor league system, was there, and as Tom began to speak, Willie felt ashamed at the thought of telling Coach McNeil and Coach Shaver why he didn't get called up.

Sommers talked like they talked, slowly and carefully, and Willie liked that.

"Willie, you are doing everything we want you to do," he said. "You got the curveball down. You're playing a fine first base. I am placing you with a team in Obregon, and you go down there and keep learning. You're gonna be a star, but we don't need stars right now. We need parts and pieces. You be patient. You're a Christian, right? Patience. One of the Christian virtues. Be patient."

I am, but I'm a ballplayer first, Willie thought. But he nodded and pretended patience at least for that moment and walked out of the office and out of the building. And he hopped in the car and drove the same way back to Seneca, South Carolina.

HE SPENT THE WHOLE of the 1978 season in Salt Lake, too, and hit .326 with 29 home runs and 110 RBIs. The steadfast believers called him regularly and cajoled him into patience. Bobby Knoop, Jimy, Sommers—sometimes he thought they set up a calendar amongst themselves to call him and coach him, these baseball ministers. He was as patient with his progress as he was with batting and fielding, and he drove slower and rejected the Mormon babysitter's advances and sent money home to Cille and called her three times a week.

And he never got called up. He played winter ball in Mexico. He did not touch a drug or a woman save for a short romance with a nurse in Mexico the second winter. He read a lot, took BP every day, and relied on his phone chats with Tom Sommers about faith and the righteous life more than ever.

He made the team out of spring training in 1979 and finished the season with 21 home runs and had 81 RBIs as the Angels edged the Royals for first place in the American League West.

But on September 18—in Kansas City—he was sliding into second base and felt his knee get trapped under his body. He needed surgery to repair the ligaments and cartilage, but one day during his physical therapy his agent Ron Shapiro called him and told him he had been traded—to Kansas City. *I could have just stayed there after I got hurt,* he thought. Then he thought something even more practical: *Get ready, Kansas City, 'cause here I come.* And then he kept humming the words to the song to himself: they've got some crazy little women there, and I'm gonna get me one.

3

Hellfire George and His Band of Merry Pranksters Are Coming to Burn Your Town Down

1980

Willie sat in the outfield in the soft Fort Myers sunlight and watched as George Brett walked out of the dugout like Southern California herself emerging to show Florida what real radiance is.

It was the first morning of spring training in 1980, and Willie felt sharp in the Royals blue.

"Mullet Head!"

Four or five guys shouted at the same time, and Brett shook his head and began to stutter step down the third-base line toward the outfield.

"Mullet Head is here!"

Brett gave a prolonged raise of his two middle fingers to his catcallers, and the players laughed, each with his own vernacular laughter—Detroit ghetto rat-a-tat and Iowa farm boy chuckle and New Jersey cackle and Southern throw-your-head-back-and-enjoy.

U.L. Washington and Amos Otis had explained to Willie that morning that every player on the Royals had a nickname and that theirs were U.L. and A.O.

"But U.L. ain't a nickname, that's your initials," Willie said.

"Some guys here ain't smart enough to realize that," U.L. said.

"So what's you're nickname, Willie?"

"Well, buh-buh-back home they call me Mick, and they cuh-cuh-call my uncle Big Mick 'cause his name's Willie, too."

Washington and Otis looked at each other, then started to laugh and couldn't stop. But then Otis patted him on the back and Washington did, too. They patted him together as if to push him to laugh with them, and he did. And they kept laughing as they dressed, and someone took out a *Hustler* magazine and they laughed some more as they passed it around.

He liked manager Jim Frey, who met Willie the day he almost hit a ball out of Memorial Stadium back in Baltimore when he was 19 and played for the Johnnies. Frey, a coach for the Orioles, felt fatherly to him then, and the way Frey walked and looked at Willie made him still seem fatherly six years later.

And he liked the vibe of the team. *Country boys with funny mustaches, black dudes with 'fros of different shapes and sizes, and California George. Waylon Jennings, Kool and the Gang, and I bet George there even listens to the damn Beach Boys.*

But he didn't like the turf. The Royals had put down artificial turf in Fort Myers to replicate the new, rock-hard turf in Kansas City. And they succeeded right down to the precise, knee-buckling hardness. It was as hard as Seneca clay in the driest days of the South Carolina summer, and just walking on it made Willie aware of the little collisions that took place inside his knees with every step.

He got up and looked at the players starting to gather around the batting cage. Players called out his name, and he felt surprised that they knew him already.

A reporter asked him about the knee.

"I'm at 80 percent," Willie said. "But that's in the field. I'm ready to be your cleanup hitter. I'm at 100 percent with the bat."

He lied. He hadn't hit all winter because the knee hurt so much. He hadn't taken a ground ball. And here the entire team was certain they had found the slugger they missed last year after the Royals had finally jettisoned John Mayberry. When the Royals traded for Willie that off-season, they knew he'd had surgery to clean up the knee. But the doctors said it was minor and wouldn't affect him on the field. Wrong.

My destiny all these days has been to be the cleanup hitter for the Kansas City Royals; my destiny was to get George Brett better pitches to hit in front of me; my destiny was to be the only hitter who could hit for power in a ballpark as massive as Royals Stadium. And now here I am with a gimpy knee.

"How's the knee, Willie?"

He tried to figure out who in the group was asking, but instead of making eye contact with the questioner he announced for all to hear.

"Hundred percent," he said.

He stepped into the batting cage after about half an hour of watching line-drive hitters, and he understood that this was really his first game even though it was just the first BP of spring training.

It felt like his heart had dropped to his knee it was throbbing so much. The cartilage and bones were making such a racket he worried the guys hanging on the cage could hear. He thought about the pickup basketball game he played last month and worried he had reinjured himself. He worried the Royals might find out. He lined a couple balls to the gaps, and then he noticed George Brett and Frank White standing together watching him.

And then it stopped. The pulsing in his knee, the pain, his whole awareness of his knee. He launched balls methodically at first, then ravenously. His teammates grew silent. They stayed silent as he walked off and flipped his bat. He walked in the path of Brett and White and waited for them to beckon him. He knew they would, and they did.

He turned on a dime even though his knee was returning to its previous place in his consciousness.

"Mr. Brett, I am your new teammate Willie Aikens," he said.

Brett threw his head back and laughed.

"Why in the world are you talking to me that way, Willie?" he said. "I know who the hell you are! Your name is Mick!"

WILLIE STAYED QUIET for the first week. He stayed to himself.

He went slowly on the field, trying to hide the knee. He fell asleep at night with an ice pack around it and thought he got frostbite. The knee stayed red for three days, and he wrapped two towels around himself on the way to the shower to make sure no one saw it.

He spoke little, trying to hide the stutter.

But the clubhouse was like nothing he had known. Crazy cats, cool cats, odd cats all. And he started to unhide, to speak. And then after another week he didn't stop speaking, stutter and all. The stutter was just another part of the cultural kaleidoscope.

His locker was between Willie Wilson and Amos Otis. Hal McRae, the team *padrino*, already watched over him—as he would do, along with George, with varying degrees of success and frustration for the next 30 years.

A reporter asked him for an interview after his best day of batting practice, and even though Jim Frey had publicly said he was thinking about batting Willie fifth or sixth, Willie told the reporter he was here to bat cleanup and he was here to help George Brett get better pitches and he was here to put the team over the top and into the World Series.

The next day Jim Frey called him into his office.

"How are you, Willie?"

"I'm guh-guh-great, Jim. I met you back in buh-buh-Baltimore, Jim."

"Yes you did, Willie. I remember your shots during BP there. I told John Schuerholz to trade for you. You're my first baseman for the season, Willie. But I understand from some writers that you want to bat cleanup for me. I think you should focus on getting your knee all healed, and let me focus on the lineup. Those sorts of things tend to sort themselves out, Willie."

Willie nodded but didn't speak. He didn't want to stutter in front of Frey. He nodded again and wanted to hold up four fingers but figured he'd show him on the field.

Three weeks later, Frey called him aside as he was jogging off the field after a final workout before heading north. Willie stopped on a dime with his bad leg leading to show Frey he was tiptop ready.

"Willie, you're my cleanup hitter," Frey said.

Willie grinned.

"Thuh-thuh-thank you, Jim."

"Now don't go talking to the writers. And sometimes against tough lefties I'm going to separate you and George and plug in Hal or Amos at cleanup. So don't go taking it the wrong way when I do."

"Ain't nuh-nuh-nuthin' you do I'd take the wrong way, Jim. I-I-I like you since the first time I met you back in Baltimore."

MY GODDAMN NAME. Why in hell did my mother and that obstetrician give me that goddamn middle name?

The fans booed and went on booing as if his name was destiny, as if his name predetermined his batting average and power output.

It had all gone wrong so quickly. He forgot to wait on the curveballs that seemed to drop a split second later and drop harder than any curveball he had ever seen. And his knee flared up. *Bitch,* he called to his knee. *You bitch, flaring up like that.* He couldn't bend to dig out balls, and George Brett would scowl at him across the diamond when the ball would spin in the dirt after Willie dropped it.

He wanted to please George as much as he wanted to please Jim Frey. Manager Frey, he called him to his face, in interviews, and with the other players. Willie always remembered who got him here.

But the Kansas City fans quickly grew frustrated with their suddenly petulant new cleanup hitter, and the press, in this case the *Kansas City Star*, took note:

So you don't love Willie Aikens? So he hasn't knocked the strobe lights off the top of the crown on the Royals' scoreboard, and he hasn't woven any silk with his defense.

So he hasn't been Maysian, as his middle name would have it. Or Ruthian, or even Mayberryish, and you don't love him for it?

If Aikens loses any sleep, it won't be over that. He has tuned out Kansas City fans. Monday night he finally did what they were brainwashed into demanding of him every at-bat, hit a home run at Royals Stadium, and the expectant crowd roared, most likely while muttering under the applause, "About time."

Dead silence after the home run wouldn't have surprised Aikens, nor mattered. "Every time I made an out early in the season, they booed," he said before the game Tuesday against the Rangers. "I didn't appreciate that. It turned me against the fans here some, to a point. I don't think it's right to boo me like that, then cheer when I hit it out of the park. So I'm not going out to play for the fans, I'm playing for me and the team. If they don't cheer for me, okay, and if they do, they can."

ONE DAY FREY approached him in the dugout just before the game.

"Willie, I know that knee is hurting you, but the doctors said it is healing fine," Frey said. "You got to believe in yourself. I ain't going to pull you because of a slump."

Jim Frey. They called him a baseball man. To Willie, that meant part father, part grump, and part pastor.

In the locker room he felt embarrassed by his stutter again. He talked less with the players and even less with the reporters.

Lying in bed one night he realized that all anyone cared about in this world was how he hit a ball.

On June 19, 1980, he was batting in Cleveland and he struck out. Not on anything nasty or praiseworthy but on junk. And he lost it. He threw his bat—after the game he would tell reporters it slid out of his hands because he had switched to a 35-inch, 32-ounce bat instead of a 35-inch, 33-ounce bat—but he really threw it. And the projectile that it became slowly somersaulted in the air, reached its summit and, gaining speed on its descent, shot straight down and nearly killed Amos Otis. *Imagine if I had killed Amos Otis*, he thought. *Decapitated the brother. A guy everybody thought should be Willie Mays decapitating Amos Otis. Imagine how Kansas City would boo me then.*

Gentleman Jim reached out and grabbed Willie.

"What the hell do you think you are doing, Willie?" he said. "Grow up, son. You are going to kill someone."

Frey never benched him, but he pulled him twice for pinch-hitters in the next few games. And Willie mastered a new walk: truculent, angry, menacing.

At the end of June, George Brett was hitting .337.

IN THE SECOND INNING of the opening game of a series against the Brewers, Jim Gantner hit a slow roller down the first-base line and Willie barehanded it. As he gripped it he thought to himself, *I just made a fine play. Let them watch that replay. I just barehanded it.*

But a ball in a bare hand to Jim Gantner was like a red cape to a bull—he charged the hand and knocked the ball loose and clapped his hands overzealously as he pounded the bag with his foot and came to a stop down the line.

The boos were mixed with laughter—and in the crowd he heard Guy Webb laughing at him, too.

Laugh, he said. *Go ahead and laugh you lawyers and truck drivers and dentists and accountants. Try to play this damn game.*

In the seventh inning Charlie Moore hit a tapper down the first-base line. Willie was holding the runner and got distracted for a second, and as the runner took off he kicked some dirt back into Willie's eyes. As he reached down for the ball, suddenly he thought about the fans laughing again, and just as he went to squeeze the ball he felt his thumb on the lacing of the ball and not on its fat middle and he felt the ball snap out. He just stood there for a second, staring at the ball and wondering if God were turning against him.

Darrell Porter made another error, and the Brewers had three hits in the inning and scored five runs.

Willie was booed as he walked off the field with his head down, and as he came to bat in the bottom of the eighth inning it felt like the whole stadium, even the women and children, were a bunch of wolves waiting for him.

They started as he stood in the on-deck circle.

"Don't forget to lift your skirt before you bend for the ball next time, Aikens!"

"Bring back Mayberry!"

"I shuh-shuh-shouldn't even buh-buh-be the duh-duh-designated hi-hi-hitter!"

He clobbered the first pitch. Just pummeled it. It went off the top of the wall and drove in a run. As he stood at second base, Royals Stadium was silent.

At least I shut them up, he thought. But then through the silence a little boy's booing triggered the laughter of what felt like the whole stadium again.

On July 20, George Brett was hitting .375.

HIS FIRST GROUPIE as a Royal sat on a stool at the end of the bar where women who sought Royals went to sit at the Sheraton. As soon as he walked in a few men grumbled, and he wanted to take a bottle and smash it over each of their heads.

Try to do what I do, he thought. *In Royals Stadium,* he thought. *Try to do what I am trying to do in this ballpark and then grumble at me. And put your ties back on while you're at it.*

He went up to the bar, ordered his screwdriver, and downed it with a gusto that he intended as a show for the people watching him, and they understood and looked away. And then the bartender gave him another. Willie looked at it and smiled.

"You'll break out of it, Willie," the bartender said. He said the same thing last week, and last week Willie nodded and winked at him, but tonight he just kept staring at the mirror trying to separate the vodka from the orange juice in his mouth before he swallowed.

"You said the same thing last week," Willie said.

Then he saw her sitting there watching him. Watching but not watching. Not watching, but watching. She had long blonde hair, a tiny nose, and a long back that was not covered by her dress.

He waited for the right song, and then the always reliable Marvin Gaye came on. There was a tiny wood dance floor at the end of the bar. No one was dancing, and as he sucked the remains of the screwdriver out of the ice in his glass he realized he could test her and say fuck you to them all at the same time.

He gently placed the glass on the bar, walked over to her smiling, and looked into her face in the mirror behind the bar as she lifted her head to meet his gaze in the mirror, too.

"Would you like to dance?" he asked. She did not smile.

"I would like to do some cocaine," she said. "We can dance first, though, if you would like to."

He did want to, though he was about as good at dancing as he was at fielding grounders. But he wanted to dance so someone would say something about him dancing on a bad knee or about his fielding being as good as his dancing or about him dancing for all to see with a white woman.

Everyone watched as she danced far better than he did. He tried to twirl her once, and that move got all screwed up, too.

At the end of the second song she mouthed the word: coke.

He took her by the hand, and she followed him with her head down as they walked past everyone and out of the bar, but as they got to the door he realized he hadn't paid.

He went back toward the bar but the bartender waved him off and smiled and Willie smiled back. And he took her home and she laid out the lines of coke for them on his kitchen table and he realized that this lady from Wichita had to work a few things out of her system, too, and that for a while this dark night they could work those things out of their systems together, and that this thing called cocaine might just help them do so.

AT THE END of the month, George Brett was hitting .390.

So easy. As Willie watched him from the dugout he noticed everyone else in the dugout sat like a fan. Normally, guys chatted or poured a cup of coffee or went into the clubhouse. The other guy was doing his job, and a few would watch but never with the steady attention of a fan. Never like this.

"He's a man on fire," someone on the bench said.

And Willie wondered where George's fire came from. The guy hit and hit and hit. He hit the nasty curves and the high, hard stuff and waited on change-ups with a smile on his face.

Willie hadn't been on fire in three months, and the possibility that the fire would never return crossed his mind for the first time. He had never had a moment of self-doubt—periods of failure were the fault of managers or his bum knee.

He had never heard the word *mojo* before, but once he heard it he knew he had lost it.

A.O. was sitting next to him as George lined a single past the first baseman.

"Vegas will get you your mojo back," he said to Willie. "Come to Vegas with me and my wife during the break."

Willie looked at George as he stood on the first-base bag. He pushed his batting helmet down tighter on his head and spit tobacco juice in a brown arc. His eyes darted from the pitcher to the catcher, but his eyes were always darting from one thing to another all the time.

HE TOOK AN EARLIER flight to Vegas than A.O. and Beverly and, after he handed the porter his suitcase, headed straight to the blackjack tables. And he lost and lost and lost. As he sat there a blonde woman occasionally rubbed her knee up against his leg, but he kept moving it away from her. *A.O. thought I would get my mojo back, but he didn't point out that my bad mojo on the ballfield could carry over here,* Willie thought. *He didn't think about that, did he?*

And just as he was about to walk away—from the table and the blonde and maybe even from the booing fans of Kansas City and baseball altogether—he won. Then he won again and again, and by the time A.O. and Beverly found him at 5:00 he had chips piled all around him, and people found out who he was, and a small crowd was gathered round watching Willie Mays take on the house.

He started to bet $500 on each hand and was playing two and three hands at a time.

At 8:30 A.O. and Beverly came back from dinner.

"I think we are going to call it a night," A.O. said to Willie.

Willie laughed.

"First take these chips and cash them for me," Willie said. "I want you to see how much I won."

Beverly helped A.O., and they came back with a receipt for $15,000.

"One more hand then I'll come with you," Willie said.

The blonde turned suddenly to face him.

"I got it back," he said. "I got to go rest 'cause I got it back now. But we'll catch up."

He played $1,000 on one more hand and won again. And then he kissed the blonde on the cheek and walked away.

In the elevator on the way to his room, he thought about what George was doing at the All-Star Game. And he knew when they saw each other again he was going to be the hitter George needed behind him to get to .400. It was back.

THE NEXT DAY before the Royals' game against Detroit, Willie walked into the clubhouse and walked up to George.

"I'm guh-guh-gonna be the cleanup hitter this half you thuh-thuh-thought I was going to be, George," he said.

George smiled, and a few reporters wrote down what Willie said.

"O-o-o-o-kuh-kuh-kay, Willie," George said as everyone laughed.

In the last game of the opening series of the season back in April, Sparky Anderson had walked Hal McRae to pitch to Willie.

Willie hit a two-run single to give the Royals a 3–2 win.

But after the game Sparky said, "I will walk McRae and pitch to Aikens a thousand times."

Someone had taped that April article with that quote to Willie's locker. He walked in and read it over and over. Then he read it out loud and didn't stutter once.

This night the game was tied 2–2 when Willie came up to hit in the sixth. The pitcher Milt Wilcox had been wild enough all night to keep the Royals hitters off balance. His ball was darting into the left-handers' knees, and Willie came to the plate wondering if Wilcox would hit him on purpose this time.

Wilcox came within a whisker of hitting him indeed, and Willie wanted to believe that he tried to hit him on purpose, even though it was just another pitch down and in.

"You luh-luh-lettin' him get away with that?" Willie said to the umpire.

The umpire grunted.

And suddenly Willie felt it. He felt like he felt two nights ago in Vegas. He looked into the dugout at A.O.

The next pitch he saw more clearly than he had seen a ball all year, and he sent it straight back over the center-field wall.

As he rounded the bases his calf felt like a bullet had hit it. On his way to home plate, he contemplated what to do about Sparky.

Pitch to me a thousand times, he thought.

But then the bullet in his calf stung more and more and he almost doubled over. The trainer, Mickey Cobb, met him at home plate and helped him to the dugout.

"Pitch to me a thuh-thuh-thousand times," he said.

"Maybe 999 from now on," Mickey said.

George slapped Willie on the back as Mickey helped him down the dugout steps.

In the trainer's room after the game, Mickey kept icing and rubbing the calf. Through the open door Willie could see all the reporters crowded around George's locker as usual.

Jim Frey walked in and nodded.

"Hey, big fellow, you're second on the team in RBIs," Frey said. "We're nine-and-a-half games up on the White Sox and 10½ on the Rangers. You're doing what we brought you here to do."

"Thanks, Jim," Willie said. "But I'm going to stuh-stuh-start doing it even better for you from nuh-nuh-now on."

THE ORIOLES WERE STARTING to meander out of the dugout as Frank Robinson stood in the batting cage on the left side of the batter's box. Willie stood behind him as Robinson twisted his hips and dug his feet deeper into the dirt.

A few Orioles paused, stared, and continued on. A few Royals watched from their dugout.

Willie said to Robinson behind the cage, "Hey there, Muh-muh-Mr. Robinson! I almost hit one out of Memorial Stadium, too."

Robinson laughed. He had been the only player to ever hit a ball completely out of the stadium in Baltimore. Willie had met Robinson when Walter Youse brought him to the park all those afternoons in 1974 to shag fly balls.

"You're still calling me Mr. Robinson, Willie. You got to stop that now. You're a grown man."

Willie was hitting .365 since July 3. He had a seven-game hitting streak coming into the night. And his overall average rose to .287.

"Huh-huh-how about a few pointers like the old days?"

Robinson looked at him and laughed.

"So you can come out and kill us in a couple hours?"

Then Robinson tightened his jaw, and his smile faded. He stepped into the batter's box on his normal right side then looked at Willie and switched to his left.

"Earlier in the year I saw this."

He made a whole body swing with his arms trailing his torso like a rag doll. Willie laughed.

"Then you started to do this."

Robinson swung more modestly, but Willie noticed his hands were still trailing his body this time.

Robinson nodded to the batting practice pitcher and stepped into the box. He drove the ball into deep left field. He nodded to the pitcher again and shot one to dead-away center. He nodded one last time and took the ball to right.

A few players from each team gathered around the cage and stared. Robinson limped. He was right-handed. And he just hit a ball more smoothly and sweetly than most of them could at half his age and from their God-given side.

"Now what were you looking at? I saw you. I saw you looking at my body. If you were smart you would have been looking at my hands the whole time.

You lost touch with your hands and wrists, man. That big body of yours is too confusing."

Robinson held out his hands like a surgeon waiting for gloves to be placed on them. He played a fake piano with his fingers.

Willie suddenly grew aware of players from both teams watching them. He took a step back. *Frank Robinson watching me like that,* he thought.

"You're still home run happy, Willie. You're not me. You're not Reggie Jackson. You got your own swing, and it should look like that. How many times has Jim told you the power will come? Huh? How many times? The power will come, Willie. You listen to Jim Frey. And swing like yourself."

Willie smiled. Not his garrulous smile, but a quiet one. He nodded back at Frank Robinson. The fans were starting to file into the lower deck. Willie walked back to the Royals dugout and felt his swing in his biceps and hips and saw it in his mind as clear as can be. All those struggles and booing and voices in his head and he finally found that swing like a lost set of car keys.

In the on-deck circle 30 minutes later, Willie held the bat loosely in his hands. Jim Palmer was not the kind of pitcher you wanted to go to the plate against with thoughts about the mechanics of your swing floating around your head.

Palmer was not his usual precise self. Willie noticed he was a few inches off all his spots today, at least here in the first inning. And he felt the temptation to try to level one, swing from his belly again like he was doing early in the year to please the fans at Royals Stadium.

But he resisted his own urges. He could feel Frank Robinson watching him.

He held the bat like a feather in his fingers, barely letting his palms touch it. He started his leg kick and dropped his back elbow less because his focus on his hands was forcing him to keep them high and not cock his elbow like he was prone to do when he wanted to hit a home run. He even pulled the bat in slightly at the last second to adjust the spot where the barrel would hit the ball. And he hit a Robinson-esque home run.

As he ran the bases, the image of the ball connecting with the bat stayed in his head. In the dugout he looked across the field at Robinson sitting next to the other Orioles coaches. *We was just talkin' baseball,* he said to himself as he rehearsed for the reporters afterward. *Just talkin' baseball. I've known Mr. Robinson a long time. He befriended me way back with Johnny's Used Cars in Baltimore. We was just talkin' baseball.*

FUZZY'S IN KANSAS CITY was hopping that night, and Willie was three screwdrivers into a conversation with two girls who said they would show George Brett their tits in a second but not him, not Willie, no way, only George.

The girls kept teasing him about his stutter. He leveraged it.

"I ain't hitting enough home runs for you either, huh?"

They took the bait and ran through their perspective on almost every Royal—performance, appearance, deserving of seeing their tits.

George, who was there for once, rarely ran with them. He could drink beer with the best of them, could out-drink even Hal McRae, who never touched drugs either. But he almost always stayed with his crowd—his brother and a few old friends from California who always seemed to be around to keep him company.

"How come you never stutter when you are talking with girls, Willie?"

Willie heard George and then felt George hit him on the shoulder as he passed on his way to the bathroom.

The girls turned and watched George—he carried his beer with him—and the whole of Fuzzy's watched him, too.

"You muh-muh-maybe should just go in there and hold it for him," Willie said.

The girls looked at him as if he had delivered a brilliant solution to a previously insoluble dilemma.

IT WAS AUGUST 18. George Brett went 3-for-5 that night and was hitting .404; Dennis Leonard and Larry Gura and Rich Gale were gazing at batters like madmen and pitching out of their minds; Dan Quisenberry was boring through the dirt with his submarine-style arm and shaving his moustache like a French aristocrat; Hal McRae and Willie Wilson were running around the bases like banshees all night long.

Willie realized that all of America was watching George's every move. Men were watching; women were watching; children were watching. They wanted to be him; be with him; or grow up to be like him.

In the locker room afterward, every reporter there gathered around him.

"I don't think it's fair that all the focus is on me," he said. "But what am I going to do?"

One reporter wandered up to Willie as he sat there rubbing Ben-Gay onto his knee and calves.

"I don't think all the major focus should be on George Brett, but it is what it is," Willie said before he even got asked a question. "George is doing something very special right now, but this is a team effort. The reporters will talk to whoever they want to talk to."

Willie thought of the girls watching for George to emerge from the bathroom.

"He got no interest in seeing your tits," he realized he should have said. "George is busy making history."

THAT NIGHT HE DROVE to the house where a teammate had taken him a few weeks prior.

It was a white rancher in a subdivision filled with white ranchers varied only by their shutter color. A white man with a potbelly answered the door. He was a different man than the one he met the first time he came here, but he had the same belly. "One gram," Willie said.

The guy was wearing boxers, too, just like the guy the previous time. He went into the kitchen, came back with a box of Chiclets, and handed it to Willie.

Willie handed him a $100 bill and turned to the door, then he turned back.

"You guys ever put cuh-cuh-cuh-clothes on or you spend your whole day in your underwear?"

The guy winked at him. No smile, didn't even open his mouth. Then he closed the door.

AS HE SAT IN HIS DEN on the ground floor, he looked at the lines on the glass table and realized this was the first time he had ever done coke alone. He could count on one hand the number of times he had done it over the past few months. But he should have been doing it alone back then, back in the dog days of April, May, and June. *All those motherfuckers booing me,* he thought. *And now I turned the corner, I'm sitting here staring at lines of coke?*

The air conditioner was chugging outside the sliding door. It was hotter than hell here, and he liked it. Seneca-hot. Humid, too. He bent down over the table, took a brown coffee straw, and slowly sniffed the first line. He sat back and looked at the condensation on the sliding door.

He breathed deeply through his nose, and the sliding doors became a video screen on which he saw a movie called *Golden Boy,* starring George Brett. There were the girls at Fuzzy's watching George; there were his darting eyes as he stood at the plate and snapped his wrists and moved into the ball so fluidly it was like he came out of the womb doing it; there he was in the locker room with press from all over the world gathered around him wrapped in one towel and wiping his wet shoulders with another, answering each question like a press secretary in the White House briefing room.

Willie liked George. Someday he would grow to love him. He had no reason to be haunted by him for sure.

He never done nothin' to me but tease me about my stutter, he thought. *George been nice as hell to me. I just failed him up 'til now, that's why it's buggin' me. They brought me here to hit cleanup and I did nothin' until now. I failed George up until July, and I can tell by the way he looked at me until recently that he felt I failed him.*

He didn't fully realize it as he sat there; he couldn't put proper words on it. But he sensed it. It wasn't George himself so much as what George was—the rampant bat, the easiness of him, not the success itself but the way he exuded success. That is what Willie saw in all those images as he drew in the lines and sat back to breathe in the remnants stuck on his nose hair—the ease of it all.

"You should do coke like most people smoke weed," one of Willie Wilson's friends said to him a few months ago. "Real slow and easy."

He sat there, feeling more alert. He poured a glass of vodka from a bottle with Russian words on it. He shot it and rested his head back on the couch. He closed his eyes to turn off the movie on the sliding door. But George kept playing out his gorgeous season on the inside of Willie's eyelids.

THE NEXT DAY and the weeks after that Willie felt buoyant. The bat was lighter than ever and his hands snappier; his wrists felt so supple that he thought he could move them like fingers; his shoulders were always loose and his knee nagged him but it didn't nag his brain; Royals Stadium felt like Fenway.

He often heard wise men say that routine is everything in baseball. He found one. He bought coke again and again. Every night after the game—solo. A driver alone on the empty roads driving to the same rancher and then knocking three quiet knocks on the door, and the guy with the potbelly in boxers giving him his baggie without saying a word.

He turned torrid at the plate. Each morning he would wake up light and free and then go to the ballpark and be happy and free and then swing free and field cleanly and see the ball better. Willie Mays Aikens was becoming what was expected of him. He was the cleanup hitter behind George. He didn't yet attribute his rampage to the calibration of the coke, but he did consciously make it part of his daily regimen. He treated it just like having a good breakfast or doing proper stretching—only it had other benefits, too.

On September 19, George Brett was hitting .400. He ended the season, after a tiny slump, at .390.

THEY SWEPT THE YANKEES in the ALCS—the first two they won in Kansas City, and the third game was in New York. Willie hit .364; Reggie Jackson hit .273. He got those questions again—the ones he got about Reggie Jackson when he was starting out back with the Johnnies in Baltimore. He liked it. But there was a difference in their approach. Forty or fifty thousand people in the ballparks and Reggie, with his swagger and self-regard intact despite his age, said with his way of walking and swinging and looking, *Watch me.*

Willie looked outward. He saw the people, he felt the power, he wanted to entertain. Willie said, *Watch this. We're having a party, people, and I'm going to host the next one, and it will blow your minds.*

GAME 1.

It was Willie's 26th birthday. He bought tickets for a bunch of friends from Seneca and told them to make sure they brought coke up to Philly with them. On the television, Joe Garagiola told the world that Willie's namesake was Willie Mays. Willie had given up trying to straighten out the story of Dr. Mays the obstetrician.

Veterans Stadium was crazed; he had some coke in his system from the night before and thought there were more than a few cokeheads in the crowd that chilly night. Most men wore coats and ties. Everyone's breath was steaming. The artificial turf was so sickly green it shocked your eyes—*65,000-some people at my party.*

He felt taller, like a giant in a sandbox. He felt like his head was the height of the upper deck and like he could reach the outfield wall with the end of his bat when he extended his arms.

He knew they would be keeping the ball low and away and staying off the fastballs, too. But he was seeing everything these days. They knew that, too, he knew. He could tell by the way the Phillies pitchers watched him. They knew he could hit anything they threw.

A toothpick dangled in his mouth. *Let me entertain you good people of Philadelphia. And you folks back home in K.C., too.*

He dug out the edge of the batter's box before he even lifted his bat. The catcher, Bob Boone, said to the umpire, Harry Wendelstedt, "His back foot is outside the box."

Willie stepped back but left his foot where it was.

"Bob, that's my foot right there," he said. "Looks like it's in the box to me."

But there was no box because he had kicked up all the chalk.

He grinned at them and twirled the toothpick. Bob Walk, the pitcher, stared at the three of them, and Willie saw him so he stepped out of the box again.

"That Mike Schmidt's a bad boy," he said to Boone. "Must be somethin' playin' with him."

Wendelstedt told him to knock it off.

But they kept jawing about the foot and the box for three more pitches, and then he hit a fly ball that the cliché-minded said was towering or smoked but that he knew and the Phillies knew better as a harbinger of deeper shots to come.

Next time up he was holding a hot water bag in the on-deck circle, and Phillies fans were razzing him about the batter's box, too.

He turned to them and said, "Where we gonna party later?"

They didn't know what to say back.

As he walked to the plate, Veterans Stadium started to play along. Boos, catcalls, but not malicious. Jive talk. He had this place in his hand.

"He gonna throw the ball over the cottonpickin' plate this time?" Willie asked Boone.

He slammed a deep foul ball.

"How 'bout that cut?" he asked, looking at Wendelstedt.

Even the announcer Tom Seaver had to admire "that awesome swing that Aikens has."

On the home run swing, his back knee touched the ground, and his hips twisted so that it looked like his torso was going to spin off his legs. He threw his bat with the same grandiosity as Reggie, but he threw it in a way that didn't say, *Look at me, I am a star.* Instead, the way Willie threw it said, *Let's party. Dig that, people. We gonna have a party tonight.*

The second homer went to deep right field. As he slowly rounded the bases, he trotted slowly and proudly. He was confirming his role as the host of the party, even in Veterans Stadium, even though the Royals lost 7–6.

The locker room afterward didn't feel like a losing clubhouse. It felt like a party, and Willie partied for real that night in the hotel when the gang from Seneca showed up with coke that was stronger than anything Willie had ever tasted before.

GAME 4.

The Phillies had won Game 2. And Game 3, the first game back in Kansas City, was tied 3–3 in the bottom of the 10th inning when Willie came to bat against Tug McGraw. It was the first time in Willie's life that Cille had seen him play—little league, high school, the minors—never. He hit the game-winning single, and as he rounded the bases he watched her sitting there dumbstruck at how these people were adoring her son. She didn't even clap or smile. She just sat there looking back at him.

Willie had flown her in with Cuda and some of the boys from Seneca again, and they got high that night in his den after he put Cille to bed upstairs.

As usual, the Kansas City crowd booed Pete Rose the most during introductions to Game 4, Steve Carlton second most, and mostly held their feelings in check when Mike Schmidt was announced. But most of them thought, *Schmidt's no George*. And when George was introduced everyone was studying his jog to see if the hemorrhoid surgery he had days before was holding up okay.

Willie felt the love of the Royals fans, but he shut out the love because he knew it wasn't true. The stadium felt like the whole of Kansas and Missouri had convened to praise their cleanup hitter. But he still resented them. He wanted to party, but not with them. Go back home, home with his home boys, the only ones who stayed true.

Here in Kansas City, he went from party host to rampager. Those Huns in Royal blue with their hillbilly mustaches and funky afros were rampaging, too, and half of them were hyped on greenies just like the Phillies. It was a madhouse chemical gathering here in middle America.

The first homer came off Larry Christenson to deep right field in the first inning. People looked at one another and said, "Can you believe it? He is on fire." Christenson didn't last the inning.

The second homer was deep right again, off Dickie Noles, and as Willie rounded the bases he kept telling himself to remember Frank Robinson's advice. *Just swing, the home runs will take care of themselves.* But deep down he wanted to become the first man to hit a home run in every single at-bat in the World Series. As he sat down in the clubhouse, he heard the PA announcer tell the crowd that he had become the first player in World Series history to hit two home runs in the same game twice.

As they got high again that night, Cuda kept imitating the second home run.

"You're a bad man," the guys kept saying to Willie. He had never felt so happy in his life. Cocaine, from that night forward, would be inseparable from a sense of happiness. The two had to go together, just like doing coke and feeling perfect at the plate.

The Royals, however, lost the Series in six games. During the final game back in Philadelphia, Willie wanted to hit more homers but went 0-for-2 with two walks. They flew back to Kansas City for a consolation parade, and people everywhere reached out to shake his hand as if he had won the Series for the Royals. At first, he wanted to withhold his hand from them, but then he gave in. And he shook more hands than he had shaken in his whole life put together.

A few days later he flew back to Seneca for a parade in his honor. He rode with Cille in the back of a convertible. He hugged his former coaches and the parents of his friends. He got high before the parade, and he and the boys got high afterward and every day that followed.

Every time they got high, Cuda told him, "Willie, you hit .400 in the World Series, man. Forget about George Brett, man. You the .400 hitter here, man."

And each time he heard Cuda say it, each time they sat around the table and laid out the lines and laughed together about the same stories night after night, Willie couldn't believe how good, how deep-down good and happy it all felt.

My mother is living clean, he thought. *I am a cleanup hitter at last. And this whole party is only just getting started.*

And crazy Clint Hurdle shouting in the locker room after the second two-homer game kept ringing in Willie's ears. "They talk about Babe Ruth," Hurdle kept shouting to the press and players alike. "They talk about Lou Gehrig. They talk about Duke Snider. Now they'll talk about Willie Aikens."

4

Somebody Tell Me What's Happening

1980–1994

1980

The water seemed clearer than the air that November day on the beach in Puerto Rico. He stopped running on the flat strip of sand and walked down the beach's slope to the calm sea. Kids were kicking a soccer ball and shouting behind him.

All those years trying to be like Reggie, he thought. *If we had won I'd be bigger than Reggie. Hell, we swept the Yankees in the ALCS.*

He turned from the water and walked back up to the flat beach. He started slowly, half-walking, then jogging past the kids, and then forcibly lifting his knees higher until he achieved a run. The beach was a mile or so long, and this was his second roundtrip.

He started to jab the dusk. Easy jabs. His shoulders felt loose; so did his legs.

People just didn't understand the injury. I came back faster from knee surgery than almost anybody could, and I still got booed. Only Jim Frey understands.

In the locker room in Kansas City as the players were clearing out their things after the World Series, Frey had told him he could be the next Willie McCovey. Willie had never heard that one and told Jim he needed to think about it, study a little bit more about McCovey. Then he told Jim he had decided to play winter ball in Puerto Rico to work on his fielding, and Jim nodded.

"Greatness," Jim said. Willie sat there with Jim's voice echoing in his head.

As he achieved a steady stride, McCovey slipped from his mind, and he pretended he was Ali. Jabbing, wiggling a little bit. Ali. *What it must be like to move like Ali,* he thought.

He remembered seeing highlights of the Liston-Ali fight as a boy. He remembered the speed of the young Ali and Liston's plodding. He remembered it like some kids remembered watching the rocket go to the moon.

He extended his arms straight out from his shoulders as he ran and tried to lift his knees up that high. Thirty times, then a minute jogging. Then 30 times. Then another minute counting to 60.

The sun had gone down and the kids were starting to scatter. But he kept at it. His hamstrings started to burn, and in one of his calves he started to feel the beginning of a cramp. Sweat was pooling in his beard. His hips got tight. But he kept at it all the way back to the end of the beach where he started.

YOU? A WORKER? He woke up one morning in the hotel and felt stunned by his characterization of himself. He always wanted to play, just play. But here in this lovely weather he was working. He was going to work. And he liked it.

The casinos still lured him—by the end of his two-month stint he lost $10,000. He took three prostitutes home one night but asked them to leave at midnight, and since they weren't stoned or drunk they responded to the extra money it took to evacuate them. He had to sleep, had to go to work in the morning.

His swing stayed—it still felt the same as in the playoffs and World Series. He wanted to maintain it but not overdo. It was here to stay, he knew. The key here was to become a fielder—not merely an acceptable one, but a good first baseman. So he took grounders for two half hours with an hour of running and sit-ups in between.

On a coolish night toward the end of November he went to the beach to run. He pulled up his hoodie and drew the strings around his neck.

There were two fishermen casting at opposite ends of the beach.

He couldn't even break a sweat, but he kept running and decided he was going to call Cille once he got back to the hotel.

"You know something, Cille?" he was going to say.

His mother would make that noise with her lips that she always made when the conversation was not going in her direction.

"You know I think that World Series game was the first time in my whole life you ever saw me play in a ballgame."

She would be silent.

"The first time ever, Cille. I mean ever. Amazing, ain't it? Not even little league. Amazing, ain't it?"

She would say, "Yes, yes. Thanks be to Jehovah, Willie."

And he would continue.

"Felt pretty good sitting in that convertible with all the people of Seneca waving at us during the parade, didn't it, Cille? Like your Willie made somethin' of himself, huh? How'd you like that parade, Cille?"

He ran harder and the wind had blown the hoodie back but the strings were still tight around his throat.

He remembered saying to Coach McNeil as his wife held Willie's hand and they stood there talking before the parade began. "How ya like me now, Coach?"

He remembered saying to Coach Shaver as he got out of the convertible and wrapped his arms around him, "How ya like me now, Coach?"

The wind was at his back now, and he was running fast, he realized. Not just fast for him, but fast.

And he realized what he wanted to say to Cille: *How ya like me now?*

He stopped running after one roundtrip on the beach and started walking back to his hotel to call her.

People were bundled up in jackets, and some people wore hats and gloves. He laughed.

The doorman opened the door for him and smiled.

"*Hace frío!*" Willie said.

"*Si, hace frío Señor Aikens,*" the doorman said back.

He got to his room and went straight to the telephone. He had to look up her number—he knew the numbers but always got the order wrong.

She picked up and gave that long, stretched-out and questioning greeting: "Heellloooo?"

"Cille," he said. "Cille, it's Willie. You know what I did today, Cille?"

She blew her nose.

"I took 100 ground balls and didn't miss one. Not a single one, Cille. How 'bout that? Real windy day, too, Cille. Blowin' the ball all around. They been tellin' me I was a bad fielder since I was six years old, Cille, and you should have been there today to see me!"

1981

It carried over into the season. He knew it had from the beginning of spring training. The first time in the cage he didn't hit a single ball out of the park but felt the strength and quickness and ease in his wrists.

But what's more, he was becoming an adequate first baseman, despite what the stat junkies and press opined.

Jim Frey hit him on the back as he came into the dugout after a great play early in the season at Comiskey Park and said, "That's gonna shut them up, Willie. Attaboy."

Some of the players thought Jim Frey was a wiseguy, but Willie's devotion grew.

Frey was batting Willie cleanup now regularly. *And I am cleaning up*, he thought. *Cleaning up and leaving no messes like last year.*

He got high with a new, methodical regularity. He started to realize that he could calibrate the highness to carry over into the next day's game. Three lines, sometimes only two. Then a vodka chaser. Then sleep—with the vodka bottle by his bed for a swig or two in case the alcohol didn't take the edge off the coke.

But he felt a new vibe in the clubhouse. The rhythm of last season was gone. The same music played on the boom boxes, but the guys weren't moving to it.

The meetings about the impending players' strike grew more frequent. He heard words he head never heard before—lawyers' words.

On February 28 at spring training, every single player on the Royals had voted to strike on May 28 if the owners did not agree to improve the free agent compensation system. They found out a few hours later that every single major league player had voted for the strike.

He took up the contagious approach: talked less, joked less.

He woke up on May 8 and picked up the newspaper on his doorstep. He didn't save any of the World Series articles. He never resumed reading the papers after he stopped talking to the press during the slump of 1980. But he read today's paper, cut out the article, and put it under a magnet on his refrigerator.

Headline: "New and improved Aikens has silenced his critics."

Top: "…Willie Aikens isn't the same person he was this time last season. Then he was scared and playing terribly. Now he is confident and playing good baseball. He is getting his glove on ground balls hit in the vicinity of first base. He is digging infield throws out of the dirt. He is hitting the ball the way he did late last season."

And the quote that explained why Jim Frey nodded to him that afternoon as he walked past Willie in the clubhouse: "'Jim Frey stuck with me when he didn't have to,' Aikens said. 'He gave me a chance to show I was a good baseball player. If he hadn't given me a chance, I don't know where I would be right now.'"

U.L. didn't think that. He had gotten benched a few times, and mocked Frey behind his back. Amos Otis hadn't thought that since January when he took offense at Frey switching him to left field and Willie Wilson to center. Frey's statement of the obvious—"We happen to have the fastest man in baseball" to play center—didn't seem sufficiently logical to Otis. The team was banding together around one thing—its disdain for Frey. Wisecracker, disciplinarian, "old-timer," "mental." All the scornful adjectives were getting back to Gentleman Jim through the press.

In the dugout in New York the week before, Clint Hurdle had sung mock-merrily along to Frank Sinatra's "New York, New York" as it played over the PA system. Then Hurdle and Ken Phelps started shouting excessively for their teammates after routine catches in the field.

"Great pitch," Phelps and Hurdle shouted with little league–like enthusiasm that might have been appropriate had Renie Martin just pitched a no-hitter. But he had merely thrown a strike to Jim Spencer of the Yankees.

Willie cringed. Frey jumped up; he'd had enough of the mockery.

Frey shouted, "Shut the hell up and grow up!"

On the next pitch, Martin hit the same spot with his pitch and Spencer hit a game-winning home run.

WILLIE WILSON SHOWED UP at the airport for the team's charter flight to Seattle dressed in suit pants, tie, dress shirt, and a blue cashmere sweater. He was one of the last players to arrive at the private lounge, and a few players looked up at him as he sauntered in. Jim Frey looked up, too. Wilson would claim he did not come to provoke, but his missing sport coat was as good as wearing no clothes at all among the mandatorily well-suited players.

Willie watched from a seat across from Jim Frey. He watched the team watch Wilson and then turn all at once to Frey.

Willie sensed a test at hand. He knew from his own encounters that Jim loved a test. He knew he was almost too eager for one. But he knew clearly that the players were irritable and loved what they were about to see.

Frey got up and walked over to where Wilson sat. He stood there in front of him.

Then every curse word Willie had ever heard started flying around the room.

And Willie thought, *Jim Frey ain't scared of nobody.*

Wilson got up and walked past Frey, past the team, and right out of the lounge.

Frey was breathing hard as he walked after him, still shouting. Then he stopped and stared just like everyone else. Wilson had split. *All over a sport coat,*

Willie thought. *Jim digging himself a big hole here. We're all digging a big hole for ourselves here. Sure ain't last year.*

The doubleheader in Seattle began at 6:05 on Monday. Frey had instructed the team not to discuss the incident with the media beforehand, but many did.

Willie heard it all and said, "Nuh-nuh-nuh-no," to reporters who asked if he had any comments, given his well-publicized blowups with Frey.

But "nut job?"—*That was damn personal,* he thought. *I had my troubles with Jim, but the next day we shook hands and Jim is an honorable guy,* he said to himself. *These guys wanna drive him out.*

There were catcalls and shouts by the lockers at the entrance to the clubhouse, and he looked to see Wilson entering at 5:45 PM.

Wilson was straight-faced and wore a suit. Somehow he had flown there by himself. He went straight to his locker. He dressed quickly and sat on the bench through all of Game 1 without speaking to anyone.

After the second game, Frey patrolled the clubhouse as the media interviewed the players.

Rich Gale got the win, and several beers into the night he garrulously recounted some of his pitches as the media entered the clubhouse.

Frey paused by his locker, and the media turned to look at Gale.

"Get a couple of beers in you, and suddenly you're Cy Young," Frey said.

Willie was sipping a Budweiser and dropped his head when he heard Frey. *You're gonna lose this club,* he thought. *What you doin', Jim? What you actin' so angry for?*

He took another sip and knew he would never say it to his mentor. He knew he should; he wanted to. *But I would just stutter and he'd take offense,* he said to himself.

He was hitting .292 on June 6. The papers called him the Royals' "most consistent hitter."

"The guy really works," Frey told reporters that day.

Willie passed by after jogging. Sweat was dripping down his entire body, down his legs and neck and back. He was working. It was all working. But the clubhouse and the strike were getting all the attention this year, as George had last year. He cared less, but as the reporters interviewing Frey in the dugout looked at him dripping wet, he stopped and smiled.

"Kuh-kuh-keep the articles coming, boys," he said. "The people of Kansas City stuh-stuh-startin' to like me!"

THE TEAM MEETING in the visiting clubhouse in Toronto on June 11 ran late and cut into batting practice. He had done his coke regimen the night before, and without BP to take a bit of the edge off, Willie felt jittery.

Then Hal McRae spoke, and Willie regained his focus. Hal did that to him and to most people. The other guys sounded like they were ranting. Hal gave focus.

"Marvin says strike, we strike," he said. "No two ways about it. So everybody stay in shape. We may be back this season. We may not. But this is a business."

They struck the next day, so instead of taking the field at Tiger Stadium, Willie went to see the Larry Holmes–Michael Spinks heavyweight title fight that night in the Motor City.

As he sat there a few rows back from the ring, he remembered all the beach running in Puerto Rico that past winter. He laughed at himself, pretending to be Ali. *You're Larry Holmes,* he said to himself. *Big and bad and slow and sloppy... but still the heavyweight champion of the world.*

THE LONGEST STRIKE in professional sports history to that point lasted from June 12 until July 31, 1981. Willie took tae kwan do classes three times a week. After the classes he went to the gym near his condo and lifted and chatted there for a few hours every day. But about 20 days into the strike, he was doing bench presses and just stopped. *Boring,* he thought. *No paycheck. No fun. No baseball. I'm done lifting. At least in the karate class I get to hang out.*

He went home and called his new friend Rita whom he had met at a bar one night. She arrived within half an hour. They took off their clothes and then just sat there laughing.

"We're naked as jaybirds!" he said.

"I dare you to play baseball this way," she said.

"You want to, I duh-duh-do it with you," he said. "We can sneak out to the batting cage one night. But you're the pitcher. And you're gettin' naked, too."

The next morning he missed his tae kwan do class. And he missed the rest of them, too. They got high three or four times a day and had corresponding sex each time.

They did go to the batting cage but fully clothed. He went several times right after he got high and hit balls off the machine. People gathered and watched. They had no idea how high he was. They asked if he were coming back tomorrow and at what time. They came back at that time, and he did, too. More and more people came—several fathers with their sons and then more boys from their neighborhoods and then half a little league team wearing Oakland A's green shirts.

After one arcing shot he turned to the crowd.

"They w-w-work this thing out and hold the All-Star Game, I'm invitin' you all to Cleveland to see me!"

They laughed and clapped, but one guy shouted, "We'll all go vote for you again, but you can't catch Rod Carew, Willie!"

"Jim Frey's the All-Star Game manager this year, fellas!" he shouted back. "You all see Jim tell him to pick his boy. No doubt he gonna do the right thing!"

He signed autographs after each session. One night after they all left, Rita got some coke out of her purse, and they sat on a bench and got high and looked at the stars.

"They settle this strike I'm gonna have to get back on my system," he said.

She laughed.

"What you laughin' at?" he said, laughing, too.

"I'm telling you," he said. "I guh-guh-got a system now for the right number of lines and the exact amount of vodka, and then the next day at the park no one can get a pitch by me."

"I could get a pitch by you," she said. "I get them by you all I want every night."

She laughed and he looked at her.

"Let's go home and do some coke," she said.

THE STRIKE ENDED on July 31 with both sides' negotiators refusing to even pose for a photograph together. And as the team returned for workouts—many players overweight and out of shape—Jim Frey grew angrier and his detractors more catty.

The league announced that the season would resume with the All-Star Game on August 9. A split-season format and other scheduling adjustments would add to the oddness of the whole thing. The Royals' Japan trip after the season was still on, too.

But the next day a reporter told Willie that Frey had picked Eddie Murray of the Orioles as the backup to Rod Carew for the All-Star Game. Frey had coached Murray for many years in Baltimore, and Willie knew they were close.

But Eddie isn't having near my year, Willie thought. *I'm leading the league in intentional walks. I'm hitting a mean cleanup. The World Series last year alone should have landed me there.*

"I know they told Jim not to pick me so they don't have to pay me my $15,000 bonus for making the team," he said to a reporter.

"He and Eddie's real close," another reporter said. "And he knew Eddie long before you."

"Jim Frey met me when I was 19, man," he said.

Other players overhead them, and his doubts turned into a big beef with Jim Frey and the Royals in the papers a day later.

Then in Cleveland on August 16 he and Jim shouted at each other for half an hour in the clubhouse.

"I'm the kind of hitter than can break up a game and cuh-cuh-cuh-carry a team," Willie shouted for all to hear.

"Then why the fuck aren't you breakin' anything but fucking baseball bats, Willie?"

They kicked things, shouted, cursed, and finally Frey walked away. But Willie noticed that the whole time Jim always waited for him to finish his sentences. He was stuttering a whole bunch, and a lot of the players were laughing, but Frey waited him out on each word before cursing him some more.

The next day Willie entered the clubhouse, and the players already there watched as he walked straight to Frey's office and closed the door. They stopped talking and listened, but there was no shouting coming through the door.

The door opened, and Willie walked out and sat at his locker. There was no detectable movement in Frey's office.

"You kill him?" someone asked.

"Man, Jim's all right," Willie said. He looked around the room at the handful of players gathered.

Everyone looked away.

HAL MCRAE REMOVED HIMSELF from a game in New York, saying he had an upset stomach; Willie Wilson said he was sick in Toronto and couldn't play; Amos Otis missed four games with a suddenly aching back.

"Mysterious ailments," one Royals official told the press.

Jim Frey was fired on August 31. Dick Howser, who managed the Yankees team that the Royals beat in the ALCS the year before, was named the new manager.

Willie heard the news from an attendant in the parking lot as he arrived at the stadium. He stopped and stood there for a minute.

"I saw him walk out an hour ago," the attendant said. "He didn't look too happy. Not crying, but damn sad. Always nice to me, Willie."

Some reporters immediately went to Willie as he walked in. He didn't even let them ask the question.

"Me and Jim had our ups and downs," he said. "But we probably had more good days than bad. He stuck with me when I was struggling last year, and I appreciate that. I feel sorry it had to be this way."

But in his head and in his heart he thought and felt much stronger things. He felt alone; he felt angry; he thought that some of his teammates had sold out Jim Frey; he thought no one realized that they were all there to play ball, just play ball, man, have fun. *Everybody is messin' that up this year. Nobody havin' any fun. And now Jim's gone. Jim's gone to play golf, and we're all sitting here waitin' for this damn season to end.*

IT ENDED WITH THE ROYALS making the playoffs despite going 50–53 on the season. Major League Baseball had established a split-season format, a five-game playoff between the pre- and post-strike division winners, and the Royals, winners of the American League West in the second half of the season, were swept by Oakland in three games, with Willie going 3-for-9 with three walks. He believed he was born to play playoff baseball and felt like something had been taken from him that was his and only his.

He sat in his locker after the last playoff game and thought about Jim Frey out on the golf course. He didn't even want to go to Japan anymore. John Schuerholz, the general manager, had given the team a lecture about the drug policies in Japan and warned them not to dare bring any drugs on the trip. He said he knew none of them were doing drugs but had to warn them anyway. And as Willie sat there after that last game, he took a pinch of Copenhagen and suddenly realized he had struck gold.

He would clear the tobacco out of the can, pop up the paper on the bottom, press some drugs in there, then refill the whole can.

HE FILLED A COPENHAGEN container with marijuana—Hawaiian Gold he got from a new dealer in Kansas City. The first night in the hotel in Tokyo he invited some teammates into his room, and they stopped dead in their tracks.

"You the craziest motherfucker in Major League Baseball, Willie," someone said.

"Damn right," he said.

He tried sushi and spit it out, went to geisha houses every night, and walked the streets laughing at all the people staring at him. The last night, representatives of a Japanese team approached him in the hotel restaurant in Tokyo. They had been sitting in the lobby waiting for him.

"You fuh-fuh-fellows ambushin' me," he said.

They told him that he had a standing offer to come play for them. They told him they would get him an apartment at the top of a beautiful building and a personal masseuse.

"What you payin' over here?" he asked with a devilish smile.

A Japanese guy rubbed his fingers together and said a few words to the interpreter.

"Mr. Aikens hits big home runs, he can buy small Japanese city here," the interpreter said.

Willie's eyes twinkled at them.

"We'll be in touch, then," he said.

1982

The two thick binders were filled with charts and diagrams, and Willie's agent, Ron Shapiro pushed them to him across the table. This off-season he was going to cash in at last.

"You led the league in intentional walks last year," Shapiro said. "You're ranked third in the major leagues among first baseman for home runs and RBIs over the past three years. John's not going to call me tonight to meet our number. But you're going to win tomorrow, Willie. The numbers speak for themselves."

In the 13-year history of the Royals franchise, Kansas City had never lost a salary arbitration case. On February 4, 1982, Willie sat in Shapiro's suite at the Wilshire Hilton and agreed to not back down.

$375,000.

"I'm worth every penny of it, Ron," Willie said.

The strike taught me this ain't all fun and games. These guys use us. I love to play ball, but this ain't all fun and games.

The next morning, Willie listened as Royals management detailed the reasons why he wasn't worth $375,000. Slow-footed. Error-prone. Weak against lefties. Streaky. And the worst one: not the hardest worker.

Sweet Jesus, Willie thought. *I was working harder than Ali all last winter. I was running every day in the hot Kansas City sun.*

But Shapiro had forbidden him. So he sat and listened and tried to think about girls whenever the bitter stuff was said.

After four hours the arbitrator ended the hearing and stepped into an adjacent room. He did not look at Willie the whole hearing.

Willie went to the bathroom while they waited and urinated next to one of Royals' front office assistants.

"What's up?" Willie said as they each stared straight ahead at the tiles on the wall.

The young man started to say something but stopped. He quickly zipped up and walked out.

Doesn't even wash his hands, Willie thought.

As they reconvened, the arbitrator finally looked at him. He knew they had won then. Shapiro had told him not to raise a fist or clap or even smile. Shake hands immediately, smile, and tell them the job you are going to do for them if you want to say anything.

He shook hands, smiled, but didn't say anything. He thought: *Jim Frey would love this one.*

HE SPOTTED VIDA BLUE the moment he walked into the clubhouse in Fort Myers that March of 1982. The pitchers and catchers had reported a few days before the hitters, and Vida was already holding court before a few minor leaguers seated around him, drinking cups of coffee.

He walked straight to Blue, and they hugged.

"I wuh-wuh-won my arbitration," he said to Blue.

Blue smiled like a man who had suffered unduly at the hands of management. Willie threw back his head and laughed.

"You fellas, too," he said to the minor leaguers. "We all goin' out for dinner tomorrow night, alright?"

Willie spotted George stretching in the outfield and ran over to tell him that he had met a girl the night before at the Ramada who he swore was the prettiest girl he had ever met in his life and whom he promised he would hook up with George if she would meet up with him after George was through with her.

"Huh-huh-huh-hey George!" he shouted as he turned back toward the infield. "How many women you slept with?"

The other players beside him laughed, and Brett faked a horrified look.

"Jeez, Willie," he shouted back. "That's not right to count something like that."

"Aw, cuh-cuh-come on, George," Willie said.

"How about you, Willie?" Brett asked.

Willie stood taller and grinned.

"I sluh-sluh-slept with 401," he said.

All the players laughed, and Brett shook his head.

Ewing Kauffman, the Royals owner, was at the game a few days later. He rarely met with the players, and Dick Howser warned them all the day before to be on their best behavior.

He sat watching the Royals a few rows from where the girl from the Ramada and her big blonde girlfriend were seated.

Unbelievable, Willie thought. *How am I going to point her out to George with Mr. Kauffman sitting right there? She's leaving in two days, and we're on the road tomorrow.*

During warm-ups Willie kept trying to find the right spot to point her out without being noticed by Kauffman.

As players jogged in the outfield he called out to Brett, "Your girl is here, George! You're gonna like this one, I puh-puh-promise you that, George!"

Then in the dugout before taking the field, he went up to Brett and hit him on the backside.

"Juh-juh-George, listen here," he said. "When we come off the field, we gonna wave to Mr. Kauffman, okay? Run right up close to him and wave. Then look three rows back and there's tuh-tuh-two blondes, okay? The real tan one is Kandy. I'm tellin' you, George, this girl is fine."

Brett laughed but turned away to face the field.

After a quick half-inning, Brett let Willie pull him back toward the front of the dugout, and Willie started waving and the girl started waving back. Then she and her girlfriend stood up and started screaming and waving at George.

Ewing Kauffman started waving back at them. Willie saw him and waved at him.

Brett took a sharp turn into the dugout and walked down to the end, shaking his head and laughing the whole way.

Willie followed him.

"Wuh-wuh-what, George? You want me to get that for you?"

"Nah, Willie, she's not my type," Brett said. He sat down and started to laugh harder.

"Willie, you're a crazy guy. Man, they don't make them like you anymore," he said.

"George, only one crazy here is you," Willie said. "You kuh-kuh-kiddin' me, right? You kiddin' me?"

After the game, Kauffman came into the locker room and made a beeline for Willie.

"Hello, Willie Aikens," he said smiling and extending his hand.

Willie dropped his head and smiled at the floor.

"Huh-huh-hello Mr. Kauffman. It is a puh-puh-pleasure tuh-tuh see you again."

He raised his hand but still did not look up.

"Willie, I just wanted to come right over and congratulate you on winning your arbitration case," he said. "I wanted you to know I hold no ill feelings, and nor will the people who work for me. If there is any ballplayer on my club who deserves a raise, it is you."

Willie smiled, nodded, and stuck out his hand. He didn't think he could say anything without one long stutter, so he kept shaking Kauffman's hand with both his own hands and tried to keep from laughing.

HIS SLUMP BEGAN toward the end of spring training and carried over into the 1982 season. One night after the game he was getting high with Rita, and she stood up and started ranting about how bad the Royals were playing.

"Why you givin' me shit, Rita?" he asked. "I come home to relax with you. You the last person I need shit from!"

She stopped and moved directly in front of him across the coffee table.

"And why wouldn't you let me come to spring training?" she demanded. "Why, Willie?"

"Rita, we're doin' good coke here, not crack," he said. "Why you actin' like a strung-out crackhead all of a sudden?"

"You got girls down there, didn't you, Willie? How many, huh? You think I'm stupid?"

He stood up and walked around the coffee table and took her by the wrists.

"Look, baby, I need you to cool out now, you hear? I'm havin' a rough time right now at the plate. I don't even want to talk about my fieldin'. And we got this guy Dick Howser actin' like a Marine in the clubhouse. He's got it out for me. So please, baby, just cool out now. I got a special treat for you tomorrow."

Rita pulled her arms away but hung her head and inhaled and exhaled deeply. She walked into Willie's chest and forced him to cradle her. She started to cry.

"What? Don't be cryin' now, baby. We're havin' a good time."

"What you got for me tomorrow?"

"Can't tell you, a surprise," Willie said.

"Tell me," she said. She rubbed her head on his chest.

"Well, this new pitcher Vida Blue, man used to throw 100 mph. Wicked fastball. He came up to me yesterday and invited us to this guy's house. This guy Mark. Says he has the best coke he ever tried. Says he gives it to us free so long as we go to his house and sit around. Real nice people go there, and they sit and get high and just relax, you know? So I want to take you there tomorrow night, okay? You come to the game, and then we'll go together and just relax over there. Vida says he's a real good guy. A white guy. Lives near you in Overland Park."

Rita pulled her head away but wrapped her arms around his waist.

"I'll come if you hit a home run tomorrow," she said.

"Shit," Willie said. "Don't juh-juh-joke about baseball, okay? I come home to relax with you. You can't talk about baseball no more with me ever again. Now let's just sit down and chill out, okay?"

SHE WAITED FOR HIM in front of the players' parking lot, and they followed Vida Blue to The Long Branch Saloon and people in the parking lot stared at the white woman getting out of Willie's car.

They walked with Vida, and a few people called to him.

"Vida, you integratin' this place or what?" Willie asked, laughing.

They all laughed as the bouncer opened the door for them and called Vida "Mister."

Willie spotted Mark Liebl the minute he walked in the door. He spotted him not because he was noticeable—6'5" and a big smile to match—but because everyone gravitated toward him. He shook hands, slapped backs, kissed one woman on the cheek, and picked up a drink waiting for him on the bar before walking to the ballplayers.

"That him?" Willie asked Blue.

Blue laughed.

Liebl gave Willie a hug and gave one to Rita, too.

"You'll get out of that slump, soon, Willie. I feel it," Liebl said.

"Tuh-tell that to her," Willie said, looking at Rita.

"Aw, now, let's just forget about baseball for a while," Liebl said. "Finish your drinks cause we're going to my place."

Willie felt like he had met the white, suburban version of Cuda. Old Cuda. He'd love this white boy. He'd just love him.

In the car Rita smoked a joint and passed it to Willie, but he shook his head.

"You hear the first thing he said to me?" he asked.

She exhaled and looked at him.

"He said he had no doubt I was gonna break out of it. No doubt. That's the way a friend talks, you see. You need to talk to me that way."

As they pulled up to Liebl's house, he saw Liebl walk to the front door and motion everyone in.

They walked in and followed him downstairs to the den. A tiny blonde woman was there, reading a fashion magazine. She smiled and stood up.

"Hi, my name is Kelly," she said.

Vida introduced Willie and Rita as Liebl walked upstairs. They all sat down and Willie looked around: bats, photographs of Liebl with famous ballplayers, baseballs signed by them, too. The place was a baseball museum. He could hear Liebl coming back down the steps.

"Your waiter is here with your meal," he said. He was holding a dinner plate full of cocaine above his shoulder.

He set it on the table in front of them.

"You come to my house, and all your problems go away," he said. "Here we come to be happy together."

Willie sat up closer to the table and stared at the coke.

"Man, I ain't tried it yet, but I realize this is like a dream, man. Getting high in a baseball museum, man. I realize it's a dream, and I never even had it yet."

TWO DAYS LATER Willie went to Kentucky Fried Chicken and ordered a bucket. He ate piece after piece and threw the remains out the window. And he suddenly realized he was driving to Overland Park. He had been thinking about Liebl all morning and supposed his thinking about him had turned into going to see him without even realizing it.

The fans had booed his two strikeouts the night before just like they used to boo him early last year. He had hit one homer at Royals Stadium all season. *But no one lets you be a streaky hitter anymore,* he thought. *No one forgives an injury either. At least not mine.*

He drove through the nice houses of Overland Park and thought about how good the coke was that Liebl gave them. Blue told him Liebl's deal—any ballplayer at his house gets free coke.

So he knocked. Liebl wasn't home. But Willie wanted more. He got into his car and looked for a piece of paper. All he had were the napkins that came with the chicken. He found a pen in the glove compartment and wrote a note on the napkin. "Hey Mark, Willie Aikens here. If you're coming to the game tonight, bring me a couple grams. Willie."

He left it in the mailbox. Liebl would save the napkin for years. He would put it in his museum.

WILLIE HIT A RARE HOMER one hot July night at Royals Stadium. He hit it with ferocity and didn't look up at the crowd because for certain several of them had been there the night before when everyone was booing him on the field and at the plate.

Liebl was waiting for him in front of the players' parking lot. Three little boys ran up to Willie. He felt them there at his waist and felt the adults watching how he would respond to them and to spite their parents he disregarded the children.

"You think these are the same people booing me last night, Mark?" he asked.

"Hey, Willie, you're breaking out of it, man. I can see it," Liebl said. "Don't worry about a few buffoons booing you. Come on. Let's head to my house."

When they got there a bunch of Royals were already there, as was a group of Liebl's friends from Overland Park.

Willie loved how these people treated the ballplayers—as if they were all just people getting together to hang out after work. Just regular people getting together to forget about their jobs and their lives for a night.

"You see my homer tonight?" he asked them as he sat down. A woman put a glass of vodka on the table in front of him.

"This is a tough baseball town," he said. "Real tough."

Liebl had come down the steps with a plate of coke and looked at Willie with the concern of a parent.

"Willie, you got to put that stuff away," he said. "You got to stop feeling sorry for yourself. You're a hell of a ballplayer, and you know what you can do. You think you got it tough? Look at Vida there. Charlie Finley put him through something you can't imagine how bad."

Blue nodded and leaned his head back.

"You know the man called him in the middle of the night one night," Liebl said. Everyone focused their eyes on Blue and waited for the first story of the night.

"Called him and said he had come up with a brilliant idea," Liebl continued. "Serious idea now. I want you to change your name to True on your birth certificate, he told that man. Change your name permanently. Will be a huge marketing deal. True Blue, baby. Woke him up to tell him that."

"Fuck," one of the suburbanites said.

Liebl sat down.

"I remember how he froze you out there during the free agency thing, Vida," he said. "Despicable man. Awful."

People were doing lines now, and Willie tried to perfect the straightness of his line by pressing his two index fingers up against it on either side.

"People don't realize," he said, looking at the line. "I never realized what this was all about."

He bent down and inhaled. No one looked at anyone inhaling. But everyone sensed when the first round had settled in, and they all sat back looking at each other sighing and smiling wistfully.

"We're all basically the same," Liebl said. "Hanging out with you all makes that clear to me. Same aggravations, struggles, same bullshit. That's why we're all here together. Everyone's just trying to get by, Willie."

They sat and talked in Liebl's little Cooperstown until dawn. They talked about Dick Howser and George and how Hal McRae was getting pissed at a lot of the players for partying too much.

Then the doorbell rang. Everyone had lost track of the time.

"It's fucking daylight out there," a suburbanite said.

Everyone looked up in shock.

The doorbell rang again, and Liebl jumped and wiped everything off the table and into a green trash bag with one swipe of his arm.

He turned toward the stairs.

"Wipe that table off with a washcloth, fast!" he said.

Willie got up and looked up the stairs toward the door.

Liebl tucked in his shirt and pushed his hair back. He smiled before he opened the door and kept the same smile pasted on his face.

A woman and a young girl were standing there. The girl peered in and down the stairwell.

"Oh!" Liebl said. "I forgot today was your day to clean. Shit! Hey, hey guys, this is my cleaning lady. This is her daughter. Come on in."

He waved them in and started down the stairs.

"Shit!" he said.

The girl looked to be eight or nine, Willie thought. She looked at him like she was scared, and then she grabbed her mother's hand as she looked at the rest of the group.

Liebl paused and turned to the cleaning lady.

"These are the Kansas City Royals," he said. "We were just getting ready to go out to breakfast. I'll leave your check on the kitchen table. Your daughter like baseball? Give her some autographs, guys. I can tell she knows her Royals."

HAL McRAE WAS NOT refined in the techniques of conversation. Willie was walking down the aisle on the plane, and Hal raised his hand and motioned to Willie to sit down beside him. The poker players had already congregated in the back of the plane, and Willie looked back at them with longing.

"Right here," Hal grunted.

So Willie stashed his bag in the overhead and sat beside him.

The plane took off, and Hal sat looking out the window. It wobbled a bit, and Willie looked to see if Hal would react, but he didn't even blink.

The plane achieved altitude, and the hostess came through with the beverage cart.

"Beer," McRae said.

Willie ordered his screwdriver but let it sit there. He felt like he had been called to see the school principal in Seneca.

"How do you think a team goes from the World Series one year to being like this?" Hal asked. He asked it while still looking out the window at the lights below.

Willie looked over at him and squinted. He knew Hal was getting frustrated with the team. He was the resident badass, a bantam rooster whom Howser now had hitting cleanup. *He was probably the tiniest cleanup hitter in the history of baseball, but the s.o.b. burns to play ball.*

"How, Willie?"

He turned to Willie.

"You're messin' with a bunch of fools," he said. "You're hurtin' the team. I'm hitting cleanup, Willie. You think that's right? You call Howser 'stupid' to the press and blame your slump on not hitting cleanup? You had an excuse ever since you got here, Willie. What are you doing? You're hanging around with a bunch of dope-smokin' fools. You see George with those clowns? You got 10, maybe 10 years to do this, Willie. This ain't even a job. They pay you to play baseball."

Willie gripped his screwdriver.

Hal was halfway through his third beer, and his nostrils were heaving and his eyes were mean.

"I know what you all are doin', Willie, and I don't give a damn about those clowns. But I ain't gonna let you go that way, godammit. I'll beat the hell out of ya, you hear?"

Willie felt himself blush. He noticed he was squeezing the plastic cup so hard that the screwdriver was about to spill over the rim. The plane was bouncing, and he thought to say to Hal that he wasn't a junkie, that these guys were just relaxing and it was only a few nights a week, that he had it under control and his sore hand was the real issue, not his spot in the order or the drugs or even his disdain for Dick Howser.

But he stayed silent and thought to himself that if Hal were in the ring with Larry Holmes, he'd bet on Hal.

THE BOOS TURNED to taunts toward the end of 1982.

"We have the fastest and slowest Willies in baseball history!" That one from an old timer seated near the dugout after Willie didn't beat out a throw to first base.

"Aikens, only thing you're cleaning up is your dinner plate!" That one from a middle-aged woman who had season tickets and who booed him every time he stepped out of the dugout.

He stood at the bar with Liebl one night and felt like he wanted to punch anyone who came too close to him.

"Willie, I know baseball better than just about anybody," Liebl said. "And what most fans don't understand is this. You think George Brett hit

.390-whatever because he's just that good? Give me a break. He hit that because you were hitting behind him. There's this guy Bill James who thinks he can turn this game into some sort of science, like physics or chemistry. Put a number on all the patterns and predict everything but who you're gonna marry. Bill James can't measure what you mean to a team, Willie. Never will be able to understand it. You're fearsome up there, man. They can't calculate intimidation. And George owes you a big part of his paycheck."

Willie bowed his head and looked at him kindly.

"You're the only guy I ever met that ever understood me, Mark," he said. "You remind me of Jim Frey the way you think."

"Fuck Dick Howser," Liebl said as he motioned to the bartender for the check.

"You know what you need to focus on, Willie?" he said. "I read Frank White in the paper saying the fans need to lay off you. Saying you're one of the best power hitters in the league and some years it just don't come. Frank White is defending you in public, man. What's worth more, a bunch of clowns who don't understand baseball booing you or the great Frank White standing up for you? I'd like to have Frank over some time."

Willie laughed. They resumed walking and got in the car.

"Frank, man, he's clean as a whistle," Willie said laughing. "Frank would never set foot in your place. His wife would have his ass, too."

They both laughed.

"Tonight, it's just you and me," Liebl said. "We'll get high then maybe take a swim. My girlfriend's away. You can stay over if you want. Then tomorrow you're gonna begin a hot streak. Believe me."

IT DIDN'T BEGIN the next day, but it began three days after that at the end of August when it got so hot that the heat was buckling some Kansas City roads.

But toward the end of August Willie went on a six-game hitting streak; he hit the first triple of his big-league career on August 20 and hustled around the bases pretending he was Hal McRae himself.

On September 30, just before the end of the dismal 1982 season, he finally felt the ease again. He woke up and snorted a bit of coke he spotted on the table in his den. He sat and sipped coffee and held hands with Rita on the couch.

Against the A's, after the three-run homer in the fifth inning and the grand slam in the seventh, he got a standing ovation from the crowd, but the booers still booed. He kept his head down and kept walking toward the dugout as the crowd stood and cheered.

He sat there without talking or blinking or even looking anywhere but straight ahead at the dugout steps. The fans finally gave up, but the booers in their section booed all the harder, and one player shouted out, "Forget about the cocksuckers, Willie!"

He remembered everyone who had teased him his whole life, and even though he didn't know the names, he knew the faces in the stands by heart.

1983

The Hawaiian water looked inviting even though he was scared of the sea. They had done a few lines of coke that morning, and he still felt queasy at the thought of a full day on the boat.

"Mark, I only duh-duh-done this once, and I got sick as a dog stuffing himself with grass," he said. "You sure you don't have one of those patches with you?"

"Willie, trust me," Liebl said. "The best cure for just about anything is a line of coke."

As the stood on the dock Willie gaped at the size of some of the yachts.

"You get your swing back you'll own one of those," Liebl said.

Willie looked back at the ocean, and the slight roll of the waves seemed to roll right into his belly.

As they started up, the smell of the gasoline filled his nostrils, and he thought he could taste it, too. The waves rolled steeper the further out they went, and he sat in the sun trying to determine if his stomach felt better when he closed his eyes or when he opened them.

After another half hour the captain slowed, and they let out the lines to begin trolling. The sudden deceleration of the boat sent his stomach into his kidneys. It stayed there. He got up and staggered toward the cabin.

"Mark, I need some coke now, man," he said. "I'm gonna puke."

Liebl and his girlfriend and the captain started laughing.

"All right, Willie, I'll get some for you," Liebl said. "Take it easy now. As soon as the lines are out we'll all do a line. Have a beer. That will settle your stomach."

"Fuck, Mark, really, I…."

Just then the captain yelled, "Marlin!"

Willie looked up, and the mighty fish jumped and twisted in the air and slapped his body into the water with rage at being hooked.

Liebl shouted and clapped.

"That monster fights like you swing the bat, Willie!" he said. "Get in that chair now! Come on, Willie! Get in there!"

Willie rushed over, and they tied him into the chair and wrapped the rod holder around his waist and stuck the rod in.

He held on and started to pull the rod as hard as he could.

"Ho, ho, not there Willie, not that way!" the captain shouted. "You give him slack, man, like this."

The captain held another rod and showed Willie how to let out the line.

"Big fish like that you got to let him wear himself out," he said. "Then we'll just back the boat down on him."

"Captain, I ain't caught nothin' but carp and catfish," Willie said. "Mark, you take this one."

Liebl laughed some more and popped open a beer.

"Willie, I brought you out here just for this," he said, smiling. "Now come on, bring that motherfucker in, Willie! Bring her in!"

After 40 minutes of tugging and easing the line he realized he had forgotten about his stomach. He asked Kelly to take his shirt off for him, and he sat there in the sun, forgetting everything for the first time in a long time.

"Hey, Mark, how I'm doin'?" he asked.

"You're the home run king of marlin fishin'," the captain interjected.

"Hey Mark, you think you can bring me a line for the last stretch?" Willie said.

"Willie, forget about coke for a minute, man," he said. "Focus on the fish. You're almost there, man. Just focus."

He noticed the fish slowing, and the line grew less tense. He felt a second wind suddenly; the fight had cured his hangover and soothed his belly and the air and a glorious feeling like the World Series games came upon him.

"Hey, Mark," he said. "This is somethin', man."

The marlin jumped less and less and then only a foot or two out of the water.

"I told you, Willie," Liebl said. "This'll clear your head. This is the best training session you ever done in the winter time."

And as the captain started to back up to the fish, Willie realized he hadn't stuttered the whole time. He realized he rarely stuttered around Liebl. *He may be the only person I don't stutter around,* he thought.

As the boat came upon the fish, the captain thrust a big hook into it and lifted it right up into the boat. It sat there, flopping softly and heaving.

"Look at yourself, Willie," Liebl said. He hugged Willie and left one arm on his shoulders. "You just caught a monster."

"He doesn't have to prove anything to me," Howser said the first day of spring training as the press sat around him, and Willie stood in the batting cage taking extra batting practice after most of the players had retired to the clubhouse after the morning workout.

"I'm not really concerned how he swings the bat now, because he's going to do his work."

Indeed, he ran and took BP and fielded extra grounders. But he didn't talk to the press and looked the other direction every time he passed Howser or Howser came near him.

After two weeks of spring training, the games began and Liebl arrived. The evening after a game, Willie went to the front desk at the team hotel and asked for Liebl's room number. He felt happy as the elevator rose. He felt safer that Liebl was here, as if Cuda or Coach Shaver or Coach McNeil or Jim Frey had come to see him.

He knocked on the door, and he heard someone bump into the wall as he approached. Liebl opened the door, and Willie could tell he was already high. He peered past Liebl and saw Vida Blue sitting at the little table with coke in front of him.

"Close the door, Mark," Kelly said. "Someone's gonna see us."

But Liebl just stood there as if he hadn't seen Willie in years, and Willie thought he saw tears dangling from Liebl's eyes.

"Mark, man, you finally made it," Willie said.

"Come on in, brother," Liebl said. "The family is together again."

Willie noticed Liebl started to slur his words more often. He had started to stagger when he got high, and it seemed like he was high all day long now. He remembered how his stepfather Guy Webb used to walk when he was drunk, and Mark was walking the same way all the time now. Only he never got mean.

Willie shook hands with Vida, and before long Willie Wilson and Jerry Martin were there, and they sat together until sunrise.

As Willie walked into the locker room the next morning, Howser was pacing in front of the lockers and saw him. He stared at Willie and his face reddened and his shoulders rounded over.

"Duh-duh-don't even say nothin', Dick," Willie said. Some players looked up.

"I been wuh-wuh-workin' my ass off, Dick," he said. "You never have a bad morning? Huh?"

He dressed and walked out into the dugout and looked at the lineup card on the wall. He had been slotted fourth. But a big blue line had been drawn through his name. No one else's name had been written beside it.

After the game, he walked out of the clubhouse and got in his rental Mercedes and drove to Fort Myers Beach. And he ran for hours, up and down the beach, not even noticing the waves or the girls or the sun. He ran like he did in Puerto Rico, and he kept seeing the image of Ali making a fool of poor Sonny Liston. *That's how Howser's treating me,* he kept thinking. *Like a dumb black mule who got here just cause he was bigger and dumber than anybody else. Never gave me a chance,* he thought. *I got to get to another team, get to someone who knows what I can do and how I need to do it.*

A FEW DAYS BEFORE the end of spring training, the FBI agent stood stiffly in front of them in the locker room. He had taken off his sport coat and kept his hand on his belt as he spoke.

An agent usually came every season along with security guys from Major League Baseball to discuss player safety and conduct. But the event usually turned into a how-to for dealing with groupies, blackmailers, and drunks looking for a fight.

This time the guy talked about cocaine.

"Professional athletes are highly prominent figures in our society," he said. Willie wondered what school these guys went to in order to all learn to talk the way they do.

He told them they were idols to millions of boys; he told them drugs had become the scourge of American society; he told them the President of the United States was single-handedly going to wipe out the drug trade. One night during a coke session in Seneca the winter before, a friend called the White House to invite Ronald Reagan to join them. Literally picked up the phone and called the President of the United States.

"Imagine doing coke with Willie and Reagan!" the guy said. "They all do coke out in Hollywood. Those guys out there in Hollywood do everything first!"

Willie stopped looking at the agent as he contemplated the idea of doing coke with the President, and he felt the agent walk in front of him. Willie didn't look up, but he was darn sure the guy was looking straight at him and reading his dirty mind.

Afterward, the players were subdued until someone shouted out.

"Hey George, man, you worried they gonna find out about your bookie?"

The guys laughed, and Brett smiled that carefree smile he flashed whenever it seemed like the circumstances called for it. But Willie didn't laugh. He felt like he used to feel when he got in trouble back in school in Seneca.

HOWSER BENCHED WILLIE for the first time on April 15. He told the press there would be a platoon at first base going forward, and that Willie weakened the lineup when left-handers were pitching.

The season was two weeks old.

And Willie broke his silence with the press.

"He thinks he's right by doing it, but I don't think he is," he said. "He's taking me, a stronger bat, out of the lineup for a weaker bat. What good does it do to take me out of the game and put Wathan at first base? John Wathan is no threat like I am to hit the ball out of the park. How can you substitute my bat for somebody that hits five home runs in a year? Really, I can't understand it. How can he make a decision after a handful of games. It's stupid."

Before the presses even rolled later that night, the quote came back to Howser with a slight turn of phrase: "He's stupid."

Willie started to skip batting practice; he skipped infield drills; and he ate. He brought cartons of fried chicken into the clubhouse and sat eating it in front of his locker. He brought spare ribs and offered them around. He brought fried fish and hush puppies, and one day he brought Mexican and it smelled so much that the locker room attendant went up to his locker and picked up each bit of trash as soon as Willie dropped it on the floor.

A reporter one day asked him about his obvious weight gain.

"I'm a big eater," he said. "When it's cold outside and there's nothing to do for two or three hours, I find myself walking up to the clubhouse and throwing stuff in my mouth. I've handled a weight problem in the past, so I know what to do."

But his nonchalance in public hid his desperation in private. He had completed the transformation from a man on the verge of greatness to a paranoid grouch. He sensed it about himself. He felt like once the fun went out of the team last year with the strike, the fun went out of his life and never came back. But he would never fully comprehend his relentless, insistent fall until he thudded on the cold, hard floor of a prison cell.

He went to Liebl's house almost nightly. Sometimes he slept on the couch there, and one morning he woke up with a sore shoulder and had to go see the trainer. Howser rolled his eyes when he saw Willie getting treatment.

Another night he woke up on Liebl's couch, and Liebl's two cocker spaniels were sleeping on top of Willie. He petted each of them and then moved them lower on the couch toward his feet.

When Mark came downstairs, Willie sat drinking coffee with him.

"Mark, man, if I get a dog, would you take care of it when we go on road games?" he asked.

"Willie, you know I'd do anything for you," Liebl said.

THE POP-UP SHOT straight into the air above the lights into the darkness. Willie lost it for a moment, but it reappeared right where it had disappeared, and he drifted into foul territory and toward the front row of seats along the first-base line. He didn't think he would be playing in this game since a left-hander was starting for Texas, so he didn't spend much time studying foul territory, but he remembered catching foul balls here before and could almost feel the distance to the stands in his feet.

As he got under the ball a hand reached out right in front of his face and snatched the ball before it hit his mitt. He hated when fans did this; it was the only time he ever wanted to fight.

"People think I'm a big mean guy," he once told a lady friend, "but the only time I ever want to pummel someone is when they interfere with the field of play."

But as anger shot through his body, he looked from the hand to the face of its owner, and there was Mark Liebl smiling straight at him.

"Hey Mark, what the hell are you doing?" Willie said.

"What the hell do you think I was doing? I was trying to catch the damn foul ball, Willie!"

"Dammit, Mark, I could have had that," he said. "I was right on top of it. You didn't even catch it. What time did you get here anyway? I kept asking Vida when you were arriving, and no one has heard boo from you."

The umpire walked closer by this point and shook his head.

"Okay, Willie, enough chatting with the fans," he said. "Let's play ball. Play ball!"

As Willie jogged back he slowed next to the umpire.

"Would you believe I know that guy?" he asked. "Crazy, man. I know that guy from Kansas City."

And as he approached the bag, he laughed at what he almost said. It almost came out of his mouth. *That guy is our team's coke dealer. Damn near came right out of my mouth to the umpire himself.*

THE HOMESTAND BEGAN with a team meeting. Willie was late and walked in with some fried chicken again, but everyone was seated and a guy in a suit was standing there, waiting to talk. Schuerholz and the coaches stood behind him, and Willie thought it seemed like another one of those talks from the FBI in spring training.

This agent took off his suit coat, too, and he hung his thumb on his belt to accentuate his pistol. *They all like to do this,* Willie thought.

Then he started in. Major drug racket in the Midwest. Dangerous dealers looking to corral athletes of all sorts into their web. Bad, bad men.

Then some gimmick like, let's just say the Bureau had wiretapped some dealer's phone and had the voices of some Royals calling him for cocaine. Could turn into a national event, couldn't it? Imagine all the parents across America—how would they explain the whole mess to their children?

Then he shocked them all by posing the imponderable: "Imagine if Willie Wilson were involved? Vida Blue? Jerry Martin? Willie Aikens? George Brett?"

Willie wondered until the wondering hurt his head. George. *Why the hell did he say George? Are they on to his bookie and our college football pools?*

The whole locker room seemed normal—no one acted guilty. None of the guys mentioned reacted at all. Except George. Willie watched him sitting there with a what-the-fuck expression on his face.

Were they using his name to trip us up? Is George doing coke, too?

Willie walked up to Hal McRae on the field before the game.

"Hal, man, I got to talk to you," he said.

McRae nodded.

"They named me cause I been doin' that," Willie said. "I been going to this guy's house almost every night of the week with everybody and getting high."

McRae frowned. He told Willie that this was probably his last chance, but that it might just as well be too late. And then he stared at Willie like a betrayed father might have if Willie had one. He stared like Coach Shaver or McNeil would have stared had they known what was going down.

JOHN WATHAN WAS HURT, and before the game on June 9 Willie nodded to the press to gather round his locker.

"Howser's gonna eat his words," he said. "I'm hitting .316, and now he's gonna see the number would be the same if he hit me against lefties, too. You don't yank a guy around like he's doing, especially when they're paying me the kind of money Mr. Kauffman is."

In the top of the seventh, the Twins' Kent Hrbek hit a smoker that Willie dove for, snagged, and threw to pitcher Bill Castro after rolling over twice on the turf.

The crowd seemed to gasp all at once. Frank White stood there and smiled. Willie kept his head down and walked back to the bag. His shoulder ached. *Who the hell invented turf,* he thought.

He looked over at White.

"Who the hell invented that stuff?" he shouted.

In the bottom of the eighth, he drove a double to the wall in left-center as the Royals came back to win 6–5.

In the locker room afterward, he overheard Frank White say, "I think 26,000 people tonight were impressed. What they don't realize is he doesn't miss many balls he gets to. People see this big, slow guy and expect him to screw up."

Willie finished his plate of food and walked to the pay phone just outside the clubhouse. He knew Liebl's number by heart and figured he had given him enough time to get home from the stadium.

Liebl picked up, and Willie heard Bruce Springsteen blasting in the background.

"Mark, turn down the music, man," Willie said. "Mark, I need some coke, man. What you got?"

"Willie, you're welcome to come over and hang out," Liebl said. "Come on over. But it's dry all over Kansas City. My man in Dodge City is completely out, too. Something funny is happening in Dodge City. But you gonna come over?"

Some other coaches walked past Willie as he leaned against the wall and faced them.

"I think I'm gonna just go to the bar at the Sheraton and have a nightcap then," he said.

"Shit, you guys only come over if I have coke, is that it?" Liebl said. "I thought you came here to relax and shoot the shit, man."

Willie chuckled.

"Mark, quit saying shit like that. I need a lady tonight, so I'm gonna head to the Sheraton. There's a guy there usually has some stuff, too. Never as good as yours, but he's reliable. I'll call you if he can hook me up."

ON JUNE 20, Liebl and his girlfriend were getting dressed after a long day in bed, and he was telling her that seeing Vida Blue pitch that night was really a privilege. He had some coke that his neighbor was able to get his hands on—they had done some in bed—and he was raving about Blue's rookie year.

"Most flamethrowers burn out," he said. "But Vida, he's still a great pitcher. His record doesn't always show it, but the guy has outlasted everybody but Nolan Ryan."

As he stood urinating, he heard a knock at the front door and shouted down that the door was open.

He had paid no heed to his neighbor's warning that morning that he was being followed.

"Half of Kansas City knows my place is the Royals' party pad," Liebl said to the neighbor. "No one cares enough to follow you, man."

But as footsteps came pounding up the stairs, he realized his neighbor was right. Several FBI agents rushed into the bedroom with their guns drawn.

Kelly started screaming and crying and fell to the floor.

Liebl walked out of the bathroom, and as he zipped his trousers the agents all pointed their guns at him. One guy walked slowly toward him with a pair of handcuffs extended, and Liebl knew to turn around and bend at his waist.

They handcuffed him and Kelly and asked them to lead them to the basement. Some agents started to search the closet and drawers as Liebl led them out of the room.

Downstairs he could hear drawers opening and being slammed shut above them.

The agents stood looking at them as they sat on the couch, and no one said a word. Finally an agent came downstairs with a bag of cocaine in his hand.

And then the questions began.

Willie Wilson?

Willie Aikens?

Jerry Martin?

Who else?

At one point the questioning officer walked slowly around his mini-Cooperstown admiring all the memorabilia. He stopped in front of a photograph—Liebl and Willie Aikens and a 314-pound marlin hanging from a giant hook on a dock.

"Nice fish," the agent said.

And then they took off the handcuffs and started walking up the stairs. All but one agent had left the house.

"You'll hear from us again," the guy who asked about all the Royals said. And then he jangled the handcuffs and walked upstairs and out the door, too.

Liebl and Kelly looked at each other and didn't speak.

"They're trying to take down the Royals," he finally said. "We have to go to the game. Come on."

Kelly was shaking, and he nudged her up and walked into the garage and started the car before she even hopped in.

"I got to get to Vida, but I can't before he pitches," Liebl said. He backed up like hellfire and dodged a couple of kids on bikes as he raced up the street.

ON JULY 24 Willie sat and watched from the dugout as Brett stepped up to the plate in the top of the ninth inning in New York with the Yankees up 4–3. Willie held his bat and twirled it in his hands.

He hadn't spoken with Liebl or done coke since Kelly met him in the parking lot after the game on June 20 and told him the FBI was hot on Liebl's trail. And Willie started to hit again, somewhat.

But Howser would never bat him against lefties, and Howser would never hit him cleanup. He knew both policies were set in stone, and as he watched Brett he felt for the first time a sense of regret. He missed the coke; he missed hitting cleanup even more.

Brett hit the first 96-mph fireball from Gossage into the stands in right field to put the Royals up 5–4. Willie watched as he circled the bases. *George, man. He's good. He's very, very good.* He shook Brett's hand, and everyone celebrated with a little more zest because it was the Yankees, man, in New York. But then Willie looked up and saw home-plate umpire Tim McClelland laying a bat across home plate. The Royals' paused their giddy romping and watched the umpires stand around the bat, seemingly waiting for it to move like a snake in the grass.

Brett started laughing loudly.

"They're checking the pine tar," someone said. "Fucking Billy Martin."

Other players started laughing, too.

"Billy fucking Martin," a bunch of players said at the same time.

Then McClelland turned toward the Royals dugout and signaled Brett out. The umps had been using the plate, 17 inches wide, to see if the pine tar extended more than 18 inches above the knob.

Game over, McClelland signaled. Willie felt Brett blow up like a hurricane. He felt him rush out there like thunder, and everyone stood up to watch him rage at McClelland.

But the game was over, the umps all insisted, and Brett had to be escorted back to the dugout and then into the clubhouse. Willie kept sitting there. He had never seen anything like it. He realized, *If Billy Martin can get George Brett, then sure as hell the FBI can, too.*

THE NEXT DAY the Royals learned that Graig Nettles and Don Zimmer had noticed the pine tar on Brett's bat in Kansas City two weeks earlier—they were just waiting, Nettles said, for a big hit by Brett to spring the trap.

Willie didn't sleep well that night. He didn't even go out. He had never been in New York City and not gone out. Then when he heard that the Yankees had waited, bided their time, he felt even more shaken. The FBI is doing the same thing, he thought. Just waiting to nail us.

But American League President Lee MacPhail overturned the umpires' decision and ruled that Brett's homer would stand. The bat should have been excluded, but the game should not have been called. The game would resume three weeks later at Yankee Stadium, and the Royals held on to win.

Back in Kansas City, Willie got antsier. He started to feel the need for coke to curb his nerves over being busted for coke. He never had thought that he was doing anything wrong, breaking any law. It never crossed his mind. But now he was afraid of everyone, just like in the movies. Guys watching him on the street, cars following him, even a funny sound on his home phone when he picked it up. It was no fun anymore; he wanted it to end; he was willing, even wanted them, to end it for him.

A few days later, Willie Wilson came into the locker room and told him the FBI had pulled him over on his way to a doctor's appointment and questioned him about Liebl. Then he heard from Blue's girlfriend that the FBI had been to Blue's house.

After a day game, Willie went to the Sheraton across from the ballpark and went straight to a guy he knew could get him some coke. Willie never knew his name, never even paid much attention to the guy every time he came up to him to talk baseball. But somehow he always remembered the time he said over a year ago that he could always get him some coke.

And he was there. The guy said, "Wait here, Mr. Aikens. I'll be back in half an hour."

And in half an hour he walked into the Sheraton bar with a big smile on his face.

"It's a sweet trap, isn't it?" he said as he put a plastic bag on the bar chair next to Willie.

"How much?" Willie asked.

"Nothing for you, Willie," the guy said.

Willie bought the guy a drink and didn't listen while he talked and then drove home like a bat out of hell.

He got high all night. Alone. He felt better. Better and better with each line but still somehow trapped. After a few hours me right image finally came to him—Jesus in the garden, just waiting for all hell to break loose.

He went to bed at 6:00 AM and left all the coke trappings on the table in the den.

Then the knock came. He got up and pulled on his robe and washed his face and knew who it was the whole time. They kept knocking as he stopped in the kitchen and turned on the coffee machine. They knocked again as he walked down the steps and stopped to look into the den.

He paused to debate whether he should even clean up the mess. He didn't.

He opened the door and two agents stood there looking through the glass in the top of the door.

"Mr. Aikens, I am FBI Special Agent Cobb, and this is FBI Special Agent Williams," Cobb said. "Good morning."

"Come on in, guys," Willie said.

They stood in the doorway, and Willie could see the table in the den from where he was standing.

"Mr. Aikens, we would like to ask you some questions about Mark Liebl. You do know who Mark Liebl is, correct?"

"Yes, I do."

"What is your connection to Mr. Liebl?"

"Muh-Muh-Mark is a baseball fan, and I met him through one of my teammates."

"Mr. Aikens, did you know that Mr. Liebl is a cocaine dealer?"

"No, I had no idea," he said.

"Mr. Aikens, we have reason to believe that you and some of your teammates are involved in a drug ring with Mr. Liebl."

"Look, Muh-Muh-Mark is my friend. But I don't know anything about a duh-duh-drug ring."

"Well, then. Thank you for your cooperation Mr. Aikens. We will probably be in contact with you at a later date."

He nodded as they walked out. He walked downstairs and pushed the remains of the cocaine on the table into a line with a piece of paper. And then he snorted it. And then he went back to bed.

In Comiskey Park, the Royals couldn't stop laughing in the dugout at the sign that a White Sox fan kept flashing at them every time one of them left the dugout: "Kansas City Royals, please don't snort the foul line!"

John Schuerholz had acknowledged to a reporter that five Royals were being investigated by the FBI in connection with a cocaine investigation and said the Royals were cooperating fully with the FBI.

The circus reminded Willie of the 1980 season when Brett flirted with .400. *But this time they want to talk to me,* he thought. *This time George isn't getting hardly any attention at all.*

He looked at George in the locker room and saw a different George. Even George wasn't smiling or joking anymore.

On August 20, they were playing the first game of a series in Baltimore on national television. In the fourth inning, the Royals had Baltimore's Dan Ford picked off first base. As Willie ran toward the second baseman, Ford suddenly stopped. Willie stopped, too. He was going to throw, but for some reason Ford's stopping made him stop. He could never explain why. He just stood there and watched as Ford started to run again and reached second. Ford later scored.

Other Royals made comedic miscues that day. But Willie's was the most extreme. Even Howser laughed as he watched from the dugout.

"Somebody tell me what's happening," Howser said to reporters after the game.

HE RARELY PLAYED after that. In Minnesota, Willie got coke and finished it by two in the morning and then drank a half bottle of vodka. He overslept and missed the bus to the stadium. He got up and caught a taxi and told the driver to take him to the closest Kentucky Fried Chicken. He ate it on the way to the park and finished it at his locker. George Brett's name was penciled in at first base.

But his hitting coach, Rocky Colavito, came over to Willie's locker and told him Howser wanted to see him in his office.

"I don't want to talk with Dick Howser," Willie said.

"Look, Willie, Dick's our manager. He is the one who gives the orders."

"He doesn't give any orders to me," Willie said.

"I think you are making a mistake, Willie."

"Rocky, I made a whole lot of mistakes this season."

Howser came out and saw them talking.

"Hey, Willie, get the hell in here!" Howser shouted.

"I don't have anything to talk about with you, Dick."

Howser glared.

"Then that will cost you a hundred."

"I'll just win it at poker, Dick."

Howser scowled.

Willie would never exchange another word in his life with Dick Howser. Just like the year before, he had a few final flourishes at the end of the season. He hit a two-run homer in the ninth inning in a game in which Dan Quisenberry tied the major league record with his 38th save. He had five RBIs on September 28 in a game in Seattle in which he also hit his 21st and 22nd home runs of the season.

After the last game, a reporter came up to him and asked about his upswing in September.

"If I get traded, I don't want it to be because I didn't get along with the manager or didn't want the other players to do good," he said.

But he was thinking very little about being traded. He was thinking about getting high as many times as he could now that the season was over. All day long, every day, as often as he could in case they were going to send him to jail.

1984

They told him famous people like Zelda Fitzgerald had come to Sheppard Pratt to conquer addictions. He didn't ask who she was. The word *addiction* didn't even register for him. Addiction wasn't yet an American phenomenon, and they also used other words like *treatment* and *program* and *therapy* that sounded way out of his league.

But he trusted his agent Ron Shapiro. The guy had become like a father to him, so when he firmly recommended this place Sheppard Pratt, Willie knew he had to go. Shapiro had a law firm in addition to his sports agency, and he told Willie that by checking into Sheppard Pratt he could possibly reduce the sentence the judge was going to hand him that winter.

The road wound up to a huge building that looked like an old mansion, the sort of place Willie had seen in the movies where rich white women walked around with umbrellas even on sunny days—the kind of old movies that were on at 3:00 AM when he was high and drinking vodka to come down so he could sleep.

Inside the building, he felt like an alien. People were walking around crazy-eyed; a woman was holding both her ears as she walked down the hall; two older men held hands and swung their arms like school kids as they walked.

The nurse walked them to another wing where another species of sufferers, gloomy but not crazy looking, sat and read books and looked out windows at the rolling hills of the hospital grounds.

He had never felt so nervous in his life. He stepped toward the window and looked out for a good while—people were sitting on benches reading, sitting on the grass reading, walking and reading. He hadn't brought any books and wondered what the hell he was going to do to pass the time.

And suddenly he thought about Paulette, how clean and righteous she was. He didn't go so far as to wonder how different his life might be if she had agreed to marry him. He just thought about how nice it is that there is a girl out there somewhere in the world who has her shit together still.

And the next day he started to pay attention—he listened to his adviser, he read the books that they gave him and underlined key passages, he spoke about getting high at the World Series and the people in his group—all white people—stared at him in amazement.

A thin teenage boy with long, greasy hair raised his hand as if he needed Willie's permission to ask him a question.

"How come you were so into coke?" he asked. "I heard black guys only did that crack stuff."

Two women tsk-tsk'd him, but his adviser brought up the kid's question in their one-on-one session the next day.

"The science isn't whole yet, but we know that crack is much more addictive than cocaine, and given its affordability, it is indeed more common in black communities," she said. "You are fortunate that your economic status as a ballplayer kept you from a far worse demon."

That night he thought about what she had said. He realized everyone at the hospital was white. He realized that except for a few Royals, everyone who went to Liebl's house was white. He had all but lost touch with Cuda and the boys from Seneca. And he thought about the only time he had seen crack cocaine— the time a dude took him deep into the hood to buy coke, and the house where they went seemed like the bottom of hell with all those people strung out and lying there.

He went to sleep thinking that for one of the few times in his life he was different because of the color of his skin. White girls never cared, coaches never cared, his teammates never cared, but this woman sure did.

He laughed to himself. He thought about how the FBI had thrown George Brett's name into the ring during that meeting in the clubhouse to cloud things up a bit. *That agent came there to help us out,* he thought. *He came there to tell us to cut it out. All these people been helpin' me, and I just kept going deeper into the funhouse. The fun is over,* he decided. *I'm gonna be a ballplayer again.*

He returned to Kansas City for the sentencing. As he arrived at the courthouse, dozens of reporters rushed toward him as he got out of his car.

The cameramen came running after them and walked backward in front of him at a speed that amazed him. *These guys must practice this in school,* he thought.

In the hallway, Willie saw Wilson and Martin and they smiled and embraced.

"Thuh-thuh-this here's a national event," Willie said.

They all shook their heads and started walking behind their attorneys toward the courtroom.

Then there were the formalities and a lot of words Willie thought seemed like a bunch of hot air before the judge finally asked Wilson to rise.

Willie heard his name called, and he stood in slow motion. He saw his mother sitting there in her high-backed seat next to the window in her apartment reading the Bible and living a clean life after all. He saw the Judge's lips moving and his eyes severe and disappointed, but Willie didn't hear a word he said.

He still didn't know his precise sentence, and he had to do all he could to keep from staggering out of the courtroom. His attorney took him by the arm at one point, and he felt the noise go away immediately.

"I get the same thing?" he asked.

He felt his attorney nod and he still couldn't hear right, so all he remembered was hearing that Martin's fine was only $2,500 instead of $5,000.

"That dude wanted to make an example out of us," he said.

His attorney nodded again as they reached the door. Willie could see all the cameras again and the way they fell all over each other reminded him of the summer Brett was flirting with .400. *All that video,* he wondered, *where does it go?*

As he got in his car and drove away, it all started to come to him, all that he thought he hadn't heard but indeed had. He was being sent to Fort Worth Correctional Institute, a minimum security place the judge called a "premier institution for the treatment of drugs."

He drove home slowly and kept mulling the notion that the Judge thought he needed to be somewhere where they treated you for drugs. He sat on the couch in his den for an hour and watched all his behaviors in that same room in his head. He decided to drive to the ballpark. The whole way he kept seeing images in his head of himself snorting coke. He parked his car near the entrance. A security guard waved at him. He turned on the radio and listened to the coverage of the sentencing. It was chilly, so he turned the heater up. The sports reporter said that John Schuerholz told the press Willie was not in the Royals' plans for the next season. Martin and Blue had already been released, and Willie would have to be traded or released by December 20.

He stared at the stadium and shook his head.

We were just having fun, he thought. *Just a place to go to get away from it all and be with people who didn't care if you were a ballplayer.*

He returned to Sheppard Pratt to finish his time in the treatment center because Shapiro was demanding it of him. It meant that he would arrive late for spring training, but so be it. And it was there that he met Pat Gillick, a meeting that he had no way of knowing would bring a future angel into his life. Gillick was the general manager of the Toronto Blue Jays and was considering trading for Willie. He wanted to do his due diligence. But Willie felt Gillick was like a visitor, a kind man asking him questions more about his life than baseball. He would never forget that kindness and would see it again 20 years later when he would appreciate it even more.

He had no conversation with anyone there for the whole month except for Ron Shapiro. Ron kept calling, visiting, urging him to get himself straight.

On December 5, Shapiro told him he was traded to the Toronto Blue Jays.

On December 15, the commissioner of Major League Baseball, Bowie Kuhn, suspended him, Wilson, Blue, and Martin from baseball for a year with the possibility of review and reinstatement in May. Blue would be the only one of the four not to be reinstated; he sat out the entire 1984 season.

THE DAY WILLIE got to the prison in Fort Worth he met Wilson and Martin— Willie started his sentence later due to his time at Sheppard Pratt—and they told him the place would blow his mind.

It already had. The taxi he took from the airport in Dallas drove straight through the security check-in as the guard waved at them without even lifting his head. As he got out of the cab he realized the place didn't even have a fence.

They had lost his bags at the airport, but when he checked in there was a bit of paperwork and then the guard just sat and looked at him.

"You can go through now," the guard said. "Just tell the woman inside the door you are one of the ballplayers."

Willie smiled at him, but the guard sat expressionless.

"My uniform," Willie said in a hesitant voice.

The guard frowned.

"The inmates don't wear uniforms here," he said. "This is a correctional and instructional institute. You are here to get better."

"But the airline lost my bag."

Then he walked into the housing section and saw some of the 200-some women who were there, too. *This don't seem like they're tryin' to teach me a thing,* he thought.

He wore the same clothes for the next three days through orientation, and they even let him go to the closest department store in Forth Worth to buy underwear. He washed them in his sink in his private cell before he wore them.

He went through an orientation that used a lot of the same words he heard the doctors use at Sheppard Pratt. Someone said the word *addiction* every five minutes.

He had been assigned to work in the kitchen cleaning plates and pushing the food carts and plate carts between the dining room and the "swamp"—the room at the end of the hall where they gave the dishes showers.

Valerie asked him during their very first shift if he was one of the ballplayers. To Willie, she looked more like a schoolteacher than an inmate. She wore her brown hair back in a bun and had those schoolteacher's glasses with a cord around them so they could hang from her neck. Then she smiled and moved closer to him at the sink where they were wiping off plates. She brushed hips with him.

She turned off the faucet and asked quietly, "So if you're one of the ballplayers, I guess you already have a walkie?"

He scraped some challenging spaghetti sauce off a plate and looked at her. "What?"

She giggled.

"A walkie. Your boys already got them. They didn't tell you yet? You get to walk in the yard and hold hands with a girl. Then maybe other things if we like each other. I'll be your walkie tomorrow if you want."

He liked the first walk—she wiggled her little fingers inside and around his and scratched gently at his palm.

The next week she took him to the love corner. It was a group of tables in the far corner of the recreation area. The guards let the walkers go there—they knew what went on there but didn't bother with it, she told him.

And they stroked and jabbed at each other's privates for 20 minutes each afternoon.

"You know," he said to her one day as they sat there. "They do all this talk about addiction and everything, but the first day I walked in here I knew they wouldn't cover my addiction to what you got between your legs."

She had the look of a woman trying to blush but no longer had it in her.

"I have something special for you in the kitchen tomorrow," she said. "Old-Timer is gonna help us out."

Old-Timer was an elderly prisoner who could have doubled for a famous blues singer. He whistled all day long. His job was to mop the floors. Willie had heard he was in for dealing cocaine but couldn't believe a guy at that age would deal.

The next morning as Willie arrived at 5:30 to take the plates and cutlery from the washers, Old-Timer winked at him.

"I got you covered, son," he said. "After breakfast you take all those carts back there and do a round-up like in the Westerns when the Indians was attackin'. That sweet thing's gonna be waitin' for you inside that bandwagon, and you get in there and get yourself some. I'll be on lookout mopping the hall. Any guard comes, I'm gonna start whistlin'. That simple. Livin' the luxury life here in Fort Worth, son."

Willie shook his head in disbelief.

"Why you helpin' me like this, Old-Timer?"

"You're Willie Mays, man! You's a fine ballplayer bring lots of joy to people. I want to give some back to you here."

Willie smiled. He let Old-Timer off the hook on the name thing. He nodded his head in thanks and started to walk away, but then stopped and turned.

"Hey Old-Timer, what song you gonna wuh-wuh-whistle if anybody starts comin'?"

Old-timer laughed.

Then in his bluesy voice he said, "'The Battle Hymn of the Republic,' son."

Willie nodded and walked to the dish carts. He started pushing them one by one toward the dining room. He saw Valerie and blew her an air kiss, and she blew one back with both her hands.

After breakfast, she stood against the sink washing dishes, and whenever he would come in with a cart she would lean over and flash him—she had slit her denim pants in her crotch from front to back, and the gaping hole so transfixed Willie the first time he noticed it that he crashed one cart into another.

As the cleanup wound down, he watched her walk toward the dishwasher room. He pushed the last cart as fast as he could, and its rattling made him worry that he might draw a guard's attention. But he hadn't seen a guard all morning, and as he passed Old-Timer with his mop in his hand, Old-timer winked.

"Ain't but one guard in the dining room today, and he's readin' the papers," Old-Timer said. "Get after it."

He lined up the last cart and saw her waiting inside the ring. Indeed, he saw her bottom up in the air waiting for him inside the ring of carts. He closed the circle and unzipped and walked right into her.

She was holding on to one of the carts as he worked away at her, and the cart suddenly gave way. Some plates smashed as they fell to the floor. He paused to make sure the coast was clear. She kept wiggling and shaking.

Suddenly he thought her heard Old-Timer whistle. He leaned over her.

"Valerie, you know that song?" he asked.

She turned and looked stunned.

"What?" she said.

"The song Old-Timer is whistlin'? You know the nuh-nuh-name of it?"

She tightened her eyes and threw her head back.

When they finished she pushed one of the carts aside herself, tidied her hair a bit, and walked right out. *She didn't even kiss me goodbye,* he thought, shaking his head.

The next day and every day after that they met after most meals so long as Old-Timer was working. As soon as he encountered him alone, Willie asked Old-Timer to whistle, "The Battle Hymn of the Republic" for him. *It's catchy,* he thought.

HIS COUNSELOR, ANOTHER WOMAN who looked like a schoolteacher, provided him with his only moment of self-reflection the whole 90 days.

"You realize that, as a ballplayer, a year away from baseball may erode your skills to a degree that you will not be able to perform at the same level as you did prior to your suspension?" she said.

"Sure I do," he said. "After the strike in 1981 I had a hell of a time getting my swing back. You should have a batting cage here for the inmates. It would be a great thing—even for softball or something."

She looked at him with disdain.

"Mr. Aikens," she said. "Our goal here is to help you realize that you need to develop a certain maturity to function as a citizen whenever your baseball career ends. Your comment makes me think you think it will never end. In fact, you may never play baseball again. You are here to develop skills in the game of life, skills for being a better player at the game that counts."

He laughed.

"You're kidding, right?" he asked. "This place don't teach nobody nuthin'. I've had a good time here with my friends. The government's just makin' an example of us since we're ballplayers. And I ain't gonna lose a bit of my game, I promise you that. Just keep lookin' for me on TV. You a baseball fan?"

"No, sir, I am not."

"Well, after meeting all of us, I bet you're gonna be one, no? At least a little bit?"

But as they sat neither realized what a waste of time it all was—the 90-day sentence, the facility, their counseling sessions. He would later admit it wasn't enough time to correct anything, nor was the time punishing enough to effect change. He would later admit it felt like the judicial system was joking around, and he wouldn't stop laughing about it until the big steel doors at Leavenworth slammed shut on him 11 years down the road.

AFTER HIS RELEASE on March 25, 1984, he reported to the Blue Jays' extended spring training facility in Florida. Major League Baseball did cut his suspension significantly—he could return to baseball on May 15. And he could travel with the team in the interim.

And the first road trip he took with them brought him right back to Kansas City.

Before the first game, he took batting practice and ran for half an hour in the outfield. He got hugs from his former teammates. He lay on the grass and looked up at the sky. Dick Howser came out onto the field and their eyes met, but only momentarily—they both looked away instantly and focused on the closest person to them.

In Willie's case, it was George, of course. He was standing over by the third-base bag, studying the field like a golfer analyzing the contours of a putting green. George looked up and raised his arms and when he hugged him, Willie felt happy for the first time in a long time.

As the game began, he undressed and showered. He stood under the water for half an hour, letting it beat against his sore back. Then he saw a bucket on the floor and sat on it under the water. He could hear the roar of the crowd, so he supposed the Royals were winning. He wanted to wait until nightfall before he took his ticket and sat in the stands. Fewer people would notice him. He dressed and pulled up his collar and went out.

As he made his way down to the Blue Jays' family section, the murmur started. He told himself he should stand up and not stutter and say, "I'm sorry." But he didn't want to, either. He really wanted to stand up and say, "They set us up, they wanted to make an example of us, and they used you as much as us. We weren't doing anything half of you don't do. Boo. Go ahead and boo."

IN HIS FIRST HOME GAME in Toronto, he had two hits in the 3–2 win over the White Sox. He got a partial standing ovation in his first at-bat. He hit a double in his second at-bat but was thrown out sliding into home after George Bell hit a single. He got a larger standing ovation, though, as he slapped the dirt off his jersey and limped to the dugout. He led off the seventh with a single, and nearly the whole stadium stood and applauded.

Afterward he said, "I've had great success against the Jays in the past, and I guess maybe the fans remember some of those times and realize that I'm with them now."

Lloyd Moseby won the game for the Blue Jays with a triple but afterward congratulated the fans for how they supported Willie.

"I don't know that they would have given him that kind of greeting in the past," Moseby said. "I think they've learned to respect baseball a lot better, and I think the fans were excellent to tell Willie they appreciate him."

He settled in. He stayed clear of drugs and the lure of the night. He had to perform two years of community service as part of his probation, so he counseled alcoholics on an Indian reservation north of Toronto. And he impressed the general manager, Pat Gillick, with his genial way and kindness on those trips to visit the Indians. On one visit, an alcoholic came up to him and told him he looked like an Indian chief. It wasn't the first time he heard that.

WILLIE WALKED UP to Gillick's office one day during batting practice. He wore his uniform and an apologetic face. He felt about Gillick like he felt about Jim Frey—just being around him made Willie believe in himself.

"Winter ball would do you good, Willie," Gillick said to him. "And I think Venezuela would be better for you than the D.R. The pitching is going to be stronger there this year. I know you are the kind of hitter who needs repetition. You need it more than most. I will speak with you after winter league ends to figure out how we can keep your swing on track until spring training."

"I trust your judgment, Pat," Willie said. "And I'm guh-guh-grateful to you still for giving me a chance."

Gillick hit him on the shoulder and smiled.

"You staying clean still, right Willie?"

Gillick already knew the answer. He didn't have spies, but he asked other players and studied Willie's eyes and watched how he carried himself sometimes instead of even watching the game from his seat in the booth.

"There's a long life after baseball, and the important thing is to keep living the straight and narrow and keep clean. Baseball careers don't end when you stop playing. You'd make a great coach someday, Willie."

"Don't worry 'bout that, Pat," Willie said with a grin. "I gonna go down there and get my swing back, and we won't have to worry about real life for a good while."

But he didn't believe himself. He knew he might get it back to some degree, but he knew deeper and truer that he probably would never be able to hit a baseball like he did those nights in 1980 when it seemed like he could have hit one the size of a pea if that were what Tug or Carlton had thrown at him. It had all gone somewhere, and he had a good hunch he wouldn't find out where.

1985

The platoon continued in spring training and his sense of looming failure did, too. This time he was sharing at-bats and first base with Len Matuszek, whom the Blue Jays acquired during the off-season, and Willie was spending nights in his hotel just waiting for Pat Gillick to knock on the door.

Three weeks into the season the reporters started to ask him about the possibility of his being released. Pitcher Jim Clancy began the season on the disabled list and was eligible to come off on May 2. Willie was earning $450,000 on the final year of his contract.

One morning in his hotel in Arlington, Texas, he heard the knock. It was gentle, polite. That meant Gillick was knocking. *Nobody's that polite in this game except Pat,* he thought.

He got up and opened the door and smiled kindly at Gillick. He wanted to make this easy for him. But Gillick already had tears in his eyes.

"Come on in, Pat," Willie said. "I know this is a tough business, Pat. Don't worry. Tell it to me straight."

Gillick looked out the hotel window. He shook his head up and down in agreement. Then he shook it back and forth in a tight berth. He trembled slightly.

"Pat, you gave me a chance, man," Willie said. "Things just didn't work out. But you don't have nothin' to feel bad about, Pat."

"The coaches just believe in Matuszek more, Willie," he said. "I have a place in the organization for you. Public relations. You can do that for a while and think about the best way to get back on the field."

Tears started to run down Willie's face. *I'm 30 years old,* Willie thought. *What the hell is he offering me a job in the front office for?*

"You can no longer travel with the team," Gillick said. "We will arrange your travel back to Toronto as soon as you want to go."

He started to walk out, then he turned.

"Willie, more than anything I want you to keep your life together," he said. "Someone may pick you up. I think you can go down to our Triple A club—we might have a spot for you there. But our coaches just don't think you match our needs as a ballclub right now."

Willie smiled at him. He wanted to say, "I'm only 30 years old, Pat. Thirty, man. My career ain't even half over." But he noticed Gillick's eyes were tearing up a little bit, too. Willie wasn't used to seeing a grown man cry, so he didn't say anything and kept trying to smile as kindly as Gillick always smiled at him.

He did play for the Blue Jays' Triple A team in Syracuse, New York, for a few months, and he hit. No scouts followed him, no GMs called, and for the first time as a professional ballplayer, Willie felt unemployed.

There was a bidding war for him among teams in the Mexican League, though, and he knew he had an ear for Spanish, so soon he headed down Mexico way.

ALL THAT FALL, though, he knew what was happening in Kansas City and what was going to happen. They were going to win. The Royals had the same energy as 1980, the same mojo, but they had one more thing—a young ace, Bret Saberhagen, who was on fire.

Willie went to Seneca during the World Series between the Royals and Cardinals, and he shot pool every night. He was still clean and barely drank during the games. And he didn't listen. He had Cuda turn down the volume on the television in the pool hall, and he never even looked up to apprise himself of the scores.

Once in a while, he took in Saberhagen mugging for the camera between inning after stunning inning, and the guy reminded him of George—sparkling, mesmerizing, and even more so on TV.

But Willie watched Game 7. They shot pool lackadaisically, sometimes forgetting whose shot was next. He drank water with lime as he leaned on his stick and took in the massacre.

And then Joaquin Andujar exploded. The first time, Willie said to Cuda, "This guy is losing it, but he isn't done."

The second time, as Andujar charged home-plate umpire Don Denkinger and Cardinals' players used all their might to restrain him, Willie shook his head.

"Let's get out of here, Cuda," he said.

"You want to go smoke some weed, Willie?"

"Nah," Willie said. "I want to go to sleep. Guys like Andujar ruining this game. Look at George and Saberhagen, out there having a ball. And guys like Andujar think this is football."

As they were walking out, Willie looked back to see the Royals hurling themselves on top of each other on the field. *I helped get them to this point,* Willie thought. *I don't deserve a ring, but some of them know. George knows. A World Series champion is a product of the teams that went before it. George and Hal know it.*

1986

They had their own spring training for a few weeks in the Mexican leagues, but in Puebla, where he had signed, the sun was so hot that it felt like summer so the players called it summer training. He was earning $2,500 per month, but his teammates already started making him buy meals since they all knew he was one of the highest-paid players in the league.

His first week he felt his heart for the first time. The Puebla altitude made it pound all night long, and he would wake up and feel it banging on his chest. He thought back to the one time the coke made him crazy. He was running up the stairs at Liebl's house to work off some coke so he could do more coke, and suddenly he felt his heart start to leap upward in his chest. He had to sit down and breathe in and out while a strange woman rubbed the back of his neck and kissed the top of his head over and over.

In his second week the rain never stopped, and they scheduled batting practice for 7:00 AM since that was when it seemed to rain least. He noticed the glorious altitude right away—ball after ball rose higher and carried further and even the bat felt lighter and faster, too.

"You got a better chance to get back to the bigs here, too," an American teammate had said as they sat in the dugout and watched the rain two days ago. "Even the scouts don't understand how much it can help you. You could hit 100 homers here, Willie."

"Get out of here," Willie said.

But he hit five in his first week, and with the 132-game season running from March through July, he already started to do the math in his head as he sat in the dugout one night.

His teammates told him they wanted him to come out with them after the game, but he knew they just wanted him to buy their drinks, too. He was getting so hot that he started jogging again before games. Then he started showing up early and doing sprints and calisthenics even during the afternoon rains. Then he convinced some bullpen guys to throw him batting practice even though they rarely took it here. He paid them a dollar a session.

After 51 games, he had hit 20 homers, driven in 58 runs, walked 53 times, and had 79 hits in 175 at-bats.

THE PUEBLA BLACK ANGELS won the Mexican Series; he ended up hitting .454 with 46 home runs and 154 RBIs. His average was a league record. And all he got was an offer from the New York Mets to join their Triple A club in Tidewater.

He spent days trying to decide if he should accept the offer; and he spent nearly a week driving his Mercedes from Puebla. Every few days he would call the Mets and tell them where he was. He would eat a big breakfast at whatever hotel he stayed at, then drive a couple hours, then eat a huge lunch, then drive a couple hours, then stop and eat a huge dinner. He felt his weight because the seat belt got tighter and tighter each day he got in the car. It squeezed his chest so much that it reminded him of how hard it was to breathe the first few days in Puebla.

One night he pulled into a liquor store in Arkansas and sat in the car. The cashier noticed him and kept walking up to the door to see what he was up to. Finally he came out.

"What you up to fella?" the guy said.

"Juh-juh-just tryin' to decide if I want a drink," he said.

"Well go decide somewhere else before I call the cops," the guy said. "I don't like selling to blacks, anyway."

Willie got out of the car and shut the door.

"Where you goin'?" the guy asked.

Willie leaned into his face.

"I decided I want a drink."

He walked into the store, and the guy followed him. He walked up and down each aisle as the guy watched him from behind the counter. He kept looking at the floor; he didn't want to look at a single bottle because the right color or label might set him off. He walked back each aisle the way he came and walked toward the door.

"I changed my mind," he said to the guy. Then he walked out the door.

He finished the season in Tidewater, never found his swing, and didn't get called up, as he suspected.

HE WAS PLAYING winter ball in Mazatlán, and two Japanese scouts kept showing up at his games. They arranged a meeting at his hotel the third week of November.

Each of the two Japanese guys bowed when they entered his suite, and he bowed back.

He motioned for them to sit on the couch. Their suits and ties matched.

"This is my boss, Samurai," the younger guy, Intramural, said.

"You make up those names?" Willie asked.

The interpreter shook his head up and down, over and over.

"So the players I guess wear those, too, when we travel?"

Intramural talked to Samurai, and they both smiled when Samurai took a deep breath and then spoke like a machine gun shooting out words. Willie started to laugh. And then all three of them laughed for a while. *They don't even know what I'm laughing at,* Willie thought, *but these guys like to laugh. That's a good sign.*

"Mr. Aikens, the boss likes you," Intramural said.

Willie looked at him, puzzled.

"You said 'we,'" Intramural said again. "When you referred to the traveling suits that our players wear. The boss like that you said 'we' already."

Willie smiled. He hadn't realized he had used the word *we,* but he liked the way these guys smiled and laughed and started to imagine himself with a roomful of naked Japanese girls smiling and laughing like this.

"You still famous man in Japan," Intramural said. "When the Royals came in 1981, the boss and his boss met you. You recall, Mr. Aikens?"

"I met lots of folks over there, and everybody seemed real nice," Willie said.

Intramural translated and Samurai took a deep breath and blurted out a bunch of funny sounding words again.

"The boss is so pleased you remember him and his boss," Intramural said.

I'll let him have it, Willie thought. *This guy is probably just trying to keep his job. Not much different than me,* he thought.

"We have been given orders to negotiate a contract with you, sir," Intramural said.

Willie had talked to a few guys who went over there for the money. *None of them ever made it back,* he thought. *So I'm gonna have to be the first one. They wouldn't sign me out of Mexico, but that's even better baseball over there.*

"I'm gonna come over and hit 50 homers for you," he said. "And win your batting title. What did the top guy in Japan hit last year?"

They both nodded and Intramural translated and Samurai stopped smiling. He inhaled but only made a sound on his exhale.

"We can pay you $250,000 for a one-year contract," Intramural said.

Willie wondered if he could hire him to interpret to Japanese women. *This guy wouldn't know how to sweet-talk, though*, he thought.

"I earned $600,000 my last year in the big leagues, so I would settle for half that," Willie said. He had expected an offer of around $100,000. He tried to do the math on the raise he would be getting from his Mexican salary, but the whole thing had him flustered and he just told himself it was a lot more.

Intramural translated to Samurai, and then Samurai took in a mouthful of air.

Willie waited, but Samurai let the air out. Then he grunted.

They both stood up at the same time and bowed and shook Willie's hand. They kept bowing.

"We will be happy to have you help bring us a championship," Intramural said after Samurai spoke.

"Well, that would be nice, wouldn't it?" Willie said. He bowed back as they walked out of the hotel room.

Then Intramural knocked five seconds later. Willie opened the door.

"We will have to clear your papers with each government and get your working visa," he said. "But we have good relationships and will be in contact with you soon."

He bowed again, and Samurai bowed behind him. *Cille don't even know where Japan is*, Willie thought. *I'm gonna have to buy her a globe to see it. And it's gonna be expensive as hell for me to fly Cuda over there*, he thought. *Hell, they probably won't even let Cuda leave the country.*

1987

Nor would they let Willie. He got a call one day the next spring before he was heading to the ballpark. The Japanese government had denied him a work visa based on his misdemeanor drug charge, a middleman in the deal told him. No way to get around it. "The Japs don't fool around with that stuff," the guy said.

Willie hung up.

The Japs don't fool around with that stuff. He kept repeating it to himself. *Half of the United States of America is going to get high tonight, and the Japs don't fool around with that stuff,* he thought.

He went to the ballpark and had a couple of singles, but the whole game long he spent convincing himself that he was going to have a drink tonight. During his final at-bat in the seventh inning, the internal debate boiled down to where it would occur: Señor Frogs or El Caracol. He lined a single past the second baseman, and as he ran to first he decided upon El Caracol. *The snail,* he thought. The perfect place for a guy who runs like me.

He got there and recognized the girl from the tourist agency at the airport who always helped him and smiled so sweetly. She always touched the tip of her upper lip with her tongue when she was listening, and when he said hello to her at the bar, she did it again.

"You have a buh-buh-beautiful tongue," he said.

"Beautiful que?" she asked.

"Tongue," he said. "*Lengua. Muy bonita tú lengua.*"

She giggled.

Her name was Yolanda, and he liked the way it felt in his mouth when he said the word. It was a word that was so fun to say he was sure he would never stutter saying it. He asked her why she liked Bloody Marys—he thought they were too spicy.

"This is tequila with tomato juice," she said. "Try one. I invite you."

He liked it, and drank five in a couple of hours. Then he drank them with Yolanda every night for the next three weeks. He liked all the vitamins. She told him tequila has no sugar so you never get a hangover. He liked that, too. And he liked her curly tongue and what she did with it at the end of the night when he felt like he was so full of tomato juice he might start pissing red and so lonely he wished he would die in his sleep.

THE SUMMER RAINS had started early, and he decided not to go back to check out his home in Kansas City before he began the summer season with Puebla. He drove with Yolanda to Puebla and spent two straight days in bed with her. At the first team workout three days before the season began, he felt sluggish. The next day, he started taking batting practice but felt like he was going to throw up, so he went home. She wasn't there, nor were her things, nor was the $1,000 he hid under the cardboard bottom of his suitcase. He went to bed and then got up to vomit in the middle of the night and vomited the rest of the night.

He called Cuda.

"Cuda, I think I huh-huh-have AIDS, man," he said as he struggled for air. "I been sleeping with this girl named Yolanda the past month, and she don't like condoms and I think she gave it to me, man."

Cuda started laughing.

"What you laughing at, Cuda?"

"Willie, you don't get AIDS in a month, man," Cuda said. "If you got AIDS, you got it from some girl before Yolanda. You don't get AIDS in no month, Willie. But you probably gave it to her if you weren't using a condom, man! So she ran off with something besides your money, man, and that's the good news here in this situation."

He got up the next morning and looked in the mirror. He was as yellow as the Mexican sun at midday. His skin, his eyes, his fingernails. Everything yellow. He started to throw up yellow bile. *I'm dying,* he thought. *I'm dying of AIDS. This is how it all ends. Even the Japanese don't want me, and I'm gonna die here in this shithole town in Mexico of AIDS.*

He pulled on his baseball uniform and staggered downstairs. The few taxi drivers who sat in the lobby stared at him and cringed.

"*Necesito ir al estadio,*" he said.

They looked at each other, and no one moved.

"*Por favor,*" he said. "Take me to the baseball stadium."

A kid in the doorway motioned to him, and he followed. They hopped in his car, and Willie rested his head on the window so he could get more air.

He handed the kid all the pesos he had as the kid helped him to the locker room. A couple of his teammates were already there. They got up and took his arms, and the kid stood there watching.

One of the teammates ran out and came back with the general manager. They all stood and stared at him.

"*Tengo SIDA,*" he said.

"*No, no tienes SIDA,*" the general manager said. "*Tienes hepatitis.* Hepatitis. Bad water, Willie. Hepatitis."

He fell asleep on the floor and woke up in a doctor's office with an IV in his arm.

HE LAY IN HIS OWN BED in Kansas City and reached over for the bottle of vodka on his nightstand and took a swig. He got up and went into the bathroom and

Willie was already speaking a little Spanish during a taped interview for a Mexican radio station during the 1980 playoffs. (AP Images)

Willie rounds third after the first 1980 World Series homer. (AP Images)

The record-setting homer on October 18, 1980. (AP Images)

The adoration: Royals Stadium reacts to the record-setting homer.
(AP Images)

Still trying to clean up for George in 1982: the cool cats celebrate at home plate after Willie hit a three-run homer in the fifth inning against the Oakland A's in September 1982. He later hit a grand slam in the seventh inning. (AP Images)

The patented lead leg as Willie watches one of his final home runs as a big leaguer in 1983. (US Presswire)

Willie weighed more than 300 pounds when he was arrested on federal drug charges in March 1994.
(Kansas City Star)

While in Estill in 1996, Willie visits with (from left) Sara's mom, Silvia, Sara, Nicole, Cille, and Willie's niece Sheba Williams. The visiting room had a platform with a tropical backdrop for family photos.

Willie, Maria, and Lucia reunited in 1998 in Atlanta. Similar platform, different backdrop.

Willie, Nicole, and Sara in 2002 in Atlanta.

At Kauffman Stadium in 2009, wondering. (Getty Images)

In May 2009, Willie (rear) and Willie Wilson helped distribute food to people in need in the Kansas City area as part of Operation Blessing. (US Presswire)

Willie and Sara in Kansas City in 2010.

Willie and Lucia at a hairdressers' shop in 2011.

Baby Sarah in 2011.

Willie and his girls in 2011. Pictured are (from left) Lucia, Willie, Sarah, Nicole, and Sara.

The legends in 2011: Willie Wilson, John Mayberry, Willie, and Amos Otis.

turned on the light. He leaned close into the mirror and looked at his eyes. They were much less yellow but still not white.

He had called Rita the day before, and she knocked on the door the next day.

He held the banister as he walked down the stairs. He opened the door, and she gasped.

"Did you bring any cocaine?" he said.

She walked through the threshold and hugged him.

"You look worse than I expected," she said.

He hugged her back then dropped his hands to her shoulders and looked straight into her eyes.

"Did you bring any cocaine?" he asked.

"Of course," she said.

He closed the door and started to walk downstairs to the den.

She followed him and asked, "Don't you want to have sex first?"

"No," he said.

He sat on the couch. She sat beside him and took out a bag of coke.

"You know, the whole flight back I felt so sick I wanted to die," he said. "And I knew the only thing that could make me feel better was this. All this medicine they're giving me and I know that all I need is this."

THAT SUMMER HE PLAYED racquetball with Rita, who always seemed to reappear when coke was around, and he slowly started to feel stronger. She would sneak coke onto the court in her panties. They would lay a racquet cover on a racquet and take turns holding it while the other one snorted. One time she told him she didn't bring any.

"How come?" he asked.

She laughed.

"Let's warm up, hit it around a bit," she said.

She walked toward the wall in front of him. He swung his arm around a few times to loosen his shoulder then planted his feet and looked toward the wall. She was bending over, waiting for his serve, but he stopped during his back swing. She wasn't wearing panties.

She started laughing and then fell to her knees she was laughing so hard.

She flipped up her skirt at him and flipped it back down. She got up and walked to the back wall and put her hands against it and bent over again.

"Which do you prefer, coke or this?" she asked.

He pondered the question while he worked on her from behind. And he knew, even as he tried to arouse a debate in his brain, that the truthful answer was coke.

By THE END of the summer he had put 20 pounds back on, but he still weighed 25 pounds less than he did before he got hepatitis. And cuts and scabs from all the snorting made the bottom part of his nose swell up and itch so that sneezing made him feel like he had a broken rib.

He kept doing coke, bleeding sometimes after he snorted. But one time a friend of a friend, a squatty guy named Ray, joined them and told him he had the solution.

"Rita told me you need to put weight back on anyway," the guy said. "So I got the perfect solution for your nose and your weight loss. Gonna give you the munchies, man."

The guy took out a cigarette wrapper and a bag of pot. He rolled a joint, then stuffed a couple of grayish pellets into it. He lit it up and passed it to Willie. He inhaled and sat back. He liked it. It went right to his head, right to his veins. He thought he could feel it going from his lungs right to his heart then spreading out through his entire body down to his toes and up to his hair. He liked it very, very much.

"How did you do that?" he asked Ray.

"You like it, huh man?" Ray asked. "You get the munchies from pot?"

"Sure," Willie said.

"Well, I'm takin' care of you," Ray said. "You gonna get high from the coke, you gonna get low and easy from the pot, and you gonna get nice and hungry."

"How you make those rocks?" Willie asked again.

"I cook the powder with baking soda and water, man," Ray said. "Real easy. Next time you come over to my place, and I'll show you how to do it. I got some chemistry sets all set up over there."

He and Rita showed up the next night and watched as Ray made the rocks. They got high and stayed up all night, and then spent the next day setting up their own little lab in his den. The first time he brewed it he thought, *It's a good thing Liebl didn't know how to do this. We would've quit showing up for the games if we knew how to do this back then. Half the Royals team would have disappeared off the face of the earth.*

And he felt himself willing to disappear off the face of the earth, too. He would go back to Mexico to play, but he knew he would never play in the big leagues again, and he knew no one really cared if he did.

1988–1991

Three virgins and their mothers witnessed the final undoing.

Maria had Chinese eyes, dreamed about having a baby ever since she was little more than a baby herself, and lived with her mother Leonora in a shack in Mazatlán; Luz had long black hair, lied more than she told the truth, and lived alone in Guadalajara but spent more time with her mother in Ciudad Guzmán; Sara was thin and shy, went to Church almost every day, and lived with her mother in an apartment in Guadalajara. He drove a cream-colored Mercedes all over Mexico to visit them. Each mother loved the car.

MARIA. SHE SAT with her mother in the front row by the Mazatlán dugout. Her mother knew nothing of the lifestyles of ballplayers. She did know that the American ones had money and could teach her daughter English and take her to live in the United States.

He winked at her mother instead of at Maria, and the old lady loved it. She started fanning herself and squeezing her daughter's knee.

After the game, he introduced himself and handed them two tickets to the game the next night.

He started taking her to games—picking her up at her mother's house and dropping her off within an hour after the game. She told him she had never been with a man the night he parked three shacks down from their shack and kissed her.

He got out of the car, and she stared at him.

"Don't worry," he said. "I grew up poor, too!"

He looked at the old men and women sitting in metal folding chairs in the street. They were all staring at his car.

"I won't stay long," he said.

Inside had nothing to do with outside. There was a dishwasher on the wall right next to a big television, and there was a big boom box on a table on the other side of the television.

Leonora, her mother, told him her name was Leonora every time she met him.

"*Llegaste tarde,*" she said. "You arrived late tonight."

Maria told her they had stopped to get an ice cream cone, and her mother asked why they didn't bring her one.

Willie shook his head.

"*Mañana*," he said.

Maria started toward the door.

"No," he said. "I don't mean *hasta mañana*, I mean we will bring her an ice cream tomorrow. *Le traigo un helado mañana.*"

Maria smiled and pushed him out the door.

"I am a virgin, Willie, but my desire for you is very strong," she said. "Tomorrow we will make love."

They did it several times in his condo overlooking the city. He did not know which of the times he impregnated her. But a little over a month later, the day Mazatlán lost in the second round of the playoffs, she told him.

THE PUEBLA TEAM folded into a team in Guadalajara, a six-hour drive from Matazlan, and during the summer of 1988 he made the trip every weekend once the Mexican summer league started. He was still hitting cleanup, and though his power was waning, he was still one of the best in the league.

She called him in the middle of the night on September 1 and told him he was the father of a girl. He snapped a crack pipe on the nightstand as he sat on the edge of the bed and listened to her.

"What do you want to name her, Willie?" she asked.

He snapped the pipe between his thumb and middle finger, and little drops of blood dribbled from his fingertips.

"Well, my mother's name is Cille, as in Lucille, so maybe I would like to name her that," he said.

"Lucia?" she asked as if she hadn't heard him clearly.

"*Si, si,* yes," he said. "Lucia."

He had a day game the next day and ran to the car in his uniform and hopped in and drove straight to see Lucia and kept driving even when his tank was running on empty. The only stop he made was to roll a cigarette with tobacco and cocaine. It gave him a headache, way more than smoking the rock, and it crossed his mind for a second that he should have tried to tape up the pipe when he broke it the night before.

As he pulled up to the house, Leonora was sitting in a chair in the doorway.

"*Mi hija necesita dinero,*" she said. My daughter needs money.

He shook his head.

"*Deja dinero aqui,*" she said. Leave money here.

He dug into his pocket and handed her a wad of bills.

"*Cuidale a mi hija,*" Leonora said. Take care of my daughter.

He drove to the hospital, rolled another blunt, smoked it like a banshee when he parked, and ran to the maternity ward. Lucia was asleep on Maria's shoulders; Maria was asleep, too. He sat down in a chair and looked around at all the babies and realized he was the only man there.

THE NEXT SEASON the Guadalajara team folded into a team in León. Willie flew Maria and Lucia there as soon as he landed. He didn't want to have them live with him full-time, for Luz and Sara were now in line to get pregnant. But he wanted to be with his daughter, or at least he thought he wanted to at those times in the day, those rare times, when he wasn't high and wasn't thinking about getting high again. Those instances in the day were so rare now that he had brought a whole suitcase full of pipes back from Kansas City with him in his trunk.

He was high when he picked them up at the airport, and he snuck into the bathroom and lit up again as Maria unpacked.

Maria sat Lucia down beside him on the bed, and she started to tug on his nose. He tugged back on hers. She giggled, and Maria started to laugh, too. And he thought, *I want to get high again.*

The next day he hit two homers and drove in six runs. Maria clapped Lucia's hands each time he did something, and each time he ran out of the dugout and ran back in, too.

His teammate Joe asked, "Who's that lady and the baby? They yours?"

"Yep, they mine," he said, laughing.

"You still gonna get high with us though, right?" Joe asked.

"You bet, man," Willie said.

That night he made love to Maria as Lucia slept beside them. He got up, grabbed a pipe, walked down the exterior hotel hall to Joe's room, and stayed there smoking until daybreak.

When he got back, the sun was shining in through the windows, and Maria and Lucia were both sleeping with their arms over their eyes.

"Why didn't you close the blinds?" Willie asked as soon as he entered the room.

Maria looked up at him as he sat in a chair. The big shard of mirror that he used to organize his coke on sat on the nightstand next to him.

Lucia woke up and started to crawl over Maria and toward him. She could almost walk now, and she was always trying to get up and stagger toward Willie wherever he was.

"You were gone all night," Maria said.

Lucia was facing him from the edge of the bed now.

"Nah, I just went down and smoked a little bit with some of my teammates," he said. "We need to relax."

He helped Lucia down and held her hands up as she walked toward him. But she stumbled. He tried to balance her, but she bumped into the nightstand, and the mirror fell and gashed her leg. She cried holy hell, and Maria grabbed her, wrapped a towel around her, and threw the car keys at Willie as he followed them out the door.

The towel got completely bloody on the way to the hospital, and Maria sat crying quietly the whole time.

The doctor at the emergency room grabbed Lucia as Maria came running up to him, but she wouldn't let go.

Willie sat there as the doctor cleaned and bandaged the leg, and all he could think about was smoking another rock. Then he saw the name "Jorge" stitched into the doctor's jacket, and he wondered what George Brett was doing right now.

"Okay," Dr. Jorge said. "The blood was bad, but that was because the glass slid down her whole leg. It is a long cut but not a deep one. She will be okay."

Willie drove them home, and they did not speak. Maria would not let go of Lucia even after they were in the hotel room.

He shook his head, sat on the bottom of the bed, lit a pipe, and blew out the smoke into middle of the room across from them.

The next day he woke up and Maria was standing at the bottom of the bed with her suitcase in one hand and the baby in the other.

"I am going back to live with my mother," she said. "I took the money from your wallet, and you need to send more next week."

She turned and walked out, and he looked at the gaps in the white, vertical blinds. The sun was bugging him. He reached over to the nightstand and lit the pipe and smoked the residue from the night before.

Luz. Of the three virgins witnessing the unfolding, she was the most of many things: wild, seductive, manipulative, rageful. She had long black hair that she slicked back without putting it into a bun or a ponytail.

The first time they met, she sat with five friends at a table on an outdoor deck in front of the restaurant. He was leaving with some teammates and spotted them. She shined in comparison; the others were bubbly and giggly, but she sat there like a woman among girls. He went up to the table, and they all looked up. But he looked only at her.

"*Como estas?*" he asked.

She tightened her eyes but did not respond.

"*Me llamo Willie,*" he said.

She ran through the names of her friends, pointing at each, but failed to say her own name.

She looked at the empty chair beside her.

"My boyfriend went to the bathroom and will be back any minute."

"*Como te llamas?*" he asked. He moved closer to the table to let her know he would not leave until she told him her name.

"Luz," she said. "It means light."

"How did you learn English?" he asked.

"It is a long story," she said.

"Cuh-cuh-call me and tell me it," he said as he wrote his number on the paper tablecloth.

She did call; she went on a date with him and told him she was a virgin and he had to meet her mother if he wanted to touch her; and she said she spoke English well because she kept going to language classes even after she graduated from college.

He did meet her mother, but the other two were fibs. He knew by the way she operated in bed. He found photographs and letters in her house. He accused her, and she relented—she had been married to a Mafioso who had been killed in a shootout between drug gangs.

Then she got pregnant. Then she aborted. She had a tummy on a Tuesday when Willie was leaving on a road trip, and when he came back she was as thin as before. It took him half an hour to notice it. She was wearing a loose white top and no bra. He walked up behind her at one point and wrapped his arms around her, and then it dawned on him that she didn't have a belly anymore. He pawed at her abdomen and then grabbed her shoulders and turned her around.

"What happened?" he asked.

She shook her head back and forth and grabbed a coat.

He followed her.

"What did you do that for?" he asked. "I kept calling you the whole time we were away. Was that why you didn't pick up?"

She just kept shaking her head, and then she ran out the door.

She never came back, nor did he go in search of her.

And he went on a tear in the playoffs. He had hit .358 during the regular season but was creaming the Union pitching in the series.

But tonight he just lost himself in the game. He didn't care. It just felt good. With the full house watching, he was just playing again—playing ball.

In the bottom of the ninth inning his teammates were all standing on the top step of the dugout with one out between them and the Mexican League championship. He got ready to run out onto the field with them Union's last batter popped up, and they all started out like sprinters at the gun.

He took three steps, but then he stopped. They were jumping up and down around the pitcher's mound, but he stood at the first-base line and just watched. He saw them but as if he were watching them through a haze. He just stood there until a teammate saw him and ran over to him and jumped into his arms. But he almost forgot to hug back. *What the hell,* he thought. *We won the Mexican League Series. I'm making fifty grand a year, but not five people north of the border are even aware the Mexican series is happening, and these guys are jumping around like they are kings of the world.*

He turned and walked back into the dugout and sat on the bench and watched. They just kept going, acting like kids winning a little league crown. He decided he wasn't going to get high tonight after all. He called an agent back in the States who was recruiting him to play in a new senior league in Florida. The guy had said a few scouts from big-league teams would be watching them, and a few would surely need a veteran presence as spring training began. *Being a veteran presence,* Willie thought, *is still way better than a Mexican League championship.*

SARA. OF THE THREE, she was the most girlish in appearance and spirit.

She sat quietly in the corner of the golf course restaurant and stared as the fat golfer with the cigar clicked up behind her on his cleats and asked if it was too late to eat.

Willie sat at the table outside and laughed when she jumped a bit.

She shook her head and stood up and looked through the glass at him. She was thin, sheepish, not his type. Her sad eyes blinked and she walked out and, as the fat golfer sat down next to Willie's table, she stood there with her pad in her hand.

"*Como estas?*" he asked as she walked past.

She smiled and started to say something but stopped. He wondered if she had a stutter. She seemed the type. She reminded him of himself, and he smiled. She smiled back.

Soon she would bear him a daughter, Nicole. She would someday—a day far, far away, marry him and bear him another daughter again. She would someday, along with those girls, help save his life.

1992

He was smoking his pipe and watching the 11:00 news in the basement den while Luz painted her toenails bright red. He was done with Mexico—fed up, disinterested—but not with the Mexican girls. He had tracked down Luz and flew her up a few months prior, and even though he had sworn off watching baseball, he had heard about George and just had to watch.

The sportscaster talked about George Brett's steady bead on 3,000 hits. He needed only 50 more, the guy said, and Willie exhaled the smoke into Luz's face.

"You know how many hits 3,000 is?" he asked.

"Sure," she said. "3,000."

He turned to her.

"You know what I mean, Luz," he said. "You know how many people done that? George is one of the best of all time. I used to play with him. I liked George."

She switched feet.

"You probably could have done that," she said. "If you didn't start smoking the pipe and screwing around so much."

"You're a smart-ass bitch sometimes, Luz," he said. And he knew it was time to show her his cards.

He got up and opened the desk drawer and laid out a bunch of the cashed checks he had sent to Sara and Nicole on the table. At the bottom of the table, he put the one that never arrived to them. And then he reached into the drawer again and took out Luz's diary.

She jumped up.

"You had it!" she shouted. "You know I've been looking all over for that. You read it, too, didn't you?"

He held up his hand for her to be silent. Then he opened the diary to a page full of writing and set it at the bottom of the table alongside the suspicious check.

"You see something different about that check?" he asked.

She kept standing there.

"Come over here and look at them," he said. He stepped over and grabbed her arm and pulled her over to the desk.

"What are you doing, Willie?" she asked.

"I'm a detective," he said. "Look at the handwriting, Luz, and then tell me the truth once and for all and we'll drop the issue."

"What are you talking about, Willie?" she asked. "Stop it. Stop what you are doing!"

"Look close, Luz, and tell me the damn truth for once in your life," he said. He put his hand on the back of her head and pushed it downward to make her look.

"All I'm asking is for you to tell me the truth, Luz," he said. "And you aren't leaving this room until you do. Just look at the handwriting, and tell me who cashed that check that went missing."

She shook her head and sat in a chair in the corner.

He sat back down on the couch and took a sip of tequila, then he took another hit from the pipe. They sat there like this for more than an hour.

"I have to go to the bathroom," she said. "I have to pee."

He was watching the movie *The Dirty Dozen. Jim Brown,* he thought, *that was a bad man.*

"Willie!" Luz shouted.

He looked at her.

"I told you, Luz, you can leave this room when you tell the truth."

She lifted her legs up and sat in a ball for five more minutes. Then she stood up and moved over in front of the sliding glass door and stood directly in front of him. She unbuttoned her jeans, pulled them down, and then pulled her panties down, too. Then she squatted.

At first he thought she was just putting on a show. But then his brain processed the sound of the urine splattering on the floor. He sat there stunned while she finished, stood, and pulled her panties and jeans back up in one motion.

"You still aren't leaving here," he said. The floor was cement because he had never replaced the carpet a few years ago when the basement flooded. The urine broke through the border of its puddle and started to roll toward him.

He got up and started to walk to the bathroom to get towels, but she grabbed the phone when he did and called 911 and started screaming.

He ran over and grabbed the phone and hung it up.

But the operator called back and said his address back to him and said the police were on their way.

Luz started laughing, cackling, as she sat back in the chair.

He started to throw his drug utensils into a drawer and was brushing the coke off the table when the knock came.

She started screaming on cue. The police busted down the door and rushed into the room and she threw herself on the floor.

"I didn't touch her," Willie said.

She started to cry.

"Look at my bruises," she said. She held up her leg—she had closed the car door on herself a few days prior.

The cops handcuffed him and pushed him toward the door.

"You're leaving her alone in my house," Willie said. "That girl steals everything, and you're leaving her alone in my house."

The cop pulled his hands back, and he decided to shut up, not because it hurt but because the instant the cop did that Willie realized they didn't notice the coke.

His crack friend George recommended an attorney, and Willie took the attorney's advice to plead guilty to a misdemeanor to avoid a felony charge. He told Willie he would be an example for a domestic violence trial because he was famous. Willie told the attorney he wasn't famous anymore. "Don't matter," the attorney said, "you'll never win it 'cause you're still famous in Kansas City, and the system is all about making an example out of you." Remember that, he said. Willie remembered it for about 30 seconds after he walked out of the office.

HE REAR-ENDED A GUY later that summer on a tequila run. He was hitting the pipe as he drove and burned his fingers lighting a match with one hand. He had mastered the skill with hours of practice: he would pull off a match with his teeth, hold the matchbox between his last two fingers, and use his thumb and index finger to pull the match head across the flammable strip. But this time he dropped the match and the box, and the whole thing caught on fire in his lap.

As they pulled over, he took a quick hit from the pipe he had in the car and got out.

The guy was spitting mad and pointing to the welt on his bumper and crevice in his trunk.

"I didn't realize I was going that fast," Willie said.

"What?" the guy said.

"I mean, I'm sorry, man, I just wasn't looking up," Willie said. He couldn't focus, but the guy said something about calling the cops and that snapped him out of his haze.

"No man, don't do that," Willie said. "I'm gonna pay cash for this. I'll get you baseball tickets, too."

"What?"

"I'll even throw in an extra $100 over the repair bill," Willie said. "Just don't call the cops on this one, man. No harm no foul."

"What did you say about baseball tickets?"

"Huh?"

"You said baseball tickets?"

"Well, yeah, I'll get you some good seats, too."

"Who are you?"

"I'm Willie Aikens," he said. "What's your name?"

The guy looked at him with concern, and then took a step back.

"You are Willie Mays Aikens, aren't you?" he said. "I knew I recognized you. Willie Mays Aikens. Man, I was a kid when you hit those homers in the World Series. You and Willie Wilson were my favorite players. Damn, I got in a car crash with Willie Mays Aikens. Wait 'til my old man hears about this one."

"You gonna let me take care of this, right?"

The guy smiled.

"You bet, Mr. Aikens," he said. "Here's my phone number. Just give me yours, or, well, maybe you don't want to give yours out. I understand. But maybe…."

"Look, I'm going to call you Monday, and I'll meet you at my mechanic's place and we'll get this all taken care of."

"Thanks, Mr. Aikens," the guy said. "Thanks a whole lot. It's a pleasure. By the way, you mind if I bring my old man with me? He's getting up there, and meeting you would make his day, you know?"

"Monday, man, no problem," Willie said. "I'll get him a ticket, too."

AT HIS FAVORITE DEALER'S house one day he met Vanessa and Kim, two lesbian friends who liked to get high, too. And they all agreed to start meeting at his house because they thought the cops had the heat on them in the hood.

After weeks of getting high every day, sleeping on the couch and the floor in the den, eating in the den, watching television in the den, even bathing at the sink in the den's bathroom instead of going upstairs to shower, they began to see themselves as a family.

A friend of theirs, Juanita, had one of her kids deliver the crack to his house every morning, and Willie gave the kid a $5 tip each time. But one morning the kid came and he had nothing left in his wallet.

"I got to go get some more cash," he said.

Juanita frowned.

"Fuck, Willie, you a millionaire and you out of cash?"

"Fuck is right," he said. "Look, you girls got to start helping me out a little bit. I think I gone through about $10,000 this week. I can't keep that up."

Vanessa got up and looked him up and down.

"Charcoal with pinstripes," she said.

Kim stood up and studied him, too.

"And I think a camel's hair top coat for winter," she said. "With his skin color he'd look good in one."

"What are you talking about?" Willie asked.

"We're boosters, Willie. We don't have no money, but we can get you a new wardrobe in a week, the highest-end stuff, Willie, like great stuff that you will look great in, Willie," Vanessa said. "All you have to do is drive us to the shopping mall in your Mercedes, and we'll come back out with the stuff. They'll never suspect boosters was ridin' in a Mercedes."

"What the hell is a booster?" Willie asked. "I ain't gonna help you steal nothin'," he said.

They left that night for the first time in two weeks. They came back the next morning carrying a rack of clothes.

Juanita walked in the door behind them laughing.

Vanessa grabbed Willie's hand, and Kim helped her start taking his clothes off.

"What you doin'?" he said. He had spent the night running from window to window looking out. He thought there were spies everywhere outside. At one point he heard a noise and went out in his boxers with his flashlight and walked around for half an hour looking for the spies. A cop car pulled up but he didn't jump because the cops weren't the spies. Someone else was. He told them he was looking for his dog, but his dog had run off months ago.

Vanessa and Kim took off his T-shirt and his pajama bottoms, and then each one put a hand on his boxers and pulled them off, too.

They took out a pair of cashmere boxers and slipped them on his legs; they took a pinstriped dress shirt and put it on him; they tied a blue tie with big black dots around his neck; the slipped black wool suit pants and a black wool jacket on him; they pushed him into a chair and put socks on his feet and then black, pointy shoes.

"He looks like a high-end pimp," Kim said.

Willie smiled. He felt sharp. For the first time in a long time, he didn't feel heavy and clunky. He felt narrower than his 300 pounds, and when he walked back and forth the shoes felt like they were pointing him in the right direction.

"Okay, we got a deal," he said.

1993

New chauffeur and constant companion Charles Taylor was another friend Willie met at his dealer's house and Charles drove Willie by Kauffman Stadium, and the lights made it look like a spaceship at first. He realized he didn't remember how he had met Charles, but that was okay. Charles was fun to be with, so he decided not to bring up the subject. Charles had agreed to be his driver if Willie would give him free drugs.

He told Charles to pull over for a second, and they sat on the highway eating Kentucky Fried Chicken and listening to the crowd.

They ate fried chicken every night; they ate bananas and watermelon every afternoon; for breakfast they ate toast and drank from a water jug filled with cut lemons.

"Big crowd tonight," Charles said.

"Coney's pitching," Willie said.

"David Cone? He from here, right?"

Willie started to laugh.

"Man, you eat enough KFC you start to realize it tastes different every day, you know," he said.

"It must be the chickens, cause they fry it the same," Charles said.

"I suppose so," Willie said. "You really think each chicken taste different?"

"I suppose so," Charles said.

Willie wiped his hands and reached below the seat for the crack pipe. It was coated with white residue, and he inhaled extra hard after he lit it.

"That tastes different every time, too," he said.

The lights from Kauffman twinkled. "Looks like the stadium about to lift off like a rocket ship," Willie said. "It felt like that sometimes, too, when it was rockin', man. Felt like big engines were roaring, getting ready to lift the whole place up in the air."

He lit one more time but there was nothing left. He threw the pipe back under the seat.

"Hal McRae's the manager, too," he said. "I'll call up Hal and get us tickets to the game sometime."

"Shit, Willie," Charles said. "We'd interrupt our schedule too much if we did that. Got to stay on schedule, man."

He threw his chicken leg out the window and started the car. Willie reached back under the seat for the pipe and for the life of him couldn't remember how he had met Charles in the first place.

THE NEXT MORNING in the den, Charles hit Willie over the head with a propane tank. Willie told him he was out of drugs; Charles didn't believe him, so he picked up the tank and clobbered him when his back was turned. Blood came gushing down his neck, but nothing hurt, not even the blow. Willie was able to register that he was so high that not even a bullet through the head could hurt him.

He grabbed Charles and threw him on the floor, then sat on him while he pondered what to do.

Vanessa and Kim came in after 10 minutes of him sitting there like that. Charles was screaming, shouting that he couldn't breathe. Kim and Vanessa dropped a brown lunch bag on the table and started kicking Charles.

Willie looked over at the bag.

"What's in there?" he asked. "You brought your own stuff?"

"We ain't cheapskates, Willie," Kim said. "We get you clothes when we can't pay, and bring the real thing when we can. You always get somethin' from us."

He laughed and then noticed three more girls standing behind him.

"That's Lori and her girlfriend Sasha, two more lesbians," Kim said. "We thought you'd like Sasha."

He studied them and focused on the shocking difference between them—Lori was a big mama wearing a spandex top and spandex leggings, and she had forearms as big as his; Sasha looked like a stripper who used to hang around with the team in Fort Myers every spring training.

The third girl was Amber—she had been there many times now. She sat in the corner alone all day and injected a mixture of heroin and cocaine into her arms and legs and side. One time Willie saw her trying to stab her neck with the needle, and he jumped up and stopped her.

Willie got up off Charles and sat on the couch.

"Get him out of here," he said.

Vanessa and Kim and big Lori sat Charles up and escorted him out of the house. They slammed the door behind him.

Willie studied Sasha.

"You full lesbian?" he asked.

She smiled girlishly. Amber was already sitting in the corner spacing out, and Vanessa, Kim, and Lori came back into the room.

The four of them got high all day and into the night. At one point Sasha motioned to Willie, and he followed her upstairs. Lori looked at them leaving and asked where they were going. Sasha frowned at her.

They had sex, and when they came downstairs Amber was strung out in the corner and Vanessa and Kim were asleep in each other's arms on the couch.

"Where's Lori?" Sasha asked.

The lesbians stirred and blinked at her.

"Where's Lori?" Sasha asked again.

"She's pissed," Kim said. "She stormed out of here. You didn't hear her banging on your door before she left?"

Willie stared at them.

"That woman could have broken down the door no problem," he said. "She wasn't banging on no door."

"She was!" Kim said. "We heard her down here. She came down cursin' you and stormed out."

Willie shook his head and looked at Sasha. She looked like she was going to cry.

"Don't worry about it," he said.

He went upstairs to the kitchen and started cutting lemons. Someone knocked on the door.

He walked down the stairs.

"Sure it's big mama," he said.

But there were two cops.

"Mr. Aikens, how you today?" the white cop said. "You wouldn't be holdin' a girl named Sasha here against her will, would you?"

"What?" Willie asked.

"We're getting calls from a friend of hers, calls from her mother, both sayin' you are holding a woman hostage here, Mr. Aikens, a woman named Sasha?"

"Ain't no Sasha here," Willie said.

"You mind if we take a look, Mr. Aikens?" the black cop asked.

"Well, yes, I was in the middle of something, and now is not a good time," Willie said. "Buh-buh-but there ain't no Sasha here."

They cops looked at each other.

"Well, thank you then, Mr. Aikens," they said at the same time.

He closed the door and walked down into the den.

"Hey Sasha, that bitch Lori called the cops and said yuh-yuh being held hostage here," he said. "You being held hostage?"

"No, Willie, I am here of my own free will, and Lori is up to her old tricks again," Sasha said. "She's a wicked jealous person, Willie."

"You'd tell the cops you are here of your own choosing?"

"Sure, Willie," she said.

"Wait here, then," he said.

He kicked off his flip flops and stuck his feet into his tennis shoes by the door and without tying them started running after the cop car. They were parked at the entrance talking on the radio.

"Hey," Willie said. "You can come back to the door. Sasha said she'd tell you she's in my house of her own choosing."

He heard the voice on the radio say his address. The white cop reached over from behind the wheel and turned off the radio.

"Mr. Aikens, you just told us no one by the name of Sasha was in your house," he said.

"I know it," Willie said. "But she's there now, and she'll tell you she's there of her own choosing. Come on back and wait outside the house, okay?"

Willie smiled at them and started jogging back to his townhouse.

But he got into trouble all by himself. He liked having Charles drive him, and he liked Charles because he was funny when they got high, so he forgave him the flare-up with the propane tank.

Charles was driving too fast one day on I-70, and a cop pulled them over and asked Charles to sit with him in the cop car and answer a few questions.

They were there for 20 minutes. Willie had thrown a big rock out the window as they pulled over right at mile marker 76 on Interstate 435. But he still had his pipe under his seat, and it had the residue from his last hit on it. He reached for it and lit it between his legs and tried to suck as hard as he could.

As the cop walked back, he called Willie "Mr. Aikens" and asked him to step out of the car.

"May I search your car, sir?" the cop asked.

"No," Willie said. All he could think about was the big rock lying behind him somewhere in the weeds.

"Well then, I am going to go get a warrant and search your car without your permission," the cop said.

And now Willie lusted for the rock.

"I tell you what," Willie said. "I got to take a piss. You go 'head and look around in there, and I'll take a piss in the weeds here."

"No, sir," the officer said. "You need to stand right there."

"Please officer," Willie said.

"Okay," the cop said.

Willie stepped over the guardrail as the cop leaned into the car and reached under the seat. Just as Willie stepped to where he though the trajectory of the throw would have placed the rock, the cop called him. He turned. The cop was holding up the pipe.

"I'll be right there," Willie said. The weeds were all tangled and damp. But he thought he spotted it. He squinted his eyes in the sun and there it was, like a pearl shining in the thicket. He dug his heels into the hill with each step and made a trench on his way back up. He stepped over the guardrail.

"There's drugs in this pipe," the cop said. He held it up in the sun. "On the sides," he said.

The cop leaned in and dug further under the seat and came out with two more pipes and a beaker all coated with residue.

"Put your hands behind your back please, Mr. Aikens," the cop said. "I am placing you under arrest for possession of cocaine."

"What about my car, officer?"

"It is state property now because it was used to transport drugs, sir," the cop said.

Willie looked back at Charles sitting in the police car. It didn't even cross his mind to think Charles might have betrayed him; his mind was already planning how they would come back to get the rock in the weeds.

IT WAS THE FIRST THING they did after Willie posted bond and got released. Charles drove there at more than 100 mph, Willie found the rock quickly, and they pulled into the garage and forgot to lower the door. After an hour in his den, he looked up and realized most of his mementos were gone from the shelves in the den.

The second home run ball from the first World Series game; the second one from the second double homer game; the signed pictures of him and George, him and Hal, him and Frank; a bat George signed toward the end of the .400 season. All gone.

Then he looked in the corner where Amber sat, slept, shot up, lived. He knew right away.

"I knew I never should have let a shooter in here," he said. "I'm going for a run."

He changed into sweat pants and put on his sneakers and ran. Up and down and up and down the stairs until the sweat felt like ice water coming down his sides and back. He started to pretend he was Ali, started to feel like Ali again. Then he got high again; ran again; got high again; and didn't leave the townhouse for a week except to go buy drugs.

HE GOT INDICTED two months later and lied to his attorney that his car had been stolen the night before his arrest and the girl who stole it had left the pipes in the car. Then he found a girl, Gloria, who came by once in a while to smoke and convinced her to testify that she had stolen the car and left the pipes. He said he would give her free drugs for the rest of her life.

He got high the morning of his trial and called his attorney to pick him up. They picked up Gloria, and she waited outside the court while Willie testified, and when her time came his attorney walked out to get her. But she was gone.

His attorney came back in and told him.

"I think the prosecution saw her and scared her off," he said. "They threatened to put her in jail, and she panicked. I'm sure of it."

The attorney explained to the judge that the witness had disappeared. The jurors left the courtroom, and Willie sat there for two hours not the least bit worried about the verdict. He simply wondered how he would get the rock in prison. He had heard it was easy to come by, but he wondered how.

As the jurors returned, he looked at each of them and wondered how many of them knew who he was. How many of them had seen him play? Just one, he hoped.

Hung jury. He found out later it was 11–1. One fan, one baseball fan out of 12. He wondered which homer the fan saw.

1993

On December 8, 1993, Karen pulled up outside his townhouse and asked for directions.

"You have a man?" he asked her.

"Kinda sorta," she said.

He told her where Cherry Street was. Then she followed him as he drove to the gas station.

He smiled at her when she pulled up alongside him as he stood there at the pump.

"You went the wrong way!" he said.

"My name is Karen," she said. That wasn't her real name, but Karen got the job done. She was no seductress, just a working girl doing her job. And he was ready now, ready to be taken away once and for all.

1994

Karen's real name was Ginger Locke, and she came to his house five times. And he still never learned her real name until it was far too late.

SHE CALLED HIM on Sunday, January 16, 1994, and left a message. Her voice sounded like it would fit right in with the girls at his house—needy, sweet, out of sorts. He liked to help girls like that; he liked to get high with them, too.

He called her back and left a message. She returned his call on Monday.

She said she couldn't call him back because she had loaned her car to a girlfriend who got pulled over driving to St. Louis, and the police found some stuff in her car.

"You mean they found some drugs?" he asked.

She said yes, that is what they found, and she had to go to St. Louis to pick up her car from the pound.

"So you like to get high?" he asked. He was getting high as they spoke.

She said she and her girlfriends liked to sit around together and play cards and get high. She said they had been trying to find a reliable dealer who didn't scare them.

"You don't need to go any further," Willie said. "I-I-I can get you all the good stuff you want. Just give me a call when you need to."

Later that evening she called. He burned himself as he lit up and stood up to get the phone at the same time.

She asked if they could play some eight ball.

"I love to play eight ball," he said. "It's the only game I play. I got the balls set up right now. You remember how to get here or you guh-guh-got a bad sense of direction still?"

She laughed. He laughed after he hung up. Amber was sitting in her corner quietly.

"Who was that?" she asked.

"A friend of mine wants an eight ball," he said.

"You got to be careful we don't make too many friends," she said.

The doorbell rang half an hour later, and he told Amber to go get it. She glided up the steps and came back down into the den with Karen. Amber sat back down in her corner and stuck her needles under a towel.

Willie stood up and smiled at Karen. She looked shocked at all the equipment and drugs in the room.

"Somebody stole my baseball memorabilia," he said. "I used to have a bunch of stuff on the walls. Good stuff."

He pointed to the bag of cocaine on the table.

She pointed to some rocks alongside it and said she'd like it that way.

"Sure," Willie said.

While he cooked her cocaine, they talked about card games. He took a few hits while he cooked it and asked Karen if she wanted a hit, too. She said she was on her lunch break and would love to but couldn't.

When he finished she handed him $200 and said she would come back real soon.

"Next time come back when you can stay and smoke with us," he said. "We have a good time here."

She promised she would.

On January 24, she called and asked for seven grams.

"Come on over," he said, but after he hung up he realized he didn't have it.

He had sex with Amber that morning, and she lay there on the couch wearing her socks and a Royals baseball jersey she took out of one of the souvenir cabinets. He looked at all the needle marks on her arms and shook his head.

"Amber, you got to cut that shit out," he said. But she was asleep, and he covered her legs with a blanket.

He filled a cup with Don Pedro and Coca-Cola and then sipped it in the doorway as he waited for Karen to pull up.

She beeped, and he went outside carrying the cup, and she smiled at him as he stepped carefully on the ice. But then he saw her smile disappear as he walked to the passenger seat and opened the door.

"We got to go get some," he said. "I already called a guy for you. I realized I got high all night and had nothin' left."

She frowned and asked why he didn't tell her that beforehand.

"You get high, Karen," he said. "You know you don't think of shit like that. Just give me $350, and I'll get it for you. You can stay in the car if you're scared."

He took her to a dealer's house, and he got out and knocked on the door. The guy answered the door and looked straight at Karen sitting in the SUV.

"Who's that, Willie?"

"She's cool," Willie said. "We get high together. I need seven grams."

The guy didn't speak and gently closed the door. He came back and handed Willie a bag, and Willie handed him the money.

He got back in the car and handed the bag to Karen. She drove him home, and as she pulled into the driveway she asked him to cook it for her.

They went in; she stood there looking at Amber as he cooked it; he handed the rocks to her in a bag; she reached into the bag and gave him a few rocks back, as if to say she appreciated his generosity and care for her.

"Thanks," Willie said.

She smiled at him and said she would see him again soon.

SHE CALLED WHEN he was in the middle of a fight with Amber. Amber had admitted she and her boyfriend had stolen his baseball memorabilia and sold it to buy drugs.

"I promise you that is why I broke up with him, Willie," she said, crying. "That was a long time ago, too. I want to be here with you, I promise."

The phone rang just as he was about to tell her she had to go find the stuff, but Karen said she wanted an ounce this time and he got an idea just as he was hanging up that made him forget about the memorabilia.

She said she wanted a full ounce this time. He realized Karen wasn't going to sleep with him, so he might as well make money on her.

"I don't have an ounce, but I'll take you back to that dealer and buy it for you," he said. "It will cost $1,000."

Then he called his dealer and told him to take out a few grams and give them to Willie separately this time and cut the coke with some baby laxative.

He took Amber with him, and she frowned at Karen the whole trip.

When they pulled up to Van's house, she put the car in park and took out 10 crisp $100 bills. She smiled at him as she handed them to him.

He went inside, put $200 in his pocket, gave Van $800, took the bag for Karen, and stuffed the other tiny bag Van gave him in his pocket.

"You learnin' now, Willie," Van said, laughing. "If you weren't Willie Mays, I wouldn't let you do this, you know. But you're the man. So keep fuckin' the bitch up."

He looked through the glass in the door at Karen and studied her.

"Just doin' what I got to do," Willie said. "Sh-sh-she ain't gonna sleep with me so I figure I might as well get somethin' out of it. Thanks, Van."

They drove back to his house, and he cooked the coke for her again but didn't cook it too much so he could have some residue, too.

She gave him a couple rocks again, smiled, and left.

Amber was already shooting up in her corner, and Vanessa and Kim came downstairs from a bedroom.

"She's a cop," Amber said. "That bitch is a cop. At least the laxative is gonna give her the shits before she arrests you."

"She ain't no cop, Amber," Willie said.

"Then how come she never stays and gets high with us?" Vanessa said.

"Cause she comes on her lunch break," Willie said. "She has a job. How else you think she can afford to buy all that coke? You should have a job like her, too!"

HIS DEALER SAID he wanted to meet them near a body shop where he was getting his car repaired.

As Willie walked over to meet him in the back of the lot where there were a lot of crashed cars, the dealer looked all around but not at Willie.

"What's up?" Willie said.

"We can't do any business today," the dealer said.

Willie started laughing, but the dealer kept looking around and had still not looked at him once. Willie noticed that he locked eyes on Karen.

"See those cars across the street, you dumb ass?" the dealer asked.

Willie looked across the street and saw lots of cars, but no car in particular bothered him.

"That bitch is a cop," the dealer said. "Look at her sittin' there. She ain't no crack head, Willie. You a stupid motherfucker. We're done."

The dealer walked away, and Willie stood there looking at Karen.

He shook his head. He hadn't gotten high all day, and he didn't feel right. He kept shaking his head at Karen as he walked back to the SUV.

"He's out," Willie said as he got in.

Her jaw dropped.

She asked why the dealer had brought them all the way out here if he was out.

"Sometimes that happens," Willie said. "He may have sold it to somebody at the auto shop who was hard up. You can't get upset about the ups and downs, Karen. Drugs are a funny business."

SHE CALLED ON February 23 and asked him to get her another ounce.

"Well, my dealer don't want to sell no more," he said. "But I found this guy named Oz. He lives here in Missouri, so we don't have to go all the way to Kansas."

She liked that idea and said she didn't have a lot of time at lunch today, so she needed to get it as rock right there from Oz.

She picked him up, and he was so high that he wanted to ask her if he could put his hand in her pants while she drove.

Karen, he rehearsed in his head, *I been thinkin'. I think I want to stick my hand in your pants while you drive. You let me do that, and I'm gonna let you pay half each time. I think that's a good deal for you.*

He didn't say it but decided he would say it on the way back.

She dropped him off at Oz's house, a dealer known for always having the right part in stock.

He went inside, paid Oz for an ounce, got a bag for himself, took a hit from a pipe in Oz's living room, and went back to the car.

He got in and handed her the bag of cocaine.

She looked pissed. She told him she said clearly she wanted rock this time, and she didn't have time to go into his house while he cooked it up.

He was going to respond, but as he looked at her he saw a guy in a car parked on the other side of the street. The guy ducked down into the passenger seat when they locked eyes.

Willie thought back to what Van had said, but the bag of coke in his pocket quickly distracted him, and all he wanted to do was get home.

"Karen," Willie said as she pulled out and drove faster than usual down the street. "I told you last time. You got to be more flexible. This ain't like goin' to the grocery store and buying chicken every time we go. You got to be more flexible."

But she was so pissed he decided not to propose the deal involving sticking his hand in her pants.

As they pulled up to his house, he swore the same guy in the same car was sitting at the end of his street.

"Who are you, Karen?" Willie asked as they sat in his driveway.

She told him she was not a cop and would never set him up.

"Well, sit here then, 'cause I'm gonna walk over there and see why that guy is followin' us."

He got out of the car and walked over, but the car suddenly pulled out and sped away. But he had that bag in his pocket, and the stress of it all made him want to get high more than ever.

They went inside and baked the coke for her, and she gave him a couple rocks back and smiled.

"Karen, I don't want you to come back here no more," he said. "I like you and all and it's been nice to know you, and I hope you ain't no cop cause I trusted you and I liked you."

She did not smile this time. She looked at some of the baseball jerseys still on the wall. He thought he saw a tiny tear in her eye, but later he would realize he didn't.

On February 26, he got a call from a man who kept saying the name "Amber" over and over, and Willie made this much out of what the guy said—"I am going to come over there and blow your fucking head off."

Amber was asleep upstairs in the same bed as Vanessa and Kim, all three nude and aligned in perfect geometry so as to have their own space on the bed.

He let them sleep and put on his jacket and drove to see a friend who he knew who could get him a gun.

The friend sold him a 12-gauge pump shotgun, and as the guy said what type of gun it was, Willie realized he had no idea what the guy was talking about but said he would take it anyway.

"Perfect," Willie said.

He went home and got high and loaded the gun and started roaming the house and looking out all the windows in the back and in the front, upstairs, and downstairs. He smoked some more and then locked himself in the bathroom with the gun. He woke up on the toilet with the gun on the floor below him and decided it was time to burn off the coke, so he did some more sprints up and down the stairs.

The door slammed open as he was just about to complete his 11th round trip up and down the five stories.

"It's a kick-in," Vanessa hollered from upstairs.

He stopped in the den and looked at the drugs and pipes and beakers all over the place. He kept running in place. He kept running in place even as a bunch of FBI agents jumped down the steps and grabbed his arms and handcuffed them behind his back.

Amber was screaming and Kim and Vanessa were shouting, and the agent pushed down on his shoulder to keep him from running in place.

"We got you this time, Mr. Aikens," one of them said.

HIS FIRST ATTORNEY negotiated him two deals.
1. "Help the government nail dealers, and you get five years."
    "No way. People already want to kill me. That would just guarantee it. I ain't a snuh-snuh-snitch."
2. "Okay. Plead guilty. They will drop the gun charge. Nine years and you will be out on parole in about six."
    "But there wasn't no gun, man," Willie said. "Look at her notes. I got the gun later cuh-cuh-'cause a guy was threatening me. The guys who broke down my door saw it. She never saw no gun. It wasn't there when she was there. Look at her notes. They added it to the notes. I ain't pleading guilty."

Willie didn't realize he was making the attorney feel the way he used to make his managers feel. He fired the guy and went to trial.

HIS SECOND ATTORNEY, who took it to trial, thought Willie had a strong case for entrapment. At the trial he hammered Karen/Ginger Locke on two front—first her failure to note a gun during any of the reports she made after visits to Willie's townhouse, and second the possible entrapment in which she had to repeatedly convince Willie to go buy cocaine for her then convert it to crack for her and only her.

Until she walked in to testify, Willie still had no idea that Ginger Locke had brought him down. His drug haze had grown so thick, and his gullibility grew alongside it.

But now, sober and clear-headed, he realized the prosecutor, Christina Tabor, was intent on nailing him. With her flat-top haircut and unblinking eyes, she seemed the perfect partner for Judge Dean Whipple, who was nominated by President Ronald Reagan to a seat on the United States District Court for the Western District of Missouri in 1987. The two of them, he thought, loathed what he had become. He didn't feel they hated him, but he felt as the drugs faded from his system that they sure did exude a keen hatred—and zero compassion—for drug addicts. And with each passing day he could more clearly hear what was being said about him.

Attorney: "Would you look in your report, please—you have testified there was a weapon—would you look in your report, please, dated 1-18-94, tell me please, where the reference to a weapon is in that report?"

Locke: "It's not in the report, sir."

Attorney: "It's omitted?"

Locke: "I made a mistake."

Attorney: "I did not ask if you made a mistake. I asked you if…"

Prosecutor: "Your honor, I object. That's argumentative."

The Court: "Sustained."

Attorney: "My specific question to you was: is there a reference in this report?"

Locke: "No, sir."

Attorney: "There is not?"

Locke: "No, sir."

Attorney: "Oh, by the way, do you know the difference basically between a rifle and a shotgun?"

Locke: "I am not very good with guns; I am not a gun expert, sir."

Attorney: "Now, you indicated to Mr. Aikens, 'Hey, I am lost.' Is that right?"

Locke: "Yes, sir."

Attorney: "Were you in the car when you made that statement to him?"

Locke: "Yes, sir."

…

Attorney: "That's when the conversation…where Mr. Aikens asked you, 'Do you have a man?'"

Locke: "Yes, sir."

Attorney: "What do you understand that to mean?"

Locke: "Do I have a boyfriend?"

Attorney: "Alright. You take it that Mr. Aikens was interested in you at that time?"

Locke: "I don't know."

Attorney: "How did you respond?"

Locke: "I said 'Kind of, sort of.'"

Attorney: "Alright. You didn't say, 'I can't see anybody now, I am living with someone,' or 'I have a relationship with someone?'"

Locke: "No, I did not."

Attorney: "You said, 'kind of, sort of?'"

Locke: "Yes, I did."

…

Attorney: "All right. Now, on the 18th, after five, at least, telephone calls initiated by you, [with] no contact between Mr. Aikens and yourself during that period of time, you were instructed to contact Mr. Aikens and see if you could get him to talk about drugs?"

Locke: "Yes, sir."

…

Attorney: "You then asked Mr. Aikens a question, did you not?"

Locke: "Yes, I did."

Attorney: "And what was the question?"

Locke: "I asked him if he knew where I could get some."

Attorney: "Okay. Now by 'some,' you were referring to drugs, is that correct?"

Locke: "Yes, sir."

Attorney: "You didn't mention crack?"

Locke: "No, sir."

…

Attorney: "Now…you nevertheless, in your report, indicated that…you made arrangements to meet with Mr. Aikens at his residence to purchase crack cocaine. Is that correct?"

Locke: "Yes, sir."

Attorney: "And that's the first time in the report that crack is mentioned is that correct?"

Locke: "Yes, sir."

…

Attorney: "Okay. Now, did Mr. Aikens have cocaine available on the 24th to convert to crack cocaine?"

Locke: "Not to my knowledge, no."

Attorney: "And in fact, Mr. Aikens had to go somewhere else did he not?"

Locke: "Yes, sir."

Attorney: "Now, did you accompany Mr. Aikens?"

Locke: "Yes, sir."

Attorney: "Were you in your car or Mr. Aikens' car?"

Locke: "I was in my vehicle."

…

Attorney: "And when he came back he had something that he didn't have when he left?"

Locke: "Yes, sir."

Attorney: "And that would be powder cocaine?"

Locke: "Yes, sir."

Attorney: "…is that correct? Did he show it to you?"

Locke: "No, sir."

Attorney: "He didn't show it to you then?"

Locke: "It was in his sock."

Attorney: "In his sock. You observed the bulge in his sock, is that correct?"

Locke: "Yes, sir."

Attorney: "What did Mr. Aikens do? Did he say, 'Let's go back to 10206 Locust, and I'll make this crack for you?'"

Locke: "He said he had to stop to get something."

Attorney: "Okay. And you did, in fact, make a stop?"

Locke: "Yes, we did."

Attorney: "And your first stop was a toy store, Brookside Toy and Science?"

Locke: "Yes, sir."

Attorney: "Mr. Aikens purchased something there. What was that?"

Locke: "A glass beaker and glass rods."

Attorney: "And that's essentially for the conversion of powder to crack, is it not?"

Locke: "Yes, sir."

   ...

Attorney: "Now, I would like to ask you a couple more questions before I conclude.

"Prior to your dealings with Mr. Aikens, were you aware of a difference in punishment between an ounce of powder and an ounce of crack, for example?"

Locke: "Yes, sir."

Attorney: "There is a difference, then, between the punishment for crack cocaine and the punishment for powder?"

Locke: "Yes sir, there is."

Attorney: "Which punishment is more severe?"

Locke: "The punishment for crack cocaine is more severe."

Attorney: "More severe. Is there a specific ratio of punishment or ratio of conversion between how much crack equals how much powder?"

Locke: "I am not sure I…"

Prosecutor: "Your honor, I don't understand the question."

The Court: "Re-ask it."

Attorney: "Let me see if I can re-ask it. You have indicated that there is a difference, to your knowledge, between powder and crack cocaine, and the crack carries a higher punishment?"

Locke: "Yes, sir."

Attorney: "Do you know whether there is a ratio of punishment or a ratio between crack and powder, how much crack…"

Locke: "Versus how much powder?"

Attorney: "…versus how much powder, yes?"

Locke: "I don't know how much powder it takes, but I do know how much approximately, how much it takes for a certain case to go a certain way."

THE JURY FOUND WILLIE GUILTY on all counts, but the night before the sentencing, he slept well. His thoughts kept flashing back to Ginger Locke pulling up to his house that day and smiling at him when he told her he would show her the way to Cherry Street. *Just follow me*, he said to himself over and over in his cell. He realized it was the first time he had led anybody anywhere in his life. But she only followed him that once; the rest of the time he was following her every instruction—all just to get in her pants. *Trapped myself,* he thought, *if that is entrapment. Self-entrapment. What's the penalty for that? Life, no? All this about crack versus coke. They're really just doing to me what I've done to myself.*

He had gone through minor withdrawal in jail, and now he felt calmer. There were a few nights of the sweats and nausea, a week of paranoia. He realized it probably affected his decision not to accept a plea deal before the whole thing started, the nightmare trial within the nightmare years within a nightmare life.

But he wanted to stand up the next day and say, "I was, and am, an addict. Have been for 15 years, to varying degrees. I was a baseball player. I am a mess. But I am not a dealer, and I would never hurt no one."

He looked Whipple straight in the eye the whole time during the sentencing, and Whipple looked right back. He heard him tell him he had once been a prominent ballplayer and he heard him say, "now look at you." He thought he heard Whipple say, "you've trashed your life and I'm here to do something about it." Or at least that is what he will remember hearing. But he had already convicted himself; Tabor and Whipple convicted him even more. A few more years, and then some, would enable conviction to achieve the level of correction. And then he would wait years more to show that the correction had occurred.

5

El Disciplinante

1995–2007

Leavenworth, Kansas
1995

Gracie Luces pulled up to the visitors' gate at Leavenworth that Sunday morning in April questioning her mission.

Recently, two inmates had sent her letters in which they requested that she send them intimate photos of herself.

She understood—these men were men, and they were mightily alone. But it meant her efforts to bring them spiritual enlightenment were not succeeding. It meant, she thought, that they were still focused on their wants and not their needs.

So that Sunday as she walked up to the big façade of Leavenworth, she wondered many things. *What the heck (she would never say what the hell) was she trying to achieve? What was she trying to satisfy? Herself, no?* She had never believed herself to be needy or self-serving. But she kept coming back to prisons all across Kansas, and she kept running afoul of such misunderstandings—and very few men were truly transforming their spiritual lives.

The holiness of the Leavenworth chapel confirmed her theory that the prison could easily be converted into a temple or monastery. Leavenworth was always her favorite place to visit—she liked the thrill of going to witness to the most dangerous criminals. She heard a line once, that inmates in state prisons robbed 7-11s and those in federal prisons robbed banks, and she believed that the criminals at Leavenworth were smarter and more intriguing.

But she also simply liked the building—magisterial, stately, oddly calming. Almost beautiful. Almost like a church.

The architecture firm Eames & Young had designed Leavenworth at the turn of the twentieth century, and it quickly earned the nickname, "Big House," because of the big dome atop its main building. It, like the federal penitentiary in Atlanta where Willie would land within a year, was a Category 5 federal prison—the second highest next to the nation's sole Category 6 facility in Marion, Illinois. They said that Category 5 was for killers, and Category 6 was for guys who had killed other killers in Category 5.

The religious architecture was no coincidence, as Gracie knew. She came to prison fellowship after she wrote a letter to an inmate serving three life sentences. She had read about him in a profile in the magazine pullout from the Sunday paper. She wrote him; he wrote back; she visited him. Then she discovered the prison fellowship ministries and threw herself into it.

She was coming off an affair with a married man. She had seen a film about the life of Jesus Christ that Easter. They stayed together three more months after the movie shook her to her core, but she knew she was living in sin and slept fitfully the whole time.

After she ended the affair, she turned to prison ministries to atone for her sinfulness.

She subscribed to a theological view of incarceration that many of the founders of the prison movement in America held—penitentiaries were meant for the penitent; corrections could be spiritual as much as sociological; and the cell could become a sort of monastic retreat in which to reform the wayward soul.

She knew from her studies that the machine of justice had strayed from the founding intent—spiritual redemption fell by the wayside as rehabilitation, then punishment, became the operative goals.

She not only lamented this slide; she rebelled against it. She was going to do her part to save souls, to heck with the prevailing prison philosophy and society's views. She could do it, one by one.

As she walked up to the gate, the sign-in guard saw the same woman he saw every time she came: brown hair, a confident gait, a polite but reserved smile, and a purposeful walk.

She had grown used to the clanging of the doors as she passed through the security gates—it was like living near an airport and adjusting to the planes roaring overhead, she told new visitors whenever they entered with her. You just learn to block it out, and your nerves settle down.

As a guard opened the door to the chapel, a dazzling red light shot through the stained glass onto the men already seated there. She felt better.

IT WAS WILLIE'S FIRST Sunday in Leavenworth, and just thinking about church reminded him of all those Sunday church breakfasts as a kid back in Seneca. He went to church with his neighbors because they heaped his plates full of pancakes and bacon and watermelon and grits, and it was all enough to make you believe in God even if you couldn't have cared less two hours before.

He laughed at the line he recalled the pastor repeating to him every Sunday— "The Good Lord will always feed you."

He sat in the pew in front of Gracie Luces and did not notice her, nor she him. She was talking to an inmate she had met before. She remembered that he loved playing softball, and she asked him how his team was going to do in the prison league this year. She remembered that his team was comprised of inmates from Kansas City.

"We gonna win it all this year if that man there decides to play for us," the inmate said as he nodded at Willie.

Willie had no trouble hearing him. He put his head down and opened the hymnal. He didn't know yet if being known as a ballplayer would help him or hurt him in here. A crazy might have it out for him just to make a name for himself; he could already tell that the Hot House was full of crazies. So for now he put his head down whenever baseball came up.

But the guy kept talking, Willie this and Willie that, and Willie himself just wanted the service to begin.

Finally he turned to admonish his admirer, but he immediately caught Gracie's eyes first and couldn't keep moving past them. She wasn't staring, just looking. But she looked at him in a way that made him open his mouth.

"I'm Willie," he said.

"Hello, Willie," Gracie said. "I am Gracie Luces. I live in Kansas City, and I am going to root for the Royals of Leavenworth."

The inmate next to her clapped and smiled widely.

"I knew you'd play," he said to Willie.

"I'm juh-juh-just the recreation specialist," Willie said. "I juh-juh-just watch and take cuh-cuh-cuh-care of the field."

He realized he was stuttering and that the inmates around him were looking at him like new teammates used to when they first heard him talk.

But Gracie did not change the way she looked at him. He wanted her to hug him.

The inmates started to giggle, but Gracie turned to them and they shushed.

"I am a volunteer," she said as she turned back to Willie. "I come in to witness to inmates. Are you a Christian, Willie?"

"I ac-ac-ac-accepted Jesus Christ when I was 13 yuh-yuh-years old," Willie said. "But I did it suh-suh-so I could eat good. I have a suh-suh-sentence of 248 months, so I nuh-nuh-need a blessing in my life."

She smiled at him as the pastor walked in, and a group of visiting singers hummed themselves into tune.

The whole service he felt her behind him. He knew she wasn't watching him, but he could feel her wishing him well with all her might. And even after chapel ended and they exchanged addresses, he didn't want to talk—not because he really didn't want to talk but because he just wanted to keep feeling what she made him feel.

THEY LOCKED THE CELLS at 10:00 PM, and each inmate had to stand and be counted. But a Spanish guy was cackling on a floor above him, and he heard the footsteps of guards above him rushing to the cell. Willie's cell faced a suspended stairwell that connected the floors and then, across an expanse of air, the concrete wall.

The whole structure felt to him like a kennel with the dogs barking or yapping or howling, depending on each man's loneliness or anger or humor at that moment. He sat back down after his cellmate did. He was a middle-aged white guy, balding, and he simply didn't talk—not just to Willie but to anybody. Never spoke a single word. They had made eye contact two or three times in a few weeks, but that was it.

The guard finally walked by and nodded at them as Willie stood up, but his cellmate didn't even look up. The Spanish guy upstairs was sobbing now, and Willie heard guards saying the guy had gotten drunk off fermented cereal.

His cellmate suddenly started laughing. He turned to Willie and laughed even harder.

Willie wondered, *Is this guy cracking up, or is it me?*

"The Spanish dude snuck cereal back from breakfast and mixed it with water and let it sit there for days!" he said. He was spitting he was laughing so hard. "Then the son of a bitch drank it! He's skunk drunk! The Spanish guy is skunk drunk!"

He rolled over and kept laughing into his blanket. Then he suddenly stopped and started snoring within seconds.

The first few months Willie did not sleep more than a few minutes consecutively each night. Noises of all sorts echoed off all the steel. The first few nights he tried to place each sound—a masturbator, weepers, the teeth-gnashers, the hummers, the prayer-sayers, the nightmare-plagued. But the worst was always the laughter. Laughter at those hours tortured him. *So out of place and selfish*, he thought.

This night he kept dozing then awakening to laughter. A guy was harassing his cellmate below them, laughing at him as he kept calling him a homo. Willie thought he knew who it was—a blonde kid who looked about 18 had just arrived, and he was literally shaking every time Willie saw him. The weaklings got noticed quickly here.

The kid started screaming for a guard, and then the whole place was soon laughing.

Willie kept trying to focus on Gracie. He actually started to count sheep to try to sleep. It wasn't working, so he started to imagine Gracie's kind face on each sheep. But other faces kept creeping up to the fence, too. Some sheep had Judge Whipple's face, and then the prosecutor Christina Tabor's face, and then random Royals fans who had heckled him.

He awoke as the first morning light filtered through the windows along the wall across from the cells. It was completely silent save for some snoring. His cellmate was still curled up against the wall, and Willie heard the ventilation system kick on and felt the air swirl in from the vent at the back of the cell next to their toilet. He got up, urinated, brushed his teeth, and wondered how guys turned toothbrushes into knives in the first place. He put on his gym clothes and sat at the foot of his bed. He reached into the box below his bunk and took out his writing paper. It was bright enough for him to see now. He wrote:

> Dear Gracie,
> It was a pleasure meeting you in Chapel. I believe I met you for a reason. I am very angry. I did not tell you my whole story, but I never did no harm to no one except myself, and the justice system has punished me far harder than people who harm other people....
> But meeting you I realize that there are ways to make it through. I hope to see you again soon here in Chapel, and until then I hope things are fine with you.

"YOU DON'T UNDERSTAND," Willie said to his prison counselor. "I'm in here with animals. Kuh-kuh-killers, man. I never hurt a fly, man."

"Mr. Aikens, I am here to help you adjust to your incarceration," he said. "But the judicial system, that I cannot help with. I am sorry. I am here to help you now."

Willie leaned into him. The tiny, white room was cool, and the air made a rickety sound as it came through the vents. The air made that sound everywhere.

"Luh-luh-look, man," Willie said. "My cellmate is crazy. There are crazy dudes everywhere. I just don't belong in this place. I know you can't get me out. I just think I should be somewhere else."

The counselor smiled kindly, closed his eyes, and bent his head downward.

"Mr. Aikens, I would like to begin counseling you on drug addiction and its role in your troubles."

Willie smiled.

"Let's start next week," he said. "My family is cuh-cuh-coming, and I need to get ready for them."

HE PAID FOR THEIR TRIP, for Sara and Nicole and for Sara's mother, Silvia, too. During the daze of the final drug years, he kept wiring them money, along with Maria and Lucia, but they rarely spoke. Kim, his old drug friend who was staying at his house in Kansas City, picked them up at the airport and drove them to Leavenworth. His bank account had more than $1 million in it—he had always been frugal, and now he knew he was going to spend every dollar to bring people here every chance he could, and then he would borrow more to keep bringing people to see him.

He sat in the visitor's room and waited. He was the first inmate to arrive, and the three guards stood looking at him as he sat at the table. The door opened, and a few women walked in. Then Sara walked in, with Nicole behind her holding her hand, and then Silvia with Kim half-holding and half-pushing her. They were all crying already.

Other inmates were sitting down in front of them, so Willie waved and Sara spotted him. She started to cry more and dragged Nicole as she ran toward Willie. She hugged him and started to kiss him, but a guard immediately walked up to them and gently pushed them apart.

"One kiss, one quick hug," he said. "It's your first time, but them's the rules."

"They don't speak En-En-English," Willie said.

"Then they got to learn it," the guard said. "And it seems like yours could use some work, too."

Willie ignored him and looked down at Nicole. She was six years old, and she looked at him like the stranger he was.

"*Que grande*," Willie said to Sara as he kept looking at Nicole. "*Mi hija es muy grande.*"

He bent down, but Nicole kept looking at him and took a step back.

"*No te procupes, Willie,*" Sara said. "*Le conte todo de ti y sabe que eres su padre. Con tiempo se pondra tranquila.*" Don't worry, Willie. I told her all about you, and she knows you are her father. With time she will calm down.

They sat down, but Willie could not take his eyes off Nicole. Silvia was still crying, and Kim was huffing and rolling her eyes as Sara explained that they did not know they would get a pat down and asked Willie why he failed to tell them what they would be subjected to.

"*Nunca he hecho esto antes, Sara,*" he said in Spanish. I have never done this before.

Then they sat in silence. He felt like they ran out of things to say; they felt so overwhelmed that they didn't know what to say. So they played hearts. Willie borrowed a pack of cards from a guard, and they played for hours. And Nicole started to come closer. She sat on Sara's lap while they played and stared at him; she crawled down on the floor and sat at his feet; she tugged on his khaki trousers; she ended up on his knee.

He looked at a few women sneaking onto the laps of their inmates. Others were watching the guards and sneaking their hands into each others' pants or skirts.

He could hear the rain starting outside, and it reminded him of the rains every afternoon in Mexico. He looked at Sara, and she looked bewildered, just like she looked then but an older, sadder sort of bewilderment now.

The guards started to move around, and he realized it was time to go.

"*Voy a salir de aqui, os prometo,*" he said. I am going to get out of here. I promise.

An inmate he sat next to at lunch a few days prior told him he could meet hundreds of women if he wanted to. They come in and visit and marry you, and you can even petition for private time with them and make a baby with them, he said. Tons of guys do it.

He wondered how many of these women met their men after they became inmates. He got up as the guards signaled for the visitors to go and kissed Sara softly on the lips. He kissed Nicole on the forehead. She wiped her head and hid behind Sara's leg. He hugged Kim and thanked her, and he ignored Silvia because she had not spoken to him and he never much cared for her anyway.

"*Mañana volvemos,*" Sara said. Tomorrow we will come back.

They did, and they had even less to say. This time the guard would only admit Sara and Nicole. Kim took Silvia shopping, and Sara told Willie she was going to have Nicole's birthday party at his house and asked him for a couple hundred dollars to buy her presents. They played cards again, and at the end of visiting hours they got up to kiss, but this time he decided he wanted to kiss her like the rest of the inmates kissed their women. He covered her lips with his and sucked them into his mouth as he kissed her.

A guard tapped him on the shoulder, and Willie pushed her gently away.

"*Me duele el corazon, Willie,*" she said. "*Lo siento en mi pecho y verdaderamente me duele como si fuera un hueso o un musculo.*" My heart hurts. I feel it in my chest, and my heart truly hurts like a bone or a muscle.

She cried as she walked away, and he stood there as everyone left the room. Two guards stood at the door and motioned for him to come. But he felt his own heart, too, and it felt like he used to feel his knee ache. It beat quickly the weeks after his sentencing when he went without drugs for the first time in years. But this hurt was different. His heart hurt like a muscle, like a bone used to hurt him. And he couldn't decide. *Does she love me, or did she come all this way for my money?*

His MUTE CELLMATE left a bunch of dirty magazines on his bed during the night. One had fallen on the floor and opened to a centerfold of a girl thrusting all her parts right at him. He wanted to tell her to cover herself up. He stashed the magazines under the guy's bed.

In addition to his kitchen duties—wrapping napkins around the plastic forks and spoons—he had been designated a "recreation specialist." And this morning and every day for the next three months after breakfast, he walked out to the ballfield to pick weeds. The prison wall doubled as the outfield wall, and he focused on the weeds at the base of the wall.

An inmate named Terry Sloan was the coach of the Kansas City team—the same guy who told Gracie about Willie's baseball glory and hounded him every day.

But as he walked the field the day before the season began, he could barely summon the energy to bend down and pick each weed. He finally sat on his rump and leaned down on his side as he pinched each weed out of the ground. He saw the guards watching him and other inmates, too, but he didn't care. He reached out for one weed at a time and stuffed it into a bag he attached to his belt. The sun was glaring off the silver dome of Leavenworth's rotunda, and he lifted his face to it and closed his eyes.

"Hey Willie, you want to help us out just let me know," Terry Sloan shouted sarcastically.

Willie kept his eyes closed because the sun felt so good on his face.

"Tuh-tuh-Terry, you are the manager, and I am the recreation specialist," he said, opening his eyes. "So yuh-yuh-you do your job, and I will do mine."

Sloan frowned at him and shook his head.

Then one day Willie gave in. He'd had enough of Gracie encouraging him to play in her letters. Some days he would hit four home runs just because he felt angry, and other days he would go easy and loop a ball softly to the shortstop so he could easily catch it and jump up and down, acting like he had caught a ball hit by Babe Ruth. And other days he would just swing and miss on purpose all game long until the Kansas City team just stopped grumbling altogether and shook their heads at the fallen hero.

"*Le importa ni fu ni fa nuestro equipo*," a Latin guy on the team said. Our team means neither *fu* nor *fa* to him.

Willie sat on the bench as the other Latin guy stared at him. He debated responding in Spanish but instead just kept staring at the sun.

"You looking for the light behind the sun?" an older black guy asked him.

Willie turned to him.

"I'm lookin' for a way to get out of here," Willie said.

The guy barely chuckled.

Willie looked back up at the dome.

"Let me tell you something, Mr. All-Star," the guy said. "I like you. You ain't arrogant. You just angry. But let me tell you something. In here you can do hard time or soft time. Hard time's when your body's in here and your mind's out there. Soft time's when they're both in here. You ain't gonna get outta here, man. You may not deserve to be here. Hell, you may deserve it more than I do, and I cut a man's throat and would do it again. But my advice is good."

On the field, a pitch sailed over the head of a Kansas City batter, and everyone started laughing.

"Can't even throw a damn softball, can he?" the sage said.

Willie snickered. He knew he was going to do hard time. He wanted to do hard time.

He said to himself, *I'm going to do hard time then. So be it. Make it as hard as you can make it.*

HE LET THE LETTER from Gracie sit on his table for two days. One night he went down to the closest television room to see if a ballgame was on. As he walked in, two inmates were shouting at each other, and groups had lined up behind them and were shouting and pointing fingers at each other—a near brawl over which TV show they were going to watch. No baseball fans. He walked back to his cell.

After lockdown he sat down and held the letter. He switched on the little bed light clipped to the steel bar above his pillow and lay there holding the envelope up to the light. It was thick enough to hold two pages, and he could not see any writing when he held it up to the light.

He looked across at his cellmate staring at the ceiling like he did all night long. He stuck his finger into the top of the envelope and slid it along the crease to open it. Gracie bought good envelopes.

He held up the letter and read. He read it over and over for an hour.

> You are where you are.
>
> Prayer and faith in the Lord can save you.
>
> An angry prayer is better than no prayer at all. Just pray any way you can; any prayer is better than no prayer at all.
>
> Only the Lord can save us, and that is as true for you in your prison cell as it is for me in my suburban home.

He fell asleep with the light on and in the middle of the night realized the glow around his face awakened him. As he reached for the switch, he heard his cellmate praying, saying the Our Father over and over, and he sat up on his elbows and looked at the mute man now speaking and Willie smiled for the first time in months.

He was still ready to follow, ever ready to do that, be it George or Hal or Liebl or Vida. Follow whoever was wanting and willing to lead. But this time he was going to follow Gracie, and by following Gracie he was going to follow God, and by following God he was going to straighten out some things. Following was what nearly killed him; now it might be what could save him.

THAT SUMMER WEEDS that looked like flowers kept sprouting up on the field. The purple blooms were tiny, and he realized they must bloom overnight because guys were running all over the diamond every afternoon and then suddenly the next morning when he went out to take care of the field there were purple flowers all around the diamond and on the mound, too.

He composed his first prayer as he bent down and plucked each weed.

> Dear Lord, please let my prosecutor Christina Tabor be the devil's prosecutor in hell, and please let Judge Whipple be the devil's judge, and let all these crazy murderers and rapists be judged by them as I was once they get to hell, and let Ms. Tabor and Judge Whipple spend their entire afterlife judging these cats over and over again and giving them sentences as unfair as mine unto eternity. Amen.

It came to him like honey, he thought, so sweet to say and easy to swallow. As he watched the game that afternoon, he realized why some of his homeboys didn't like baseball. The game was slower than picking weeds. *I understand why some people can't sit through baseball games,* he thought. As he said the prayer over and over, he thought he saw the weeds growing on the diamond right there in front of them in the shadow of the dome.

God must have heard his prayer fondly because Willie got word from his counselor that the state had dropped its case against him, and although this did not mean a reduction in the 20 years of his federal sentence, it did result in a reduction of his security level.

"Where would you like to go?" his counselor asked.

He felt like answering with the obvious sarcasm, but it was too easy. He listened as the counselor described the various medium-security prisons for which he was eligible, and then when he said the word "Estill," Willie raised his hand for the man to be silent.

"Estill?" Willie asked.

"Yes, Estill, South Carolina," the counselor said. He started to thumb through Willie's file.

"If I recall correctly, you are from...."

Willie raised his hand again. The last time he was in Estill he was chasing after Paulette. Now here he was trying to imagine what his life would be like had he been able to convince Paulette to marry him. Paulette. *I never once thought of her during all my drug years. Paulette. She knew what she was doing, that girl. She could see straight into the future, couldn't she? She must have had a crystal ball, that girl Paulette.*

"I would like to request Estill," Willie said.

A month later, he was filling and labeling a few cardboard boxes with books and clothes, and inmates in the hallway were asking him if he could give them the magic marker he was using so they could sniff it.

THAT NIGHT HE FELT like he had made one of the worst decisions of his life. He had only met Gracie once. But she was all he had right now. And she was terribly close. Even though Sara and Nicole came, even though the visit went great, he felt this strange woman was the only person in his life who could help him get through this. He took out his little writing board from a box, switched on his night light, wrote a few sentences, tore up the paper, then took a deep breath and started to write again.

> Dear Gracie,
>
> I write you with good news… They are transferring me to Estill, South Carolina, and I will be much closer to my family there… I know you have been praying for me, Gracie, and I believe your prayers had something to do with this… I will be praying for you every day, too. I am sorry I will not see you again, but your letters are almost as good and I hope we can keep in touch that way.

Estill, South Carolina
1995–1996

You pull it, or you fill it. That was what Willie knew about the dentist in prison. Two options.

An abscess in his left rear molar made his whole cheek swollen. He had been waiting three days for the dentist to come, and one inmate said the infection could go to his brain.

He got up early because his head was throbbing. He couldn't brush his teeth because he couldn't open his mouth. He heard the guard unlocking the doors downstairs for breakfast. Today he would lose a tooth but have a new cellmate.

He waited by the door and walked directly to the dentist's office as soon as the guard unlocked him. There was already a guy there, and another came up right after Willie. All skipped breakfast.

The guy in front looked fine—Willie studied the sides of his face from behind and saw no swelling. He tapped him on the shoulder.

"What you got, man?"

The guy turned to him and stared.

"What?"

"What you got? Wuh-wuh-what you need to see the duh-duh-dentist for?"

"A filling."

"Let me ask you a favor, man. I guh-guh-got an abscess. It's killing me. Three days now. You mind if I go in first?"

"Yes."

Willie thought it meant a good yes and moved forward. The guy stuck out his arm.

"I said 'yes.' That means, yes, I mind."

"What?"

"I mind. I don't want him touching my mouth after he touches a nigger mouth."

For a moment, Willie forgot the pain, but then it came back worse than ever.

"You did not have to engage me in conversation. I came here early to be first, and I am going to be first."

"Good luck being first then, brother."

Willie fell back in line as the dentist arrived. The dentist motioned to the guy in front, and he followed him in.

Willie started to gently hit his forehead against the cinder block wall as he waited. The guy behind him put his hand on his shoulder.

"You're okay, man. A few more minutes. You're okay."

"Thanks," Willie said without looking at him. "You know that guy?" Willie asked.

"Yes and no. Know who he is, don't want to know him."

Willie turned his head.

"Most white guys here aren't like that," the third guy said.

"Most white guys everywhere aren't like that," Willie said.

By now there were five guys behind them.

"He's AB, man. Why don't you sit in that chair? I'll make sure you go in next."

Willie held his hand to his cheek.

"Uh-uh-Aryan Brotherhood's here, too?"

The guy behind him laughed.

"You came from Leavenworth, right? We all know you're the ballplayer. Well, lots of guys come here from Leavenworth. AB all over the place, man."

Willie forced a smile, but it hurt his head more.

The guy came out, closed the door, and walked past everyone without looking.

The guy behind Willie walked over and helped him up. The dentist opened the door and stood in the doorway.

"My buddy here is in trouble. He's getting sick. Take good care of him, doc."

"He cut in line," the dentist said. "He goes to the end of the line."

Willie looked up.

The guy half pushed him into the room.

"The previous patient said he cut in line."

"The previous patient is a horse's ass. This guy was second, and I told him to sit down 'cause he's hurting. You take him now, or I'm gonna pull all your teeth out one by one."

"Do not threaten me."

"Take him now. This guy is Willie Mays Aikens, a great baseball player. I'm sorry I threatened you. Be a Christian, friend."

The guy carried Willie and helped him sit, then walked out.

The dentist closed the door.

"Please don't ask me fill or pull," Willie said.

The doctor did not smile.

The needle in his gums reminded Willie why he never tried heroin.

The dentist tugged and twisted, and then leveraged his leg on the chair to get better leverage. The sound of the roots tearing in his ear made Willie wonder, *Is this it? Is the final punishment and then it will all go on the upswing?*

As he staggered out of the room, his new friend smacked him on the backside the way ballplayers did.

The guards help him up the grated stairs, through the cell door, and onto his bed.

"You got a prescription for antibiotics here," a guard said as he placed a piece of paper on the top of the table. "And your new roommate will be here this afternoon. His name is Mike."

Willie nodded and folded his arms over his face to shut out the light.

MIKE AWAKENED HIM as he dropped a box on the floor in the middle of the cell. He was wearing a skullcap with red beads on it, and a tattoo of a dragon ran the length of his forearm.

Willie considered extending his hand, but he thought twice and reached for his Bible.

Mike sat his box down at the foot of his bed and took out his own book. *A reader at least*, Willie thought.

Mike reached into the box and took out a pair of orange slippers and stuck his bare feet into them. His toes were huge and each seemingly of an equal size. No big toe, no little toe—just five blocky toes all the same size. He sat completely straight and set his book in his lap.

The Koran.

Willie lifted up his Bible and turned from Jeremiah to the New Testament.

Mike and he sat there in their book duel until lunchtime.

Willie watched Mike leave the cell, closed his Bible, and lay there for a moment longer. He once shared a locker in A-ball with the filthiest man in baseball. The guy stunk even after taking a shower. His clothes stunk so much that Willie used to bring plastic to wrap around his clothes when they were playing so they wouldn't catch his locker mate's contagion.

He stood up and slipped into his flip-flops.

At lunch he saw Mike sitting at the table with guys who were either Crips or Bloods, he could never keep them straight. They all sat together the way the black guys used to do when minor league teams went out to dinner together.

Willie drank tea and tried to eat some bread, but his mouth still hurt too much. He felt Mike and his buddies looking at him. On the way back to his cell, he asked permission to see the counselor. The guard directed him toward the office and Willie knocked.

"I need to make a cell change, sir," Willie said.

The counselor looked up immediately.

"Give it time, Willie. You know I can't get anything through for you this soon."

Willie nodded and headed back to his cell.

Mike walked in seconds before lockdown that night. He sat facing Willie and started reading the Koran.

Willie covered his eyes and started to doze. He could hear himself start to breathe deeply and then snore.

Later that night he felt hungry. He had taken some bread and peanut butter and jelly back from the mess hall, and he got up and unwrapped it from a paper towel.

In the dim light he felt Mike look at him for the first time.

"You can't eat when I'm in here with you," Mike said.

Willie slowly looked at him.

"There ain't no rule about not eatin' in your cell."

"It is a rule for my cell, ballplayer," Mike said. "And my brothers will back me up."

"Don't be bringing your gang shit into this to try to scare me," Willie said.

"Stop eating," Mike said.

"I haven't eaten in days, and I'm guh-guh-gonna eat. And this is my cell. You're the new guy. You should act with suh-suh-some manners here."

"If I find even a crumb on the floor I'm gonna kick your motherfuckin' ass, ballplayer."

Willie finished his last bite then wiped a few crumbs onto the floor as Mike watched.

He left them there when they went to breakfast, and he went back to the cell after recreation and decided to leave them there still.

Mike returned to the cell that night just before lockdown. They lay on the beds, and soon he heard Mike stand up and roll his prayer rug onto the floor.

Mike finished his prayers, rolled up his rug, and sat down across from Willie and stared at him.

"You wanna see me?" Mike said. "If you wanna see me, you come see me right now."

Willie didn't look up. Suddenly Mike pounced on him. Willie wrestled him off his bed and onto the floor, but Mike hit him in the chest, knocking Willie's head against the sink.

Willie grabbed him and held his arms around Mike's neck.

The Muslims in the cell below heard them and shouted up through the vents.

"You all right, Mike? You got him, Mike?"

Willie tightened his hold when he heard their voices. He knew they all knew this was going to happen, and even as he tried to keep Mike from killing him he knew they all would be trying to kill him soon. He threw Mike across the room.

Mike charged him again, and Willie thought he saw a knife in his hand. Willie pushed him away and started to shout, "Open up! Open up! Open up!"

The inmates started shouting, and Mike rushed him again from behind.

Willie grabbed him by the throat again, and Mike kept hitting him in the kidneys as two guards arrived. The guards rushed in and pushed them apart, then Mike started shouting and screaming and crying.

"He tried to kill me, man. The ballplayer kept callin' me a Muslim and tried to kill me! Kept callin' me a crazy-ass Muslim!"

The guard looked straight at Willie.

"That ain't true, man," Willie said. "This guy been t-t-trying to get at me since he got here."

The supervising guard arrived as one guard stood beside Mike and the other beside Willie.

Everyone was hyperventilating, and the inmates were raising hell all around them.

"Aikens, that just don't make sense," the senior guard said. "Mike has six months left. He ain't gonna go startin' no fight. Now you're both going to spend the night in the Hole until we can talk to each of you separately tomorrow and fill out an incident report. Get them out of here."

One guard took Willie by the arm and nudged him out the door. They walked past all the cells with inmates whistling and shouting and jabbing their fingers out. They walked down the long corridor that led from the jail to the Hole, the special housing unit.

"I didn't do nothin' to provoke that, man," Willie said to the guard. "That guy and his guh-guh-gang set me up. I'm tellin' you."

"Mr. Aikens," the guard said, "Why would a guy with six months left start a fight and increase his points? You got to explain it in the morning, but you got some problems here."

The guard opened the door to an empty cell, and Willie looked at him as he walked in.

"You ever know you're getting screwed and know you can't do anything about it?" Willie said.

"My whole life," the guard said as he closed and locked the door.

FOR 23 HOURS A DAY for two months he sat alone in the white cell, slept alone, paced alone, did push-ups alone, and went to the bathroom alone.

Mike was down the hall in the Hole, too, but only for two weeks. Willie could hear him saying his prayers. He heckled Willie when the guards escorted him past for his shower.

The day Mike was sent back to the main house, a guard told Willie he had to stay in the Hole because the Muslims would kill him otherwise.

"You read about the Holy Wars centuries ago?" the guard asked. "Well, the only place they're still going on is in the prisons of America. Forget about the Aryan Brotherhood, man. They hate you niggers, but they ain't gonna start no war with you. But the Muslims want to kill you Christians, Aikens."

"I ain't a Christian, either," Willie said. "I ain't nothin', man."

"But you ain't a Muslim, so you might as well get hot for Jesus real fast to get somebody to protect you."

He wrote. He wrote to Gracie every day, sometimes twice a day. He wrote to Sara and Nicole but didn't tell them what happened. He wrote to Ron Shapiro and a financial adviser, Charles Baum, to Frank White and Hal McRae, he even wrote to Mark Liebl, who was long out of prison now after serving two and a half years for the 1983 bust.

One guard was a baseball fan, he could tell. He never asked Willie, but Willie could sense he knew who he was. One day he decided to shave his head, and he knew this guard would help him.

"I need a razor," he said.

The guard laughed.

"You can stay with me while I use it," Willie said. "I ain't going to kill myself. I'm guh-guh-gonna shave my head. Like a monk. You can sit right here while I do it in front of the mirror."

The mirror wasn't a real mirror but a heavy-duty piece of glass that it would take a cannonball to break. His reflection was blurred and magnified in it, and he kept cutting the crown of his head with the blade.

"I only did this for you cause you were a ballplayer," the guard said. "So stop cutting your fucking head so much or they are going to fire me!"

Willie finished and wrapped a towel around his head like a sheik.

"Muslim enough fuh-fuh-for you?" he asked the guard as he turned to look at him.

They both laughed. Little spats of red speckled the towel. When he got up later to take it off, his head had scabs all over the top.

THE GUARD HANDED HIM his mail that day, and along with another letter from Gracie and *Sports Illustrated*, there was a big manila envelope from Mexico. He didn't recognize the handwriting.

His scalp was itching, the water was dripping in the sink, and he had never felt so alone in his life. He pulled out a 12"x6" photograph of a girl, maybe 10 years old, sitting in a white dress on the beach in the sun. She was beautiful. He pulled out a letter, recognized Maria's handwriting, and knew the girl was his daughter Lucia.

He didn't read the letter; he just kept looking at the photograph. He stood up and staggered to the sink. He vomited, and the guard came to the door and called to him as he kept vomiting.

He rested his head on the bowl of the sink and ran the faucet over his head. The guard unlocked the gate and stood there looking at him.

Willie wiped his head, walked over to the bed, and picked up the photograph. He held it up to the guard at eye level.

"This is my daughter, Lucia," he said. "God sent me her picture today."

HE STAYED UP ALL NIGHT looking at the photograph. They told him if he stayed in Estill the Muslims would kill him, so he was being transferred to Atlanta. In the morning he slept. He waved off his breakfast and slept until lunch. Then he took out his pen and began to write Gracie. He told her how he hadn't heard from Maria or Lucia in years. He told her how Maria had tracked him down after writing the names of every friend she knew he had and making up addresses in Kansas City, hoping some angel would pass it on to its proper addressee. Willie told Gracie he needed to wire them money because they were having trouble making ends meet. He told her he felt blessed to be Job, to be cursed and cursed because surely God would reward him for all the cursing he had suffered. At the end he wrote:

> "And here I was in the Hole and for the first time I didn't believe I could make it, Gracie, and then this package arrived that very minute of that very day. And I believe you now. I believe the Lord is looking over me and he sent me this photograph.... I have found my way back to the Lord through you, Gracie. Thank you, and praise be to God."

And he realized for the first time that he deserved what he got, or some of what he got, and that he needed what they gave him. The judge and the prosecutor had none of this in mind, he knew. But the time they threw at him was the same time that was cleansing him. They surely didn't care if it turned out that way, but he was turning it into something that way through his own will and grit and he was temporarily and for the first time proud of something utterly unrelated to a home run. His most enduring creation, he realized, was his own self-destruction. He wanted to change that.

Atlanta
1996–2007
Eres una vergüenza. You are a disgrace. The Spanish words—each of the mothers of his daughters said it to him at various times, and their mothers, too—ate at

him on the bus ride from Estill to Atlanta just as they did on the plane ride from Leavenworth to Estill a few months prior.

The federal prison system had its own airplanes and buses to move inmates among penitentiaries across the country. He sat in the bus thinking about how he used to travel with baseball kings in fancy planes that buzzed like New York nightclubs. He sat on the bus this day thinking, too, of the minor league bus rides—seven hours, ten hours, overnight—and how he didn't ache a lick even though the seats sometimes didn't recline, and the Spanish guys left their music on during the night, and sometimes the air conditioning broke and he drank water the whole ride and never had to go to the bathroom.

It was heaven then, and you are a disgrace now.

He got framed for the fight with Mike just as he typically got framed for everything. He always heard some guys say they got framed because they were black, but Willie now thought more theologically than that. *I got framed because it is God's plan,* he thought. *And one mean S.O.B the Good Lord is. Every blessed day some sports star is raping teenagers or beating his wife or shooting up a nightclub. I just wanted to disappear, and the system is hitting me harder than any of them fools. That's the funny thing about this country,* he thought. *You hurt someone else, they might let you off easy. You only hurt yourself, and they blow you to kingdom come.*

In this bus there were five guys in chains and a guard at the front and at the back, each with a shotgun. The bus was getting close to Atlanta. They had left Estill at 5:30 AM, and he fell asleep with his face against the grating in front of the window. When he woke up he could feel the imprint on his cheek. As they came upon the Atlanta pen his jaw dropped. It looked just like the entrance to Leavenworth—the big walls, the central tower with the marble stairway up to it, its self-presentation somewhere between a stadium and a cathedral.

They drove to the side and into a tunnel. As they ambled out of the bus, the guard motioned to him with the barrel of the shotgun, and it brushed Willie's shoulder.

The inmates lined up and got strip-searched and orifice-checked, and then they changed into prison attire.

Then they walked single file to the Hole—Atlanta's version of solitary confinement. Each new inmate had to pass what they called Captain's Review before they were allowed to enter the general population. The captain's reviewing of Willie would take longer because he was coming from another Hole, so he had to remain in a new Hole here until the review was compete.

He spent a month there under the same regimen in Atlanta as in the Hole in Estill—23 hours in the cell, one hour in a small yard, his days reading and napping and writing and lamenting.

He received many letters from Gracie, the last one on his last day in the Hole. He was nervous. Atlanta had as many hard cases as Leavenworth, and just a few years ago Cubans from the Mariel Boat Lift had rioted and damn near burned down the place.

Her writing was as soothing as ever, its calmness and neatness and the smell of her paper.

> Just think, Willie. You are going to be freer soon. When you leave the Special Housing Unit, you are taking a step toward freedom. Keep that taste in your mouth to remind you of what awaits you. Time will pass faster with your faith in the Lord. We all have freedom inside us.
>
> Your anger will fade, Willie, but not before you turn it on yourself. Repentance is what God requires of you. You have a right to be angry at your prosecutor and at the system, especially when you see men all around you who have done severe harm to others. But you have harmed others, too. You have hurt your daughters. You have hurt their mothers. You have hurt your fans. I know very little about sports, but I am sure there are some little boys in Kansas City who cheered for you like their lives depended on it, and now they are teenagers still wondering why you did what you did.

He barely slept that night, and the words kept ringing in his ears. *Why you did what you did.* This little white woman he was following now was saying things to him no one had ever dared say before. And she was right, and he wanted to keep following her wherever she was leading him.

That morning the guard brought him breakfast, and he stood there while Willie ate the dry scrambled eggs and toast.

The guard had never said a word to him, but this morning he seemed intent on saying something.

Willie handed him the tray through the cell door, and the guard smiled at him. It wasn't a friendly smile, and Willie sensed he was being laughed at.

"You Willie Mays Hayes, man," the guard said.

Willie looked puzzled.

"You know, the movie, *Major League*," the guard said. "That crazy dude, Willie Mays Hayes. That's you, right? I mean, they based that guy on you, right?"

As THE GUARD walked him through a concrete corridor and out into the yard, Willie stood still and breathed the air deeply a few times until he heard shouting and saw a white, bald inmate waving a steel pipe as he chased a black inmate across the recreation yard. The white guy caught the black guy and started hitting him on the head with the pipe. The inmates around them scattered as alarms sounded and guards came rushing out. The guard behind Willie started, then stopped.

"Don't move," he said to Willie.

"I duh-duh-don't intend to move," Willie said.

Fences subdivided the yard, so guards locked the spot where the beating was going on, and as Willie watched he imagined what it would have been like if they had built cages around boxing rings and just let guys fight to the death.

Even as guards clung to his arm and chest and legs, the bald guy kept bashing the fallen inmate in the head. Blood splattered with every blow, and finally they got the bald guy handcuffed as a nurse came rushing across the yard and kneeled beside the beaten man.

"Okay, let's move," the guard behind Willie said.

Willie looked at him, then looked back out at the nurse holding the victim's head in her lap as guards dragged away the lunatic.

"Okay," Willie said. But he walked as slowly as he could to keep breathing and feeling safe in this spot for as long as he could.

As they wound through the prison and walked up a metal stair to his cell, the guard announced to two inmates standing outside the cell next to him, "Your new neighbor Willie Mays Hayes is here!"

He smiled like he had come up with the funniest line of his life.

Willie looked at him, thought of Gracie, and said quietly to himself, *I forgive you.*

IN MEXICO HE HAD SEEN them on television, marching in formation on a humid Easter Sunday. He went with Sara to a village once to watch them in the flesh. He had been getting high the night before, so he was still juiced to the point that the whole spectacle gave him nightmares even while awake, he told her.

They whipped themselves. The blood slowly stained their backs as they marched down the street beating themselves.

Gracie said in her last letter that the real point of incarceration, if he intended to grow, is the establishment of self-discipline with regard to the human appetites and the transformation of those appetites into signs of God's grace.

He now agreed. He saw himself as a victim not so much of a craving for drugs as a craving for company. He didn't miss drugs; he didn't miss sex all that much, either. But he missed sitting around the den with the coke crew, laughing with them, waking up and having them there. He missed the team, the sweetest team he had ever played on. He missed George, too, getting teased by George and teasing him back. And for the first time in his life, he missed Sara. She was always the quietest, the sweetest. She wanted things, sure, and her mother sure wanted money. But beyond her want he realized she had a need for him. And suddenly he had a need for her.

He was always an early riser but decided to become a dedicated one; he made his bed before he even brushed his teeth; and he read Scripture for half an hour every morning, afternoon, and evening. In the gym, he did what they told him to do years ago with the Angels—alternate cardio one day with strength work the next. Within six months, his weight would drop from 270 pounds to 225.

And he beat himself. His favorite way was to bench press free weights until his arms started to shake, and his spotter could barely get the bar back up to its brace. As the whole system—bar and spotter and his arms—shook above his head, he offered himself up to God so that if the bar fell and crushed his throat, he knew his punishment would have been God-decreed.

And it all suddenly seemed to pay off, this change in lifestyle and attitude. In the prison library one day he heard about some guy named Bailey in Washington, D.C., who had a gun charge overturned recently because the appeals court said a gun had to be within reaching distance for a person to have used it in the commission of a crime. In Bailey's case, the gun was in another part of his own house, but he had been charged with using a firearm during the commission of a crime nonetheless.

Willie devoted Tuesday and Thursday afternoons to the law journals in the library, and the precedent-setting Bailey case seemed like a gift from God.

Indeed, his attorney back in Kansas City told Willie his gun charge was overturned accordingly. *Even the judicial system of the Unites States of America,* he thought, *is suddenly turning a kind eye on me.*

But then he got another letter from his attorney saying that when his case had been remanded back to Judge Whipple for a new ruling, the Judge reinstated his gun charge based on testimony from Ginger Locke saying that the gun was sitting on the arm of Willie's sofa.

He read that letter on a Thursday afternoon and stayed in bed for the rest of the day. He tried to write a letter to Gracie but couldn't. *That is the funny thing,* he kept thinking. *They don't have no way to measure your progress. They think you are the same you today as the day you did all the bad things you did. And there is no way to show them I ain't that guy no more. They don't make a way to measure that.*

He ate a few meals over the next two days but didn't go to the gym and skipped his counseling.

That Sunday he skipped breakfast. He had grown aware of his stomach, its shape and emptiness. And the idea of a hunger strike had crossed his mind. He had read about the Cubans here who had done it a few years back, and he read about other cases and it always seemed to work.

His buddy and Christian brother, Tyrone, knocked on the bars of his cell door and walked in.

"You got to get up, Brother Willie," he said. "We goin' to Church."

Willie looked at him. Brother Tyrone saw the tears in his eyes.

"You can't be takin' this like a non-believer, Willie," he said. "Get yourself up now."

He got Willie's pants and shirt and put them on the bed and tapped him on the shoulder.

Willie obeyed. His stomach pinched him from the inside as he dressed. He followed Brother Tyrone down the hall, and as they walked down the stairs Brother Tyrone kept looking back at Willie to make sure he wouldn't fall.

Pastor Oakley was there that day and a group of 10 or so gospel singers from an Atlanta Church. The service was a haze, and the singing hurt his head.

But after an hour and a half they sang "Amazing Grace," the women and men alternating lines. The women all sang the words that struck him: "…a wretch like me."

He cried. Brother Tyrone handed him a handkerchief. Willie sat there covering his face while everyone else stood and sang along. *Such a famous song, and everyone thinking of the amazingness of grace. And what word sticks with me? Wretch!*

He gathered himself and leaned on Brother Tyrone as they walked to lunch. He ate, but he didn't speak. At one point Brother Tyrone rested his hand on Willie's leg to urge him to eat more.

That afternoon he wrote Gracie. He took a nap halfway through the letter, and his stomach hurt more even though he had fed it. He half-slept and tried to dream about the Disciplinantes but couldn't get to sleep deeply enough to dream. So he sat back up and kept writing to Gracie.

"YOU SPOKE WELL AGAIN today, Willie," Pastor Oakley said.

He had talked about baseball in his testimony—how God had given him this gift that he always took for granted and never saw as a gift until it had been taken away.

They wanted him to play ball here, too, and Gracie had urged him to treat the game as a gift and see his Brothers cajoling as a sort of, well, grace.

"I really mean it, Willie. When you speak about your relationship with the Lord, you lose all self-consciousness," Pastor Oakley said. "You catch on fire, you catch the fire for the Lord, and you don't look back. The Lord harnesses your tongue."

I wish the Lord had harnessed my genitals, too, Willie thought. He thought about relating his thought to the Pastor for a moment then decided to keep it to himself.

"Muh-muh-my other daughter Lucia is coming this week with her muh-mother," Willie said.

"What is her mother's name, Brother Willie?"

"Her name is Maria," Willie said. He noticed that he said the sentence without a glitch.

"The name of the mother of God," the Pastor said.

Willie felt like he had been ambushed. He had never thought about that coincidence.

"I wire them a couple thousand dollars a month," Willie said.

He knew he was holding his own here. He was speaking flawlessly; the success from his testimony was carrying over.

"Vulgar, Willie," the Pastor said as he stepped closer and jutted his jaw out close to Willie's face. "Your obligation is to provide, and provide you shall without counting dollars and cents."

Willie wanted to tell him that he was blowing through close to $5,000 a month; that the mothers of the mothers of his daughters were coaching them on how to ask for the money and then probably spending most of it themselves; and how at this rate he would no longer be able to meet his obligation to provide even if the Lord did indeed obligate him to do so.

But he couldn't. He felt his tongue get tied down with an unwillingness to say it. He would keep providing until he went broke.

THEY WALKED THROUGH the door into the visiting room with looks of terror on their faces. Maria had always been tougher than Sara, less timid in bed as in life. But here she looked like she was about to be thrown in the slammer herself. Lucia was nine years old now, and she was obviously mature enough to be terrified, too.

Lucia tripped as she followed her mother. Willie kissed Maria on the cheek, but a little boy kept tugging at her hand and then tapped Willie on the knee.

"*Willie, este es mi hijo,*" Maria said.

Willie felt his gut sink. She had never mentioned this, not once. It was impossible. He could not have had a second child with Maria.

Then she told him the boy was from another man, and she had to take him with her because that man had disappeared, too, and Willie realized immediately the trip had cost so much because he paid for the boy's ticket, too. But Pastor Oakley's words came to mind, and he said nothing about the money.

Maria said the boy's name was Saul. He sure smiled a lot, this kid.

Saul took Lucia by the hand and half-dragged her up to Willie.

"I am your father," Willie said. She looked at him curiously. "*Soy tu padre.*"

Maria smiled. Lucia looked at Willie's bald head.

"*No te conoce, por eso no te habla,*" Maria said. Willie translated the obvious for himself—she doesn't talk to you because she doesn't know you. Maria was always good at stating the obvious, he thought.

They talked about her mother, about Mexico, about Saul, about how beautiful Lucia was and how well she was doing in school.

And he couldn't wait to tell Gracie about the wave of happiness that came over him for the first time in years. He felt an elation he had felt years ago on the ballfield, only this time he was aware he was feeling it and felt blessed in the moment.

Then he saw Lucia's leg. The sight of the scar cut through his happiness like a shard of glass. The night came back to him in an instant—he was just bending down to snort a line off a piece of glass, and Lucia came running across the room and tripped right into the shard of mirror leaning against the wall.

He couldn't stop staring at the scar, and Lucia realized it and pulled down her skirt to cover it. Willie looked up at her. She didn't know, he realized. She looked at him blankly, not with anger. *But someday she would know. Someday. And she won't forgive me. She will someday get teased at school or get touched by a boy who will ask her about it, and she will despise her father with her whole body and soul.*

He touched her on the forehead, then she reached up to his bald head and patted it.

HE STOOD UP AFTER CHAPEL one Sunday and made the announcement. He would be coaching the Christian Brothers team, and they would welcome anyone, even non-Christians, who wanted to play for them. His brothers let out a holler, and Pastor Oakley clapped his hands.

"And our goal will be to win," Willie said. He did not stutter. "We will be a Christian softball team and I expect everyone to act accordingly, but our purpose is to win."

The ballfield in Atlanta had a short left-field fence, but the right-field fence tested even Willie's power. He realized he would have to try to go to the opposite field and laughed that he was finally listening to all the things people like Pat Gillick and Tom Sommers had said to him back when he played.

By the third practice he realized he was coaching a bunch of hard-heads. One pudgy guy named Marcus had the most power on the team, but he insisted he knew as much about hitting as Willie. *He could be the guy to hit behind me if only he would listen,* Willie thought. So he set out to coach the prison softball version of himself.

He pulled Marcus aside one day before the game. He had rehearsed his speech and delivered it like a father to a son. But Willie saw himself in Marcus' response.

"You got your own style, Willie Mays Hayes, and I got mine," Marcus said. "Just 'cause you played big-league baseball don't make you no superstar softball player. They's different games, Brother Willie, and different games take different swings to succeed."

Willie looked at him like he had kicked him in the shins.

"Think of it this way, Brother Willie," Marcus continued. "You threw a baseball all your life, right? So think of it this way. I'm going to take you out in the yard tomorrow and throw a football with you. And you'll see that if you throw a football the way you throw a baseball, you'll throw it right into the ground 10 feet in front of your receiver. Totally different release point. I was good enough to play Division I football, so I know these things. I'm going to prove it to you tomorrow. Then you'll understand, Brother Willie. A baseball swing and a softball swing are as different as throwing a baseball and throwing a football. 'Morrow you'll see. Now let's get out there and win this game!"

HE WROTE THE DAYS away, pages at a time in a long, slow book. The recipients became the days: Gracie Mondays, Charles and Patti Baum Tuesdays, Cille Wednesdays, his old Angels coach Tom Sommers Thursdays, Ron Shapiro or

Frank White or Hal McRae when he had not written them in a while and thought another letter wouldn't bother them. Behind the scenes, Shapiro and Baum, who once managed some of Willie's money and took a liking to him, were working with a host of lawyers and politicians nationwide to try to get Willie's sentence reduced. Willie, however, was more interested in how they were helping to sustain his soul.

He wore his spectacles and sat tall and square. He turned each word like he used to twirl the bat at the plate.

Days and weeks lost their meaning. The name of the month sometimes mattered, but the years became the only significant markers of time. He went to work out or eat or shower without even realizing he was doing so. His body led him around when he was not writing, and it was only then, on his tiny chair at the tiny white table at the foot of his bed, that he felt and thought and remembered that there might someday be more to his life than cool metal and concrete.

He succumbed to soap operas in the afternoon.

He dreamed about the episodes at night, about the girls in the episodes. But he resisted that, too, for Gracie had told him over and over that women were people and sex was a gift and he had to fix himself in that category, too.

As he awoke one night, his bald head touched the steel bars at the top of his bed and he must have been sweating because for a few seconds his skin was stuck to them and he had to detach his head with his fingers for fear of ripping off his scalp.

HE GOT UP the morning of January 20, 2001, feeling the love from President Clinton way up north in the White House that very morning. People had warned him that his gun charge might complicate the pardon effort that Ron Shapiro was spearheading, but his attorney thought that Willie's case had reached the desk of Eric Holder, the deputy at the Justice Department responsible for Clinton's pardons list. And Shapiro and Charles Baum had worked all their connections to try to get him on Clinton's list. *And they'll know Judge Whipple is a hanging judge,* Willie thought. *They'll understand the man was out to get me, lynch me. Reagan appointed him; he wanted to punish people. Clinton would know that. Holder is a brother; he'll get it.*

Willie had wanted to write Clinton himself when he heard Clinton called the first black president of the United States. He wanted to tell him the gun wasn't there, that they were framing him. Clinton would understand what it felt like to be framed, Willie thought. "For a white dude, Clinton sure can talk black," someone said in the TV room once.

He lifted with verve that day in the weight room; he ate less because he had the butterflies. He went up to the TV room during dinner and sat down right in front of the television and waited. They started to file in from dinner before the national news, but Willie crowded in front of the TV.

"Yo man, this TV is ours," a guy said.

Willie decided to try to be reasonable.

He turned to the inmates seated behind him.

"Look, I need to watch just the beginning of the news, okay? There's somethin' important on here and it's going to affect my life, so just this once I got to ask you to let me watch this."

The D.C. boys grumbled, but slowly their faces softened when they saw how desperate Willie's face looked.

The news came on, and all the newscaster kept talking about was the scandalous pardon of some guy named Marc Rich who had fled to Switzerland years ago. Clinton was friends with his wife, she had raised a lot of dough for Clinton, and this, it was clear to Willie, was the payback. The next story had to do with Clinton's pardon of his brother and some other guys convicted for drug trafficking.

Willie shook his head and stood up.

"Thank you," he said to the D.C. boys. They stared at him.

He barely slept that night and rushed to the library to be first in line the next morning after breakfast.

The newspapers were calling the pardons a travesty; his attorney said the gun charge could have been overcome because people were pardoned for far worse crimes. Willie just couldn't offer the *quid pro quo*. He didn't know what that meant, but he did know what it didn't mean.

He ground his teeth.

"I thought this guy understood," he said to anyone who sat next to him. "I thought this guy would get it."

"YOU A DAMN FOOL," Darrell, his new cellmate, said as he did push-ups on the floor below Willie's bed. Willie realized there was a pattern in how certain wise men addressed him.

"Ain't no president of the United fucking States gonna pay no heed to your crack ass. You got to get practical, man. You think you a famous guy, but nobody give a shit about you no more, man. I ain't seen no Major League Baseball protestin' the tragedy of Willie."

"Man, Darrell, I like you, but stop callin' me a damn fool. I'm starting to get tired of it."

Darrell stopped in mid push-up and lifted himself higher on one arm.

"You threatin' me?"

Willie turned on his side so they were face to face. Then they both started laughing, and Darrell fell on the floor.

Willie felt for the first time like he had met a real friend. He realized he felt the same feeling he used to feel in Mark Liebl's house—not the feeling he got from the drugs but the feeling he got from being together with all those guys and laughing all night long. Darrell was red hot for the Lord, too. His father had been a minister, and he recited Bible passages for Willie every night after the lights went out. And when Willie would wake up in the middle of the night and hear Darrell breathing, he would pray for his soul.

A FEW WEEKS LATER Darrell told Willie to take out a pen and tablet.

"You become a scholar here writin' and readin' all the time, so you gonna write my story for me," he said.

Willie was sitting at their table reading the newspapers. He looked up and tried to formulate the wisest response he could.

"Muh-muh…"

"Shut the fuck up, Willie," Darrell said. "Start writin'."

He thought he heard Darrell say, "I'm going to get you out of here, you damn fool."

Willie wrote for weeks. Every evening after dinner they sat and he wrote. They got a rhythm—Darrell spoke more slowly, and Willie developed his own sort of shorthand.

He wrote the stories but often stopped just to listen because they were so good. "Keep writin'," Darrell would say.

Willie obeyed. It was better than going to the movies, he thought.

There was the robbery of the armored truck outside the casino in Vegas that Darrell and his brother decided to do the old-fashioned way—a stickup—only the guards came out of the truck firing. Darrell's brother shot one, and the other ran out of bullets, so they grabbed the bags of money and when they got to their hideout they just spread it on the floor and lay on top of it, drinking rum and laughing.

There was the Arab jewelry dealer who paid them in buckets of cash— literally cash in buckets—for the jewels they were robbing from Atlanta clear down to Miami. He filled a 5,000-square-foot warehouse with the stuff they were bringing him. Then he told them to start robbing his own stores in Atlanta, and they would show up and stick him up for all the security cameras to see and a few hours later meet him at the warehouse and hand him his own jewels and walk away with a bucket each. Darrell gave him dates and addresses, and at one point Willie asked him if he had a photographic memory, and Darrell started laughing.

"That's only when you read somethin', dumbass," Darrell said. "This here's memory. But yes, since you ask, I do. How you think I remember Bible passages without even pausin' for a second? God gave me many gifts."

The last one was how he was the mastermind but his brother was a cold-hearted killer, and the owner of a jewelry store cursed him as he was opening the glass drawer, so his brother just held a gun to the poor guy's head and blew his head to bits, but the guy's body kept spasming like a chicken with no head as Darrell just stared, the jewels twinkling in the blood on the glass counter.

By that time, Willie had stopped. He was writing out Bible passages instead of what Darrell was telling him. He knew what Darrell was up to, and when Darrell asked for the pages Willie laughed and handed them to him. Darrell read for a couple hours then got to the Bible passages and stood up and threw the pages on Willie's bed.

"I ain't gonna snitch on you, Darrell," Willie said. He stood up, too. They both stood there a foot apart, and neither blinked for more than a minute.

"I ain't gonna do it, Darrell, I just ain't," Willie said.

Darrell didn't talk to him for two days, and he stopped reciting Bible passages out loud at night, too.

Finally, in the middle of the night, he knew Darrell was awake, and he opened his mouth to speak but Darrell cut him off.

"You're gonna do it, Willie, otherwise you'll be lettin' me down."

Willie turned away, and into the wall he said, "Okay."

And he felt love come over him again. He forgave Clinton and Holder and all the fat cats in D.C. Willie could tell the difference—Darrell was trying to save him because Darrell could tell he was trying to save himself.

THE PROSECUTORS IN ATLANTA contacted Willie a couple of months later and arranged for him to come downtown for questioning. Two guards came to his cell that morning after breakfast and shackled him.

"Willie, don't worry about hurtin' me," Darrell said as they led him away. "Ain't nothin' can hurt me. I'm on fire for the Lord, man, and ain't nothin' gonna hurt me no more."

Willie wanted to cry.

As they drove, the guard in the passenger seat looked back at him.

"You want to drive by the new Braves ballpark?" he asked. "There are two ways to get downtown, and we can pass by it if you want."

Willie still wanted to cry, and the guard about put him over the edge. He didn't respond at first and then just nodded. The driver saw him in the rearview mirror and took the stadium route.

"There it is, Mr. Aikens," the guard in the passenger seat said. But Willie had already seen it in the distance, and the tears had already started.

"That's one hell of a ballpark," Willie said, and the two guards looked at each other as his voice cracked.

THE PROSECUTORS QUESTIONED him for several hours in a conference room, and Willie had a hard time thinking clearly because the chair was so comfortable that he wanted to sleep. They read paragraph after paragraph out loud, asked him questions as if he were part of the crimes, and took turns looking sideways at him when he couldn't answer.

At the end of the meeting, one of the prosecutors put his head in his hands.

"I can't believe this guy only got 10 years," he said.

Another prosecutor looked sternly at him and then at Willie.

"We will contact your lawyer soon, Mr. Aikens, to relay our decision," he said. "Thank you for your time and your truthfulness."

Willie turned to them as he stood.

"You know my sentence, right?" he asked.

They looked at him as if he had said something he shouldn't have said.

He licked his lips and thought about how he spoke during his testimonies in chapel.

"I got 20 years and eight months," he said, looking at each of them. "I have served almost 10 of those years. And I will serve the rest if I survive them. But juh-juh-just think for a moment about what we've been talking about here. This man Darrell. He's a good man. Killed a bunch of people, though. And I'm livin' next to him right now, you know. Doing hard time with him. I'm not gonna ask you to answer, but I'm just gonna leave you with a question. You all think that's right?"

As the guards came up to Willie, the exasperated prosecutor asked the same question he had asked an hour and a half ago: "How did you get him to tell you all this stuff?"

"He's on fire for the Lord," Willie said. "I couldn't get him to stop talkin', he wanted to tell it so bad. Guess he just thinks I got screwed, and he wants to set justice straight."

The prosecutors looked at him blankly.

A FEW MORE MONTHS and they both stopped talking about it. Darrell kept wanting to hear baseball stories, and Willie knew he had to oblige even though he didn't want to think about baseball anymore.

Then the letter from his lawyer came, and Willie waited to open it until Darrell came back to the cell from the yard.

Willie held it up for him as he walked in, and Darrell clapped his hands and smiled wider than his ears.

He grabbed the letter and opened it, but his face filled with rage, and Willie thought right away that he had gone and got his friend the death penalty.

Darrell threw the letter on the ground and turned away. Willie picked it up. The prosecutors did not want to pursue any of the cases. On some, the statute of limitations had expired. He didn't know why they elected not to pursue others.

Willie went up behind Darrell and put his arms around him and hugged him. Darrell turned and hugged him back. They held each other, then sat on the floor and didn't say anything at all.

IN THE MEANTIME he had met a far different Willie. Ron Shapiro had told him on his last visit to the prison that he could never stop believing and that he was telling Willie's story to anyone who could help. Shapiro had bumped into the ESPN reporter, Jeremy Schaap, at the Dodgers spring training camp in Vero Beach in 2002. He told him Willie's story, and Schaap told it to his producer, the tireless Willie Weinbaum, and Willie's television tag team was born. Their reporting and Weinbaum's dogged devotion would become his lifeline to the world. They would come to interview him in Atlanta twice for segments they did on ESPN; and Weinbaum was the only person to ever speak with Ginger Locke, albeit via telephone as she stood them up for an on-camera interview. Willie realized television—television of all things—might help bring him some sort of justice by raising awareness of his plight.

But deep down, Schaap and this other Willie, this indefatigable guy from New York City who reminded Willie of Hal McRae on constant injections of caffeine, seemed like one of those sudden gifts that Gracie kept telling him about. Just when he was about to stop believing, there arrives this guy whose ferocious devotion made up for all the other forces working against him. This guy could single-handedly make you believe. *These guys, Baum, Shapiro—Gracie told me I am blessed, and the blessings have names.*

THE INMATES WERE ACTING up every night that April of 2004, and Willie just didn't want to deal. He was on autopilot, except for his testimonials and softball.

All those years he had learned that the rage goes in waves. It starts with one guy who feels stir crazy or has been set off by a letter from a lover or by the snoring of a cellmate, and sometimes it spreads and then takes hold. Guys called them prison wildfires. A little spark, usually unintentional, grows into an inferno.

That April guys were talking about the Cuban riots in Atlanta a decade before. There were still inmates there who remembered the feeling the weeks before, and the edge was the same.

A few weeks prior in the TV rooms, inmates turned *The Shawshank Redemption* into a knee-slapping comedy. They were laughing at almost every scene.

They could never make a great baseball movie, he thought, *and they sure can't make a great prison movie.*

A Vietnam Vet inmate told him the same thing about the war stories—everybody loves them but the ex-soldiers. That piece of shit called *Platoon,* the guy said. Piece of shit.

Shawshank, Willie mused to himself. *Piece of shit.*

It all started with his favorite guy on the team, Ruben Blanco. Ruben was on fire for baseball and had been ever since he was a kid in Puerto Rico.

Ruben was in for murder. He was due to go home in less than a year. He was the only guy who really listened to Willie when he gave batting tips. "All those hardheads think they know it all," Ruben said, "but you Willie Aikens, and I'm here to soak up your knowledge, *hermano.*"

Another time Ruben said, "*Hermano,* you know the difference between me and the rest of your team? Baseball hit me in my soul, man. The game hit me in my soul. These guys don't understand the game, the spirit of the game. You have to let it hit you in your soul to play it well."

Willie smiled at him. He was standing behind him adjusting his arm height. And he stepped back and just smiled. Tom Sommers, his old hitting coach in the minors with the Angels, flashed across his brain. So did Jim Frey and Gentleman Pat Gillick and Coach Shaver and Coach McNeil. All the teachers.

Ruben sucked. He said he almost got signed by a team to a minor league contract back in Puerto Rico, but he was blushing when he said it, and Willie let him go.

But Willie said to him a few days later, "Your love for the game will drive you. You are going to start hitting home runs with that new swing, I promise. Don't try too hard, Ruben. Just swing easy, and you'll get it over that short fence."

One day he did. The pitcher lay the ball in the center of the plate, and Ruben held back then swung right at the perfect instant and the ball carried over the wall. Ruben ran the bases like a wild man, his feet barely touching the ground. Willie thought, *The man is on fire for the game.*

Ruben's cellmate, a guy named Chen whom everyone called Chink, got sent to the Hole several days prior for using drugs.

Ruben had told Willie he was scared of the Chink, and when he got sent to the Hole Ruben's whole body seemed to loosen and grow taller.

But when Chen came back some 60 days later, some of his stuff was missing. The cellmate code says that when one guy gets sent to the Hole, the other guy guards his stuff with his life. A bunch of vultures sweep in trying to steal stuff, and the cellmate has to beat back the vultures because that is how the code says you do it.

But Ruben couldn't keep track of his own stuff, let alone Chen's. Ruben was scattered. And Willie reminded him several times to watch the Chink's stuff cause the Chink would kill him if he came back and anything important was missing; he was that mean.

Well, Chen came back and noticed some things missing and demanded Ruben pay for them. Ruben refused, and the next day Chen killed Ruben with a knife made out of a sharp stone from the yard. He stabbed Ruben over and over, and Willie heard that finally the stone got stuck inside Ruben's chest and they didn't even try to operate on him. They just let him die with that stone sitting there inside his chest.

CILLE AND SARA AND NICOLE walked in holding hands. He watched them look across the visiting room for him, and he ducked lower so he could keep watching them for a bit longer. I guess I love them, he thought. I guess that's what this is. And I guess that is the word for what they got for me.

They spotted him, and Sara raised Cille's hand so that they looked like victors celebrating together.

He got up, and Sara pulled Cille into him, and suddenly the three of them were hugging. Nicole stayed off to the side, as she would make a habit of doing. But they kept hugging for more than a minute.

He had never hugged Cille in his life that he could recall. She didn't really hug back, either. But it counted still, sort of like a ball that barely wiggles to the right of the third base bag, allowing a heavy-legged bull like himself to run out an infield single once in a while.

They all let go at the same time and sat down, Willie and Sara blushing a bit and Cille looking like she had just been plowed over. No one spoke.

Then he looked at Cille.

"You got yourself a funny family here, Cille," he said.

She squinted her eyes.

"I mean, look at it," he said. "All that bad livin' you did and I did and here you are with a granddaughter from Mexico. "

"Praise Jehovah," Cille said.

Willie frowned.

"Praise the Lord Jesus Christ," he said back. And he took Sara's hand in his.

THEN THE D.C. BOYS got Pinkston. He was Willie's favorite recreation specialist, a real baseball fan who encouraged Willie to keep fighting for his release. He was one of the few guards who ever told Willie he thought he got a bum deal.

A D.C. transfer named Mark was chatting up a female recreation specialist, and Pinkston put an end to it. The next day Mark showed up in Pinkston's office and struck Pinkston in the head over and over with a paper hole puncher. Everyone knew Mark had multiple life sentences for murder, and two inmates working that day with Willie went running toward the office as they heard Pinkston shouting.

"Mark getting him," they shouted to Willie, and before he could figure out who Mark was the two inmates were dragging Pinkston out of the office and blood was all over his face and shirt.

Willie got there and held Pinkston while one of the inmates took Pinkston's walkie-talkie off his belt and called for help and the other fended off Mark.

As the guards arrived, they pinned all of them, even the Good Samaritans.

The guy who called for help from the walkie-talkie was pinned to the floor screaming in pain.

Willie just held up his hands and begged off.

"It was Mark," he said, "only Mark. These guys was trying to help."

And he realized, as the guards dragged Mark and everyone shouted for more help for Pinkston, that he didn't stutter. He spoke clearly, and the words just came right out even as all hell was breaking loose.

The two main Good Samaritans had to be relocated. Willie worried that the D.C. boys would think he fended off Mark, too. He wanted to get even lower under the bed and hide from the D.C. boys until they came to tell him he had fully served his 20 years and 8 months and was free to go home.

That night he sat writing Gracie and felt a warmth coming out of his writing light. He looked at it, right into it, and held his eyes without blinking as long as he could. He kept his pen on the paper. He looked until his eyes could take it no more. Then he closed them and kept writing:

> Dear Gracie,
> I am just about an old man now. I thought I would die in prison when I met you. I never thought I would live out my term. But your faith nourished me, and though I get sore like an old man in my body, my soul feels happy. I have seen so many men succumb over the years, get angrier in here. But they did not meet you.

THIS TIME HE GOT the pants right. Like Charles Baum and Ron Shapiro before him, Gentleman Pat Gillick had broken the rules and worn khakis his previous visit—the same color as the prison uniforms. He had to walk down to the Army Navy store to buy some blue sweatpants before they would let him see Willie.

Once he got the attire right, Gillick entered and saw a glummer Willie limp into the room on this hot summer day in 2006.

They talked about Cal Ripken Jr., writing a letter to the first President Bush to urge the second President Bush to pardon him.

"You know, Ron Shapiro was knocking hard on Clinton's door, too," Willie said. "But they figured Bush is a baseball fan, so that might make a difference."

They talked about the segment on ESPN's *Outside the Lines* that Schaap had done. Willie hadn't seen it, but Gillick told him the world knew about him now and about the unfairness of the crack cocaine sentencing disparity.

They talked about the day Gillick had to cut him in Toronto, how it was the hardest thing he ever had to do as a baseball general manager.

Willie wanted to hug him like he did that day. He would still follow Pat anywhere.

"Pat, you know, my body's startin' to hurt," Willie said. "I was doin' pull-ups the other day, and both my hips just felt like they exploded. They won't do no X-rays here, but they hurt so bad I can't sleep."

Gentleman Pat was a listener by nature, and his whole demeanor made Willie talk more.

"I think I might get killed in here, Pat. There's a real possibility," Willie said. "They murdered my friend, assaulted a guard I like, and the whole mood of the place just swings back and forth so fast I can't tell how the day's gonna be when I wake up."

"I think they turned their backs on you, Willie," Gentleman Pat said. "Ron Shapiro and Charles Baum and some of your attorneys are fighting like dogs for you still, but MLB, well, you're just not on their radar."

"That's the truth, ain't it?" Willie said.

"How comes Darryl Strawberry gets off easy every time he does somethin', Pat? How about Doc Gooden? Hell, I ain't never hit no woman. Ain't even kicked a dog before. Only person I ever hurt's myself, and I'll be the first to say it, my family. But they lock me up forever, Pat?"

Tears started to drip down Willie's face.

Gentleman Pat was a hard softie, and his eyes welled up, too. But unlike the day he cut Willie in 1985, he caught himself.

"Willie, you still have some loyal people fighting for you, and up in Washington I hear that the tide is shifting toward sentencing reform. You were never a quitter. I offered you a job with the front office way back when, and you wouldn't quit. You wanted to play ball. You have to realize how strong you are. Your strength gives us strength."

They both looked at each other, startled at what Gillick had said. *We look to you for strength.* Willie sat up straighter. He lifted his head.

Gentleman Pat rubbed his sweats.

"You like this outfit?" he asked.

Willie cracked a smile.

"I'm practicing for retirement," Gillick said.

"Me, too," Willie said.

AMEN. BUT. AMEN. But. No, no "but" this time. Amen. He learned in a letter that his security level had dropped to low based on his years of good behavior. D.C. guys were filling Atlanta because they were closing prisons in Virginia, and Willie had started to think his fate was to be murdered by a crazy dude from the District of Columbia. He no longer prayed for his pardon; he prayed every night to be transferred.

He selected Jesup, Georgia, when they gave him his low-security prison options. He wanted to be as close to his sister and mother as possible. There were five other guys headed there on the bus with him the morning of his transfer. They left at 5:00 AM, and as the sun was breaking he kept looking for the Braves stadium again but couldn't spot it.

He dozed the whole trip, but the guy next to him started elbowing him as they arrived at Jesup.

"It's a chain-link fence," the guy said. "Just a chain-link fence."

Willie tried to focus his eyes and there it was like a miracle in the soft summer sun. No wall. No guard towers. Just a waist-high chain-link fence like any you would see around a little league ballfield.

And as they entered, he prayed for the faithful.

Lord, bless Ron and Charles for standing by me, bless Charles and his wife Patti for visiting me and sending me all those letters, bless Gracie for taking me to you, bless them all for helping me come to a place that I never would have considered paradise before, bless Tom Sommers and Hal for standing by me, and bless me for standing by me, too."

Jesup Low
2007

The cells became open cubicles, but his cubicle neighbor was a white-collar criminal who masturbated three times a day.

He wondered, *How do you ask a guy to masturbate more quietly?* He was going to ask the prison counselor for advice. But in a few days the guy was gone. He had served three years of a five-year sentence. *I'd rather be in the Hole in Leavenworth,* he thought whenever the guy acted on his habit.

He gave up softball forever. It hurt too much. He felt like he had played football after playing a game of softball. His hips were shot; his knees were shot. He felt like a geriatric case. Some of those old guys you saw in every prison—let them go, man. Just let them live the last years at home 'cause they couldn't even hurt a kitten. He felt like one of the old timers. Even his jowls were drooping when he looked in the mirror one morning.

Chess and soaps were easier on an old-timer. He had seen a few guys play chess back in Atlanta, and he had learned the game a bit. But here it was the rage. And he always liked to follow the rage, so he took it up with a vengeance. He surpassed the playing skills of most of the inmates within a few months.

One day he sat in the sun playing a guy doing time for fraud. The guy was a banker, and Willie was working him into a corner with every move. They both knew it.

"I'm gonna talk for a second," Willie said.

The guy looked up from the board.

"This game might have saved my life," Willie said. "It makes you aware of consequences."

The guy nodded and smiled sheepishly at Willie.

Willie leaned his head back and looked at the board. *So slow, like baseball,* he thought. *I could have learned the same damn thing from that game, so what am I saying?*

THE THIRD WEEK of his luxury imprisonment, a memory from years earlier clobbered Willie. He was on a road trip with his Mazatlán team to the edgy town of Culiacán. He carried coke and marijuana in his bag. He wore sunglasses all the time, even at night. He was at the end of his time in Mexico, and, that night, close to the end of his life. He got high alone after the game and went to a whorehouse with some teammates. He took a girl home. She wore a fake fur coat and underwear underneath. When they got to his room, he went to the bathroom and got high again. He came out and she was standing there naked.

"Two hundred dollars," she said.

"Dolares?" he asked.

"Si," she said.

"Muy caro," he said. Very expensive. But he set the money on the table and went back to the bathroom to get high again. He closed the door and turned on the bare bulb overhead. It hummed, and he watched the metal cord keep swinging as he sat on the toilet.

He took off his clothes while he got high. The door creaked so loudly when he opened it that it hurt his ears.

She was gone. Her bra was still on the chair and her high heels were on the floor, but her fake fur coat was gone along with her. And the money was gone, too.

He sat in a chair looking out at the city, and kept chugging from a bottle of Don Pedro. Then a hard knock at the door, and another, and by the third he was pissed off but kept sitting there.

"*Quien es?*" Willie said.

"*Soy el manager,*" a man said.

He limped to the door and opened it.

Two pistols pointed directly at his face. He stood still and focused so that one eye looked down one barrel and the other eye looked down the other. The man was not the manager of the hotel.

"*Muevete,*" the man said.

Willie backed up and the man motioned with the guns for him to move further back against the window.

"*Donde estan?*" the man said.

"*Quien?*" Willie said.

"*Los otros?*" he says.

"*No entiendo,*" Willie said.

"You rape a girl, you and your friends, you rape one of my girls," the man said.

"*Amigo, no, no paso nada, we were here alone,*" Willie said. He felt his stutter start to well up.

The man came closer.

"Look, look at the bed, a-a-amigo," Willie said. "*No paso nada, amigo.* I am Willie Mays Aikens. I picked up this girl, I paid her, I went into the bathroom, I came out, and she was gone. I nuh-nuh-never even touched her."

The man walked closer still so that the guns were a foot from his face.

"*Como te llamas?*" he asked.

"Willie Mays Aikens."

The man slowly dropped his arms and stood there still looking at Willie.

"Willie Mays Aikens," he said back to Willie.

"*Sientate, amigo, no paso nada,*" Willie said. "Sit and have a drink with me."

The man surveyed the room again and turned to Willie.

"*Bien,*" he said, and sat down.

Willie slid the other chair over to the table and put his shirt on. He poured the booze into two glasses and placed one in front of the man.

"Why did that girl lie to you?" Willie said.

"*Olvidate de la chica,*" the man said. Forget about the girl.

They each took a drink at the same time.

"*Como es que llegaste a estar aqui, Willie Mays Aikens?*"

Willie felt surprise at the question.

He repeated it to himself aloud.

"Como es que llegue a estar aqui?"

This guy and his tough questions.

How is it that I arrived to be here?

Details of the dream filled his head for days. He walked around asking himself that question over and over again. He had never asked it of himself in Leavenworth, in The Hole, or even in Atlanta. But he couldn't stop asking himself here: how did I get here?

SARA AND NICOLE were coming the next day. But they never came. He waited, almost eager to show them his new home, hoping they would see him in a better light, imagine him someday at home with a chain-link fence in the backyard.

But they didn't show. He had bought their tickets through his travel agent in Kansas City. He FedExed the tickets, and Sara wrote him that she had received them. He was counting the days, not least because here they could even walk around outside together and hold hands under the sun.

He felt betrayed, but then he said to himself: *what do you expect? You think it is normal for a woman and her daughter to keep coming to see you from Mexico because they love you? You think they don't have an agenda? You think they don't want your money? Give me a break, man. You ain't stupid! They stood you up. And you had it coming, relying on them.*

And instead of his bad dream, his anger consumed him. He thought he had conquered it years ago. But now he was acting like a new prisoner again: slamming his fist into the wall, refusing to eat, looking for fights.

But he did now what he did then: he wrote Gracie. And the very act of writing eased his anger, tempering it back down a few notches into frustration. He told Gracie the whole story, how he finally let himself believe in them and then they stood him up.

A few weeks later she wrote back, and she began by saying something he had never thought of: maybe something happened to them. And suddenly concern supplanted frustration. He couldn't call them; they couldn't call collect. So he wrote a letter to Sara each day and prayed that he would soon get a letter back from her.

He had to play a guy named Wall Street in the finals of the chess tournament the next day. Wall Street made a bunch of money on Wall Street, but it turned out he stole a bunch of money, too, but he was the chess champion of Wall Street and a big talker, to boot.

Willie picked up the game as quickly as he learned to hit; he was a natural. But he had avoided playing Wall Street until this tournament because he didn't need the aggravation. Wall Street didn't respect the game. All he cared about was winning, and he would talk and curse and tease any opponent when they played just to distract them.

Now, a few months into his stay, Willie heard that Wall Street had sent out the message that he expected Willie to show up to play him the next day.

Willie didn't go.

"Tell him I don't play with talkers," Willie told the intermediary. "Tell him I play to relax."

BUT, ON THE LEGAL front at least, the luck kept coming. Several times the Sentencing Commission had recommended to Congress to start narrowing the gap between cocaine and crack cocaine sentence requirements. In September 2007, they recommended again. This time would be no different, Willie assumed, but even in the newfound luxury of Jesup Low, Willie followed the issue like he looked forward to the World Series. Shapiro was working with an attorney in Washington, D.C., named Margie Love who for several years now had been pitbulling his case and the whole reform issue, and she kept updating him on her progress.

But on November 7, the deadline for responding, Congress didn't respond. That was the way it happened—no response meant they were at last responding.

But he couldn't think about that. He was walking in the yard all day back and forth, wondering what the hell happened to Sara. He had no money left, a million dollars down to zero. What wasn't spent on attorneys he had sent to his daughters and their mothers in Mexico. He had just taken a home loan to keep paying for their trips and wiring them money each month. He couldn't afford the collect calls anymore. *And they weren't calling much anyway, so why the hell am I thinking about collect calls,* he thought.

Months passed and all the crack guys were talking about the crack laws, but Willie was going crazy thinking about Sara. Had she really stiffed him after all these years of support? He took a computer course so he could learn how to search for her on the Internet. He scoured the Mexican papers to see if their connecting flight had crashed; he read every paper to see if there had been a kidnapping somewhere nearby; he called 30 or 40 times in a row to her house.

Then one day she picked up. She was already crying before the phone came to her ear.

"*Lo siento, Willie, me dio mucho miedo todo,*" she said. "*Me paralizaba el pais alli. Le dio mucho miedo a Nicole tambien.*" I am sorry Willie, it all made me very scared. The country there paralyzed me.

He couldn't even get angry. He didn't believe her, but he was so hurt that the hurt kept the anger from arising. He wanted to hug Gracie, to have her tell him it was all part of the test and that he was on the proper track and love would come to him one day because he was coming to love.

AND SO HE WAITED some more. Laine Cardarella, his new attorney back in Kansas City, thought the adjustment would reduce his sentence. Then she said it might just well get him out altogether. The weeks passed as slowly as the years used to. And his only distraction from the waiting was his anger at Sara. The hurt had passed; he hadn't felt anger in a long time, but he felt it again now.

He wondered if they came at all. He wondered if her mother helped her bilk the money from the airplane tickets. He wondered how, at the point of being set free, he had relied for hope and strength and love on a woman who, along with her clever mother, might just have been robbing him blind.

Even when the call came from Laine, he kept fixating on the girls' abandonment of him. Your sentence has…*why didn't they show?*…you are free…*and now that I need them most*…within a week…*after all I have done for them*…halfway house in Kansas City.

He hung up the phone and thought he would feel like it was 1980 all over again, but realized he felt a whole lot more like it was just another day.

6

Terrible Love

2008–2011

He wonders if he will stutter during the interview. The camera crew from ESPN has to wait a mile down the road, so a prison guard gives him a ride. The reporter is there, and the camera is zooming in as they pull up and he gets out of the car.

And then the question that he knew would be the first question—how does it feel to be a free man?

He had worried about stuttering, not speechlessness. He had focused so much attention on his response that he hadn't contemplated not being able to respond at all.

For a second, that seems to be the problem. He looks as if he has been asked the most private detail of his personal life. He stares at the reporter and then looks off into the distance for a second and sees Seneca as if it was not miles and miles away but right there—his little town set up in a field right in front of him.

Speech then comes fluidly—he thanks the Lord, his family, and his friends—but the whole time he is seeing Seneca.

When they shut off the cameras, the reporter from ESPN, Malinda Adams, asks him what his plan is. He has to report to the halfway house in Kansas City the next night by 10:00 PM. It is now 8:00 AM. But he wants to roll the dice. Seneca is pulling at him. He doesn't know why—it is not specifically to see his mom or Cuda or his sister nearby in Greenville. He knows he wants to walk around Seneca.

"I have to get a bus from Atlanta. Would it be okay if I rode with you there?"

She has no idea what he is up to, what she is participating in. As of 10:00 PM the next day, he will be in violation of his parole, and until then he is at the mercy of the American transportation system.

Soon there are fast food joints and he sees a KFC on the right, and he turns quickly to Malinda and smiles.

She smiles back. She knows.

"We had chicken once a week in prison," he says. "But it wasn't KFC."

"Praise be to God for fried chicken," he says, and they both laugh out loud.

He had called his sister to ask her to pick him up in Greenville on the bus from Atlanta. It is late afternoon now, and he realizes he needs to check the airline schedule to Kansas City as soon as he arrives.

THE PEOPLE ON THE BUS around him are talking on cell phones. He wonders what else he will see that didn't exist before.

It is worse in here than in prison, he thought. Louder, less respectful. People now say anything at all in the presence of others. One lady was talking in Spanish about how last night a raccoon had appeared through a hole in their house and looked around at her and her kids while they were watching television. They called the police, but they wouldn't touch the raccoon, so they called the animal shelter, but they were closed, so she and her kids had to sleep at their neighbor's house until the morning when the animal control people came to evacuate the raccoon.

He also thinks, *My Spanish has gotten even better in prison, writing all those letters to my girls and talking on the phone with them. I bet there isn't one person on this bus other than me that knows that lady let a raccoon take over her house last night.*

He looks at the middle-aged man next to him in a yellow, short-sleeve shirt.

"Feels good, don't it?" Willie says.

"Yes sir, it does," the man says. "Never understood why they keep these buses so goddamn cold. So cold and chemical-smelling."

"You should smell the air in prison," Willie says.

The guy snaps his head toward him and then quickly away. He moves a few inches more to his side of the seat.

Willie laughs.

"Don't worry," Willie says. "I'm all good. Never was violent. A big misunderstanding, really."

The guy looks back at him and nods but his leg keeps shaking, and Willie can tell he is looking toward the front for empty seats.

"I never hurt a fly," Willie says. "Except my daughters."

He keeps thinking about what went wrong after Seneca and if it all would have gone wrong if he stayed or if Paulette had stuck with him. *Hell, Cuda's a mess and he stayed, drugs and tons of jail time for him, too.*

Indeed, Cuda had been busted for drugs and various other misdemeanors, though his jail time was more of the local type.

Coach McNeil and Coach Shaver are dead now, but Willie imagines them meeting him at the bus station and just standing there staring at him, shaking their heads back and forth like they did the time in a playoff game when he threw to get the out at second instead of nailing the runner going home.

He is breaking the law already. The last instruction he received from the exit interview was to go straight to meet his probation officer in Kansas City. And it isn't as if he loves his mother the way some guys do. He isn't sure he even loves her at all. That is just where you go and who you go to see at a time like this.

He wonders if she will even get up to hug him. *I bet she will act as if I saw her last week,* he thinks. *She'll be sitting in her chair by the window reading the Bible, and she will look up and nod, and I will have to speak first cause she never speaks first. And I will have to bend down to hug her.*

He chuckles and shakes his head, and he can tell the man next to him has registered his conversation with himself.

He is dozing as the bus reaches the outskirts of Greenville. His back hurts because the seat won't recline; his knees hurt from being jammed by the reclining seat in front of him. He realizes that cells are everywhere, and that is a funny feeling after 14 years. *I'm free,* he thinks. And then he thinks, *To do what?*

The bus bounces over speed bumps as it pulls into the Greenville station, and he notices a small crowd waiting.

Willie waits his turn as the line slowly moves. He sees his sister Jean, who used to be called Hattie, and a woman with a camera next to her and a television crew with their equipment, too.

She done gone and called the press, he thinks. *I'm gonna end up back in jail tomorrow for violating parole, and all I wanted to do was see my mother. Why did she go and call the press?*

And he wants to get under the seat.

Everyone gets off the bus, and the bus driver stands and looks at him.

"Whoever you are, I think they are waiting for you," he says.

Willie gets up, and the driver walks down the steps in front of him to force the reporters back a bit.

As he steps on the South Carolina ground, a female reporter sticks a microphone in front of him and asks it again, "Mr. Aikens, all of South Carolina wants to know, how does it feel to be a free man?"

CILLE'S APARTMENT IS the same as it was when he used to be a free man—the paintings of Jesus; the piles of Jehovah's Witness pamphlets, only this time higher; her velvet chair in the corner by the window with her sitting in it as if she had never moved.

"That you, Willie?"

The door is open, so he walks in, and he can see her looking hard. At first he thinks she is scrutinizing him, looking to see if he has gotten fatter and balder since she last saw him. But then he realizes she can't see. He moves closer, and she still can't see. She looks up at him as he moves closer then holds up her arms.

"I have prayed too many nights and many days that this day would finally come," she says.

She has a tissue in her hand already, and he can see there are dried tears on her cheeks.

"I got you some fried chicken in the refrigerator," she says. And soon Cuda is walking through the door—big, smiley Cuda hugging the dickens out of Willie and then sitting down to eat the chicken with him.

The bones are piling up on a plate in the middle of the table when Willie says to Cuda, "I'm gonna violate my supervised release if I ain't in Kansas City at the halfway house tomorrow night by midnight, man."

Cuda stops eating and stares at Willie.

"You got a flight?"

"I just got out of prison after 14 years, Cuda. How am I gonna have a flight?"

A friend takes him to the Verizon store, and he talks on a cell phone for the first time in his life the next morning. He buys a ticket for a flight from Atlanta to Kansas City that lands at 9:00 PM; after that he calls all the people he can think of, so amazed that he can hold a tiny phone in his hands and walk anywhere he wants and talk to anyone he wants at the same time. He thinks, *Man, this must make a drug addict's life a whole lot easier today.*

His sister drives him halfway to the airport, then a friend meets them on the highway and takes him the rest of the way.

The airport is full of women, women everywhere. They brush up against him, they push past him, they see him staring at them and frown.

At the security gate he waits in line and wonders what is taking so long for people to enter the terminal. At the counter, the ticket lady studied his prison ID with a face that betrayed either bewilderment or disgust, he couldn't tell which. She finally nodded and handed him his ticket. But here the TSA guy looks at it alongside his ticket and calls over a colleague.

"Please come with us, sir," the colleague says.

Willie follows them through the crowd and stands there as four of them huddle and study his ID.

Then they go through a door and leave him standing there with his bag.

Finally they all come out and walk toward him.

"This way," the original guy says, motioning Willie to the first line where only a few pilots are passing through.

Willie follows him, puts his bag on the conveyor, and starts to walk through the X-ray.

"Wait!" the guy says. Another guy holds his hand up from the other side of the machine.

Willie holds up both hands in the air.

The guy on the other side drops his hand and looks at him as if he is the craziest man he has ever seen.

"Take off your shoes and belt, please," he says to Willie.

Willie turns and looks at everyone doing just that, nods, and obeys.

"Things change," he says to the guy as he passes through. The guy grunts.

HE SITS IN A ROW with two women on the plane, and the one next to him falls asleep and her head slowly and surely slides toward his shoulder. He can see down her blouse and looks a few times, then he looks back out the window.

Her hair is touching his shoulder now. He pushes his eyes down and looks at it. It is brown, but he can see gray roots in her part. He wants to touch her hair so badly that he forgets even about looking at her breasts.

As the pilot announces the descent, her head bounces off his shoulder and she sits up straight and shakes herself awake.

She looks at him and slides closer to her neighbor.

Kansas City is all lit up and clear, and he looks for Kauffman Stadium somewhere in the distance but the airport is too far away. He looks at his watch. It is 10:07. His attorney Laine Cardarella and her husband are picking him up, and he imagines them drag racing through the streets of Kansas City to get him to the halfway house.

As the plane approaches the runway, he thinks how great it would be to just land and drive straight up to George Brett's house in the airplane. He heard George built a new palace out in the suburbs, a Spanish-looking place with a moat around it. He wonders what George is doing right now.

And as the plane bounces lightly on the runway he wonders what Gracie is doing. Making a cup of tea, reading a book. He will reach out to her in due time without realizing that Gracie believes her work is done.

As he walks into the baggage terminal, Laine is there waiting. He has never met her, but he wants to kiss her.

She walks up to him, and he starts to thank her but she raises her hand.

She introduces him to her husband. Then she turns, and her whole tone of voice sounds like she used to sound on the phone when he would call her from prison.

"Get your bag, and let's get out of here," she says. She turns to her husband.

"Go get the car," she says. "Hurry." She looks at her watch on and off while they drive.

At 9:55 they pull up to the halfway house.

"Call me tomorrow, Willie," Laine says as he gets out of the car.

He stands there as they drive off. The halfway house is a huge brick building that looks like a rich man's house back in the day when rich men lived in town. He drops his bag on the curb and just stands there.

This is more than halfway, he thinks. *Way more.*

THE MEN SLEEP in rows of bunk beds, and Willie has been half-awake for hours, and he realizes he will probably be half-awake all the nights he sleeps here because there is so much racket. *Worse than prison,* he thinks.

The objective today is to get Nicole to talk to me.

The fat black guy on the top bunk two rows down had the volume on his Walkman up too high all night. The skinny white guy across the passage snores through his beak nose. Someone keeps passing gas.

The room starts to brighten, and Willie rolls onto his good hip and puts his feet on the cold floor.

I will call her at 9:00. She will be awake then and getting ready for school. That is 8:00 her time.

He slips on his work trousers, bad leg first. He ties his boots loosely for now; he'll tighten them once they get to the job site. The back of his neck hits the bar of the bunk above him as he stands. The sting turns into a tingling down his spine.

The guy grumbles something that Willie doesn't try to understand. He walks down the row of bunks and hits the feet of the guy with the Walkman as he passes.

The guy jerks off his earphones and jumps up on one elbow.

"You motherfucker!" the guy says.

Willie stands above him, leans into his face, and whispers.

"You need to get some courtesy to be a part of society. And curse less."

The guy looks befuddled.

Willie backs up and keeps staring at the guy. He raises his finger to his lips and holds it there for a second as he turns.

He walks to the kitchen and pours a whole can of Maxwell House into an industrial brewer. He goes downstairs to get the newspaper while the brewer chugs.

It is drizzling but not enough to cancel work. The paper is wet, and Willie takes it to the kitchen and dries it off with a paper towel.

He pours a cup of coffee and takes out the sports page. He walks to the small table by the window where no one can sit with him. Morning is for quiet. And he knows he is ready to call George. At first he was ashamed, after all these years. Hal was always more approachable even though he dug deeper into my life. But George, man, he might just ignore me altogether.

He takes out his spectacles and turns to the box scores.

He sips the coffee, and he keeps seeing her phone number in the box scores.

She is sleeping still in the room in the back of her mother's house, but the roosters will wake her soon. I wonder if she ever thinks of me, if I am ever the first thought that comes to her head when she awakens. No. That is too much to ask.

The halfway house residents start drifting into the kitchen, and a spoon clangs to the floor. He folds the paper, swallows the last quarter cup of coffee, and looks out the window. He smiles.

Her face is in the window.

She will wake up in half an hour. How can my one daughter accept me and forgive me and love me, and this one wants nothing to do with me? It must be their mothers.

ON HIS WALK to the company garage, he stops to watch a couple staggering down the street. The man has his hand on the woman's backside, and he falls to his knees every few steps but then bounces right back up again. Willie stays far behind them and thinks to pray for them for a moment. As they pass the garage, the men gathering for work stand and shake their heads.

Willie walks into the parking lot, and the foreman is sipping coffee as he directs the crews to their destinations for the day. Hal McRae has been calling him once a week since he got out, acting like a job agency for ex-cons. And Hal landed him this gig, telling Willie digging up manholes is better than flipping burgers and emphasizing that he has to build up a clean record of work if he ever wants baseball to let him back in.

The foreman calls Willie over.

"Shoot straight with me, pal," the foreman says.

Willie looks at him blankly for an instant before he gets it.

"I kicked it, coach, ain't doing nothing," Willie says calmly. "How can you accuse me? Look in my eyes, coach."

"I don't mean that, Willie. I mean your hip. You hide your limp here in the morning, but I hear that on the job site you can hardly walk by the end of the day. This job has one thing in common with baseball, Willie. It's a young man's game. The job is yours if you keep showing up. But I recommend you get that looked at. And think about what you are doing here. These are young men, Willie."

"I been resting for 12 years, Coach. Like they froze me in a block of ice. I'm still good to go."

The foreman raises one eyebrow at him and takes another sip of coffee.

"I know a doctor you need to see. I'll make an appointment for you. He'll see you the first time as a favor to me."

"Thanks, Coach."

Willie nods at him and walks over to his truck.

She is waking up now. I will let her have her breakfast then call her from the job site.

He sits in the back of the truck with four Mexicans. They are talking about the ballgame last night. He closes his eyes and listens, visualizes Mike Aviles smothering a sharp bounder to the second-base bag and throwing over his shoulder to the first baseman.

That is a young man's game, not this. $250 a day. A year of this and I'm back on my feet. I will call her as soon as we stop.

The mansions on the boulevard remind him of the homes of famous ballplayers. The Mexicans do not notice them.

"Amigos," Willie says.

The four guys turn and smile.

"Mira estas casas, esto es como Paris."

"Paris!" They say and laugh. *"Tu has estado en Paris!"*

"No," Willie says.

They laugh harder.

"*Tu hablas espanol?*"

"*Si,*" Willie says.

"*Como es que hablais espanol?*"

"Because I lived in your country for six years, man!"

The Mexicans smile and say, "No way."

Willie turns and looks at the house that has huge white columns and a white and red brick façade.

That could have been my house. I could have been walking into her room to wake her up right now. Nah. If I had never been banished to Mexico, I would never have met her mother so she would not have existed today. Can't think that way. Got to think going forward not backward.

He turns and walks back to the truck where the men are gathered.

"*Amigos, voy a llamar a mi hija en vuestro pais. Esperame un momento. No quiere hablar conmigo pero voy a llamarle.*" Pals, I am going to talk with my daughter. She lives where you are from. She doesn't want to talk with me, but I am going to call her anyway.

The Mexicans stop and stare at one another.

Willie walks onto the big lawn of the brick house with white columns and takes his cell phone out of his pocket. He dials slowly and notices his finger twitching.

Her mother picks up.

"*Soy Willie,*" he says.

"*Si,*" she says.

There is silence for 10 seconds.

"*Esta despierta la hija?*" Willie asks.

I could hear her voice in the background when Sara picked up. I know she is awake. I am going to tell her about Obama and how this country is going to be great again.

"*No, no esta despierta.*" She is not awake.

He paces on the front lawn, and the workmen look up at him then look at one another. Willie stops and looks back at them and shakes his head. They frown back, one gives a half smile and motions to Willie to come back and join them.

He walks to the truck and takes out a steel bar, then walks over to the manhole that the men have surrounded with barriers. He wedges the bar into the manhole and pops it up. He rests the bar on a barrier and bends deeply in his knees to lift the cover. It weighs more than 100 pounds, and the pain shoots straight up his leg to his hip, but Willie stands slowly and carries it to the truck.

The other men assemble the jackhammer and begin to smash the area surrounding the manhole. They cover their ears with big orange headphones, but Willie does not feel like putting his on. The earth all around is shaking with the two jackhammers hitting the road now, and the vibration actually makes Willie's leg and hip feel better. He walks closer to them to feel even more of it.

It is okay if my daughter ignores me forever. It is her right. I have to prove myself. And that could take 20 years and 8 months, but I will keep trying. And I will pray that she will at least pray for me. If she prays for me even once at night when she goes to sleep, the wait will be cut in half. And in half again the second time she does it. I believe that.

AND ONE NIGHT he calls George, and it feels like they spoke yesterday. George invites him to his house, and they hug as if they had hugged yesterday, too.

"Mick, you remember the time…."

George says this five or six times in an hour. He is sitting behind his big wood desk in a big office with wood walls and wood floors. And he keeps talking about the old times, and Willie keeps smiling like a little kid and it is clear that Willie would still follow George Brett anywhere. But at the same time, Willie realizes George lights up around him. Always manic, George just lights up.

"I do a ton of speeches, Willie," George says. "They pay big money. And yuh-yuh-yuh you could do that, too, you know? People would love you."

George still imitates the stutter, and Willie still laughs. George was always the only guy whose teasing never bugged Willie. It seemed like he wanted to be able to stutter, too, the way he did it, malice free and fascinated.

"I'm going to see what I can do to get you some work like that, Willie" George says. "You got to stutter some more though. Not like you used to, but a little bit more just to keep things interesting."

HE HAS TO GET PERMISSION from his probation officer to go to the wedding of Ron Shapiro's son, and he half-begs to go because Charles and Patti Baum will be there and Ron and others who wrote him letters and visited him and fought for him all those years.

The first thing he realizes is that there is no dancing yet, yet everything persists in dancing. There are two pastures for show horses, and they skip around each other and jog along the fences. There are two ponds, one on the top of the hill and the other at the bottom, and fish jump in sequence in the top pond then bottom pond then top again. The baby chickens hop in a line along their coop; two swans spin their heads, bob, and then pose.

He sees Nicole on a farm like this on her wedding day, her skin much darker against the white dress, her hair pulled back in a bun. He wants to ask Ron if she can get married here someday.

A waiter hands him a glass of champagne, and he does not know what it is at first so he takes a sip and that sour taste triggers a deeper sour taste. *I may never have this for Nicole. She may never let me give her away. I cannot blame her. These families acted like families, and I acted like nothing of the sort. You can't just plan a day like this and perform it. You live up to this day, and then all you lived takes shape in it. What did I live up to? What day did I lead my family to except a sad day?*

He sets the glass down on a table and looks for another waiter. A black one smiles at him and walks up.

"You got anything without alcohol?" Willie asks.

"Sure do, sir," the waiter says.

He looks over at the horses again for a second. They are galloping now, working off their meal as Charles Baum comes and hugs him and smiles at him as if he were his own son home after a long, prodigal absence.

"I don't see many Orioles here," he says. "I remember Ron used to represent just about the whole team."

The people ask him about his job, and he describes in precise detail the process of paving around a manhole.

They ask him about his apartment, and he says yes, it is the same place where I got busted.

"My neighbor watched over it for me as if I were an upstanding citizen," he says and then laughs to give them all permission to laugh, too.

They ask him if he used to like to come to Baltimore to play, and he talks about coming here at age 19 to play for the Johnnies.

"Ate hard-shell crabs almost every night I was here," he says, and someone claps as he laughs.

Then they ask him about his daughters, and he smiles and looks off at the torches lining the field.

"They are too young still to get married," he finally answers. "They're at the problem age. Causin' me problems mostly. But my one daughter, Lucia, she won a beauty pageant, Miss Mazatlán. She actually brags about me. I read the article in the computer when she won, and she told them what a great father I am and what a great ballplayer I was. She even fibbed a little bit about me!"

A woman makes a sad face, and Willie looks right at her before she can speak.

"But then I guess I caused them a bunch of problems, too," he says.

As THEY LOOK at the X-ray on the wall, the surgeon, Dr. Steven Joyce, the Royals' team physician in the early 1980s, points at the hip with his blue ballpoint pen and tells him he has the hip of an 80-year-old man.

"And I bet it is more due to your few years playing football than all your years playing baseball," he says. "The other one is bad, too, but not quite as bad. And your knees are shot; you'll need new knees soon, too."

"At least my heart is good," Willie says.

"Well, we'll have to test that, too, before surgery," the doctor says. "You have any history of smoking?"

"What?"

"You ever smoke?"

"Smoke what?"

The doctor looks at him funny, then a sense of recognition comes across his face. Then he smirks.

"Tobacco, of course," the doctor says as he shuts off the light behind the X-rays.

Willie laughs.

GEORGE HAS ARRANGED for Willie to speak about drugs at his son's school, and he has arranged for a representative of the Royals to be there, too. He wants them to hire Willie. He told Willie he can't last long on that chain-gang job, but he also told the Royals he worries about his stutter like they do. This will be a good test, they agree.

As Willie walks into the gym, George hugs him, and holds him for a second longer than he usually does. And Willie can sense that he is trying to calm him. *But I don't need it,* he thinks. *Wait 'til George sees the homer I'm gonna hit.*

And he does, he knocks it out of the park. The kids are mesmerized at the stories about prison even more than the baseball ones. He stutters a few times, he notices he does this when he looks at George or George's son, but he knows a little bit of stutter adds to the whole show.

And afterward when George hugs him, it is Willie this time who hugs George a little longer than normal. He says, "I hit it out of the park, didn't I George!" And George, it seems, is speechless for the first time in his life.

HE CALLS SARA for the fifth time in five days. He has to squeeze the surgery in now while work is slow so he can rehab and get right back to work as soon as the weather improves. He has been begging her to come to Kansas City for months now; she has been resisting. He thinks her mother has been resisting for her. He can't travel out of the country. He wants to have her there—walking around the townhouse, cuddling with the puppy he bought for her and named Mickey, even getting angry at him for being sloppy around the house.

He hasn't touched a woman, really touched one, in 15 years. He debated calling an escort service—he found their numbers in his sock drawer still. The numbers had been there for all these years. Two of them hadn't changed. A girl answered; he hung up.

Her mother picks up when he calls Sara this time, and Willie hangs up on her, too.

He calls back an hour later.

"*Te necesito,*" he says. I need you. He explains why. He can't think of the word for hip, but she comes up with it for him. In her voice he senses progress.

"*Pero mi madre me aconseja…*" she says, and he shuts off his ears as she finishes the sentence. But my mother thinks…

He doesn't curse anymore, never did curse all that much. But he wants to say bad things to her mother.

He calls her again two days later. He tells her he needs her. He tells her he can't do this alone. She rebuffs him once more. He hears her mother in the background.

Three days before the surgery, he calls her after having refrained for a week.

"*Por favor,*" he says. He is sitting alone in his townhouse, and he hates himself. He sees his old behaviors everywhere—snorting here, cooking there, fucking here, collapsing there.

"*Por favor,*" he says. "Please, Sara. *Por favor.*"

She calls back the next day, and he can tell by her voice that she is coming. He has taken out a home-equity line on the house, and he buys her ticket with that.

As he lays in the bed in the ICU, he comes out of his sleep and sees her face over him. *She found her way this time,* he thinks. *She didn't get stuck in Jacksonville. She found it.*

She cups his bald head in her right hand and holds his shoulder with the left. She smiles, and for a second he thinks he can hear her say, *Te quiero, Willie.*

But then his stomach turns suddenly, and he pukes.

A nurse comes and holds a blue plastic bin under his chin, and Sara takes hold of one end of it, too.

He can feel the vomit on his chest, and before he can ask them to clean him Sara is already wiping him with a warm, wet towel.

SHE BATHES HIM at home, too, and even after the exhaustion and anger he feels during physical therapy, her touch excites him.

His third day at home he asks her to sit on top of him.

"*Muevete despacito,*" he says softly. Move slowly. But please sit on top of me and move even half the way you used to.

The first time they sleep together, afterward he cannot sleep because the Holy Ghost convicts him. The Holy Ghost looks like a ghost from a comic strip when it visits, but it points its finger at him, and with his prosecutor Christina Tabor's voice it says, *You have sinned.*

The second time, it points with even more vehemence. *You are convicted,* it says. *I have seen you and your behavior is a sin, and I convict you of that behavior before God and his son Jesus Christ who have witnessed it, too.*

The third time they do it, it arrives in the middle of the act and points a straight arm at him and says what his prosecutor Christina Tabor said during the ESPN show—*You are a "pathetic individual."*

The next morning his hip is on fire. He tells Sara, and she puts a massage cream on it and moves her hand slowly back and forth over it.

In the kitchen later he steps in front of her as she is crossing to fill up her cup of coffee. "*Tenemos que casar,*" he says. Literally: we have to make house, but he doesn't realize the literalness of the statement. He is asking her to marry him.

"*Si,*" she says. "*Nos tenemos que casar.*"

She blushes. He is leaning on his walker, and he bends down to kiss her. He kisses her with conviction.

They don't sleep together again until the day arrives when they have made the appointment to be married by the judge downtown. Literally. They sleep in separate rooms, and he sleeps better. She still comes in to help him get up to go to the bathroom when he calls her and to help him turn in bed. She has bought him a little bell that he rings when he needs her. He shakes it like a tambourine when he needs her; he shakes it with so much conviction that she comes rushing in and tells him the neighbors will complain.

He laughs. He laughs so hard his hip hurts.

His DOG MICKEY has walnut brown hair and black trim around his ears, nose, eyes, tail, and feet. He poops beneath the dining room table with such steadfastness that he will break down the barrier that holds him in the kitchen to do it. Yesterday when they were out he managed to jump three feet high and snap a rubber band that held the doors together.

And every time Willie says the same thing: "I'm gonna give him a whuppin' that he won't forget!"

And every time Sara looks sadly at the dog, looks sadly at Willie, and walks into the family room to sit as Willie rolls the paper, shakes it at Mickey, rubs Mickey's dog poop in the dirt, and then smacks him.

On this day, Sara shakes her head and holds her left hand to her stomach.

"Que?" Willie says as he walks into the family room with the rolled newspaper in his hand and Mickey following behind him as if all Willie's bluster were just that.

"Va a ser difícil," Sara says. It is going to be difficult.

Willie stops. Mickey stops alongside him and looks up at him.

"But we love each other and God will let it happen if he wants it to," Willie says.

She smiles as small a smile as her tiny lips will betray. He smiles wide and flips the newspaper in a somersault and drops it as it descends. It plops Mickey in the head, and the dog ducks belatedly.

Willie stoops and pets him then lifts him up in one big hand.

"Lo siento, Mickey. I'm sorry fella."

And he kisses him on the forehead where his black hair and brown hair blend in confused furrows.

He takes Mickey back into the kitchen, closes the doors, and builds a barricade of extreme proportions: a thicker rubber band, two chairs, and a block of wood at the base of the door.

"Dejale," she says laughing. "He's going to get out no matter what."

"No he ain't," Willie says smiling back. "Not this time he ain't!"

He puts one last rubber band on the tiny door knobs and snaps it as he lets go.

"Quiero otro hijo contigo, Willie," she says. I want another child with you. Despite her lupus and age, and despite his finances and ailments, they have talked it through. His only fear, he tells her again and again, is how Nicole will react if it happens.

Mickey is already raising hell, his bark that of a dog far bigger and older. He and Sara look at each other and start to laugh together more deeply and togetherly than they ever have. Mighty Mickey is, by the sound of it, body-slamming the barricade just above them.

He puts his arm around her shoulders, and her face grows stronger.

"Seguimos intentando," she says. We will keep trying.

"Damn right," he says.

He calls George that night and tells him they are having a hard time pulling it off.

"You got to keep plugging away at it, Mick," George says, laughing. "Sometimes it takes a while. Just keep plugging away, Mick."

LUCIA COMES THAT CHRISTMAS. A few weeks prior, he got a call from an old friend in Mazatlán saying how Lucia would show up at ballgames and tell everyone about how great a ballplayer her daddy was. He picks her up at the airport and can't wait to ask her what she says, but the first thing she says is that she wants to go shopping before they go home.

They shop that day, and she spends the evening trying on the clothes he bought for her. Then she wants to go shopping the next day, too, and the day after that. By the fourth day, he has had enough.

"You come here to go shopping or to visit with your father?" he asks.

She is way much less hard on him than Nicole, but she is hard in her own way. She seems to forget I exist, he thinks. I'd like to tell her how much I have spent on her over the years, clothes and school and trips for beauty pageants.

That night she cooks for him, and they sit at the dining room table.

"Tell me some of the nice things you say about me to your friends," he says. She laughs.

"I tell them how great you were," she says. "All the home runs that year. I tell them you could have been one of the greatest baseball players of all time."

He smiles, ignoring the subjunctive.

"You know how much it means to me that you talk about me like that?" he asks.

But she is looking at her new shirt, admiring it. He lets her go. She gives me what I need, and that is enough, he thinks.

THE SKY IS OVERCAST all day in Kansas City, but it never rains. After a week of sick heat, the cooler air comes through the car window like a soft kiss, and Willie and Sara are both moving their faces to feel it on them as they ride. R&B

is on the radio, and as Willie pulls into the stadium parking lot, the old timer collecting parking passes gives him a big smile and Willie gives him one of his big smiles.

There are not many cars—journeyman Bruce Chen is pitching for the Royals, and the Royals manager, Trey Hillman, will be fired in a day—but Willie circles a couple times, looking for the closest spot.

And then they limp in together. Sara's lupus makes her the perfect walking companion for Willie with his bad hips and knees. A fan walks in near them, and Willie calls out to him. He is white and young but has a limp, too.

"Look at us, a Mexican, a black cripple, and a white boy all strugglin' in together," Willie says and laughs.

The white guy laughs and pats Willie on the back.

Willie wraps his pass around his neck, and each of the attendants at the VIP entrance gravitate toward him as he walks up.

"What's up, fellas!" he says.

Three of them pat him on the shoulder, and in his excitement he barrels through the door as Sara stands there and watches him.

The night gets chilly, and there is little camaraderie here in the section reserved for players' families and friends. Three women sit two rows in front of them and chitchat, but other than that the families and friends stay within their groups. Willie pulls his Royals hoodie up. Sara's knees are bopping up and down and she shivers. Her eyes are tired but lively, and she comments on the action while he smiles at her enthusiasm.

By the fifth inning one of the three women in front of them has gotten up, she twists and twirls and tugs her jeans provocatively, all the while chewing a wad of bubble gum with which she keeps failing to blow significant bubbles, before sitting down again. She has a bubble butt and bubble boobs and even bubble lips, and Sara and almost every other woman nearby scowls at the spectacle.

But Willie stares at Bubbles, and then Sara executes him with her eyes. He feels like a schoolboy under her deadly gaze.

"*Que?*" he says.

"*Este es vergonzoso,*" she says. This is shameful. "*Esto es La Ligas Grandes? Juegan como si fueran en las Ligas Mexicanas.*" This is the big leagues? They play like they were in the Mexican League.

After a moment, Sara starts to shiver again and moves closer to him as his shoulder and left chest seem to carve out a space for her.

THE FEDERAL BUILDING in Kansas City resembles most federal buildings in its unrelatedness to its surroundings, its devotion to concrete, and its vast but empty rotunda.

Willie realizes he is running low on gas as he pulls into the parking lot on a side street in the shadow of the federal monolith. There is an honor system for payment, and he only has a $5 bill in his wallet and even though it is double the fee he stuffs it into the slot that corresponds to his parking space anyway. But as he walks past he car, he realizes he is parked in Lot 5 and he stuffed the money into Box 4 because that was the number he saw on the ground when he opened his door. He stops, slaps his hips with his hands, and wonders if his probation officer could ever get wind of this.

Gusts of wind blow across the park in front of the building as he walks through it. The steps here are steep and numerous and his hip clicks each time he lifts his leg up. The guard nods to him as he walks through the sweeping door, and the two guards at the metal detector say, "Hey, Willie," at the same time as he walks up to them.

"How you all doin'?" he says back.

He has his hands inside the front pocket of a royal blue Royals hoodie, and the hood covers the back of his head.

"I have to take off my shoes here?" he asks.

The older guard has a kindly smile and a soft voice.

"They have metal in them?" he asks Willie.

"No, but I got metal in my hip!" he says back.

"Me, too," the guard says. "Just put your wallet and phone in the box, and we'll sweep you through."

The detector doesn't beep as he passes through.

"I always wondered 'bout them things," Willie says.

Both guards study it, look at it as if they want to kick it, and then shake their heads.

"I'm sure I got metal in there 'cause it goes off at the airport," Willie says.

The guards look at each other and shake their heads again.

As Willie laughs three people walk through the main doors that lead to the elevators and the air shoots through the rotunda, and Willie feels it blow the hoodie off the back of his neck.

He turns and looks at the three people—a white woman, a short white man, and a black woman with short, shiny hair in the middle.

"How 'bout that?" Willie says to the guards. "How 'bout that."

The black woman with the same crew cut as before is Christina Tabor, his prosecutor. He stares at her, and she stares back. Her eyes are calculating who the familiar bald man in royal blue might be. She seems to be flashing all the faces of all the men she has prosecuted here and she can't quite place this one, but Willie can tell she knows. Like Willie, she is 15 years older now. Willie has been changed utterly by the intervening years, but he is amazed to find she still looks the same.

"Ms. Tabor, you don't remember me?" Willie asks. He smiles big and bright and pushes the hoodie back further off his head.

"I-I-I'm Willie Aikens," he says. "Willie Aikens. The ballplayer from the Royals. How you doin'?"

He smiles even bigger and she freezes and starts walking backward to rejoin her colleagues, who've gone on without her.

"You got a minute to talk?" Willie asks.

She frowns.

"I was just wuh-wuh-wonderin' if you had time tuh-tuh-tuh-talk," Willie said.

He had come with two intentions. One to get permission for his probation officer to approve a trip to Mexico to visit Lucia. Two he wasn't quite sure—perhaps to ask some sort of forgiveness, perhaps to show her she was wrong, or perhaps to show her she was right and wrong.

But the guards stiffen and step toward the prosecutors, and Tabor manages to collect herself and smile.

But I just blew you away, he thinks. *I just rocked your world, didn't I? You who said on national television that I was a disgrace more than 10 years after I really was a disgrace? You didn't believe I could change, did you? Did you? Well, I did. And here I am.*

"We are heading out to lunch," she says. "You know where my office is. We will be back in a little while."

"Uh-uh-uh-okay," Willie says. He is angry with himself that he has stuttered again; he wants to show her his steady speech, too. He wants to say what he thinks. *But you win some and you lose some,* he thinks. *This one I still won.*

He turns to the guards and nods.

"Sure seems awful easy to get in here!" he says and laughs. "I'm heading up to see Judge Whipple."

"Okay, Willie, seventh floor," they say in unison.

He nods again and walks through the glass doors to the elevator. *How the hell they keep Al-Qaeda out of here,* he wonders. *Anybody and his brother could just wander in and take the elevator up to exactly whatever justice they want.*

The buzzers are in a wooden box on the wall beside a big, thick wooden door. Willie reaches for the buzzer next to Whipple's name with his forefinger, then pauses and switches to his thumb. He hears strong clicking heels and imagines a middle-aged brunette opening the door and jumping slightly at the sight of him.

But the big door opens slowly, and Judge Dean Whipple himself stands there eye to eye with him, a tall, aging guy with a pointy chin who looks like he could have played Wyatt Earp in the movies. He, unlike Tabor, looks older. He is still tall but has silver hair and his face seems even more pointed; he wears the same finely polished cowboy boots that gave him a cowboy tilt as he walked into the courtroom.

"Judge!" Willie exclaims. The man who sentenced him to 20 years and 8 months in prison, who followed the letter of the law A to Z but caught none of the nuance of the alphabet once words gave it room, whom Willie liked even then even though he should have hated him.

He smiles, and Judge Whipple smiles back. For a moment they pause, and it is as if they are each contemplating a back slap or a brief, masculine hug.

"You remember me, Judge? I'm Willie Aikens!"

"Of course, Willie, of course," the Judge says. "Come on in here! How you been?"

Willie follows him through the door, and they walked with the goodwill of longtime whiskey drinkers reuniting for a few reminiscent sips.

"I'm livin' with the mother of my daughter now, and I got a job!" Willie says as they turn into the main office area.

A secretary looks up and smiles.

"How you doin'?" Willie says.

"Just fine, thank you," she says.

"I'm Willie Aikens," he says to her, and she smiles and nods once and then tries to wipe her smile away but can't.

The judge's office feels the size of a major league locker room—couches, a big long desk, a wall of bookcases, memorabilia from Russian military campaigns.

The judge sits in a chair and stretches out his legs so that his boots point up to the ceiling. The tips of them shine, and he twists his ankles back and forth so that the heels click into each other.

"So when did you get out, Willie?"

"Last year, Judge. I been workin' on a road crew. And the mother of my daughter moved here from Mexico. My daughter's comin' to live with us this summer."

"And you're staying away from bad things? You were doing some bad things back then, Willie."

"I know it, wasn't I. You know Judge, I can honestly say it don't call to me no more. I know what I done, and it was all wrong and hurt a lot of people. But I don't think I deserved what I got."

"You did a lot of bad things, Willie."

Willie tugs down on the strings on his hoodie and blinks.

"Judge, I was wonderin', I have a daughter in Mexico, and I'd like to go down there to see her. I was wonderin' if maybe you could help me out, if maybe you could tell my P.O. it's okay."

"Willie, I don't even know that I should be talking with you here."

Willie puts his head back and belly laughs. The Judge twitches his nose, and his eyes tighten.

"Judge, Bin Laden could of made it up here to talk to you. Ain't no security at all here. It was harder to visit my buddy across the way in prison than to see you."

The Judge cracks a smile.

"Willie, I'm going to dig up your case and look at it. That was a long time ago. But your P.O. is really the guy you need to convince."

Willie grins.

"I'll have him give you a call."

They stand, and the Judge extends his hand across the coffee table.

"It's good to see you again, Willie."

"It's good to see you again, Judge. Good luck with everything now, ya hear."

"Good luck to you, too, Willie. I'll dig up that case file."

On the way out, Willie feels like in another place and time he and the man who locked him up and locked a mighty deadbolt on him, too, could have been friends. *That is how much the world changes when you leave it for as long as I did,* he thinks. *It changes so much that it will shock you if you come back.*

He stops into the prosecutor's office. The receptionist says Tabor is back from lunch. Willie asks to see her, and the receptionist says she will check. She returns and hands him a card with the name of the office's public affairs person.

As Willie walks down the hall toward the guards they seem to be waiting for him. They are smiling.

"You forgot your wallet, Willie."

He stops and laughs.

"Second time I done that this week," he says.

They all laugh as the guard hands it to him.

"Ain't much in it anyway," he says, and they laugh again.

As the wind slams the glass doors shut behind him, he looks up to the top of the tower where Whipple's office looks out over town. *I forgive you*, he says to himself.

"I NEED TO DO the test before we go to pick her up at college so we can tell her if it is true," Sara says.

"I don't know why," Willie says.

"Because I think it is true this time, I'm sure it is true this time, and she deserves to know before we begin the summer," she says. "She can't just be here and see my tummy growing."

He laughs.

"She already don't want to come home, and you're gonna tell her first thing in the car that she's gonna have a little brother—cause you know we're due for a boy, Sara. I don't think that's too smart, Sara."

He didn't think a lot of things they did were too smart, but that never seemed to stop them. He imagines Nicole hitting him and grabbing the steering wheel; he imagines her screaming and pulling her hair out; he imagines her growing silent and not speaking another word for the next three hot, long, crowded months in Kansas City.

"*Bien*," he says. "*Vamos a la clinica.*"

He turns on a rap station while they drive to the clinic, and he turns it up louder the first time Sara looks over at him and starts to speak. The rapper is singing about his well-bottomed girl, who also seems to be the girl of several of his acquaintances.

Mi hija, he thought to himself. *De edad*. My daughter, of age now. *I hope she ain't messin' with no dude who acts like I did at that age*, he thinks. I *hope she is with someone who is treating her right.*

He shakes his head, and Sara shakes her head at him.

ALREADY HE HAS GROWN accustomed to the reliability of a body next to him. They do not make love, but she offers herself up to him whenever he wants, and he cannot tell her how grateful he is for that. But deep down he thinks, *No way. A 42-year-old woman with lupus. There is no way we will ever have a baby again.*

They did make love once, though, and in the middle of it all he told her he loved her and they clenched hands. That day she had rubbed the spasm in his back for more than an hour and he realized she really did love him, and so the words just slipped out.

Today, though, they are back at the clinic, and all signs point to a minor miracle. But Willie is getting used to those. Good things are happening, and he thinks he could make a go of a life like this.

"You are pregnant," the doctor says.

Sara smiles and looks like she is going to lift off from the earth on a rocket ship.

Willie starts to giggle.

"Well, it should be a boy after two girls," he says.

She laughs and he lifts his eyes and smiles the sort of smile he has not smiled toward a woman his whole life.

"Okay, *voy para el camion,*" he says. I am going to pick up the van.

He stands up and starts to walk past her but pauses next to her.

"You sit and rest," he says. "We have a long trip tomorrow. And let's wait to tell her until she settles in, okay? I want her to settle in first."

THE VANS ARE PARKED on curbs and on the grass, and he feels like he felt when he went to Japan or when he walked into Memorial Stadium in Baltimore to catch batting practice for the Orioles. These people are different; these people are not like Sara and me.

It is a warm, sunny day. The place seems like one massive rich man's garden, the sort you see out in George Brett's neighborhood in Kansas City.

Nicole is standing in front of her dorm, and she does not realize it is them until Sara pulls down the window and calls to her. Nicole lifts her arms in surprise and runs over and kisses Sara. She does not look at Willie. He rolls down his window hoping she will come around and kiss him. She still does not look at him. He turns off the engine right there in the middle of the road, and she jumps a little bit.

"You can't park here," she says. "You are blocking the road."

Willie frowns.

"You tell your friends they gonna meet me?" he says.

She frowns back.

He starts the van and follows her as she walks around the building.

"She didn't say nuthin' to me," he says.

"Please, Willie. Please."

He spends the next two hours taking the handcart back and forth between her room and the van. *She has more stuff in this little room than I have in the whole apartment,* he thinks. She is sitting with Sara on the bed; each time he opens the door they get up and knee a box into a different place, but he knows they are sitting back down as soon as the door slams behind him and talking some more. *I guess I got to get used to that,* he thinks. *That is what girls do.*

THE FIELDS ARE already green, and the sunlight is softening so that the horizon extends, he thinks, to the Mississippi. He looks in the rearview mirror at her sitting there in the middle of the seat between them. She rolls her eyes.

"How come neither of you talk around me when you're together?" he asks. "You scared of me or sumthin'?"

Sara puts her hand on Nicole's knee.

"*Tu papá te quiere mucho,*" she says.

Nicole seems to be looking for New York on the horizon now.

"I need to translate that for you?" Willie asks. "She said your father loves you very much."

"Ha, ha," Nicole says.

"I got news for you, too," Willie says. "I filled out applications for you at McDonalds, Wal-Mart, and Price Chopper. You need to learn how to earn a living, and this summer's best time to do it. You can save some money since you'll be livin' with us."

Nicole starts to shake her head, then shakes it faster as tears come down her face.

"I am not working in any of those places," she says.

"Yes, you are," Willie says.

"I am not," she says. "*Mama, dile que no. Que no. No voy a trabajar en esos sitios.*"

"Keep shaking your head like that," Willie says. He starts to push harder on the pedal and looks down at the speedometer. He is going 90 mph.

"You are going to learn what it is to work this summer," he says.

As THEY PULL into the driveway Mickey starts to yap, and Nicole looks up at the kitchen window.

"What's that?" she asks. "Is that our dog?"

Willie smiles at Sara, and Sara giggles.

Willie hits the button on his keychain to open the garage door, and he can see Mickey jumping up above the windowsill. They walk through the garage, and Nicole races up the stairs and snaps the rubber band off the knobs of the two doors to the kitchen.

Mickey jumps up to her and knocks her back into Willie.

She grabs him and lets him lick her lips then turns to him and Sara.

"Why didn't you tell me we had a puppy?"

They both laugh.

"We wanted it to be a surprise for you," Sara says.

"It is a German Shepard Chow," Willie says. "His name is Mickey. That was my nickname. He is going to be a big dog."

Nicole sets Mickey down and kneels down on the floor. He rubs against her legs like a kitten.

"You know what, Nicole?" Willie asks. "Dogs cost money, and this is your dog, so you gonna have to work this summer and learn how to manage your lifestyle."

Nicole looks at Sara and starts to shake her head again, back and forth so fast her cheeks shake.

She grabs Mickey and pushes between Willie and Sara and runs to her room. Willie turns and calls after her.

"And you gonna have to unpack your own stuff like a normal person, too."

Sara slaps him softly and scowls.

"We are going to unpack, and she will help us," she says.

"Neither of you know what I done for you," he says. "Neither of you. You know how much money I had in the bank when I went to prison? You know how much I spent on you?"

"Well Willie, maybe if you spent a little less on drugs you'd have more to spend on us now," Sara says. She stares at him and walks toward the stairs.

He suddenly sees a room full of mounds of cocaine several feet high and prostitutes walking all around him as he sits on a chair in the middle of the room.

He snaps out of it and hears a door slam upstairs. He cannot move. He feels paralyzed there in the doorway to the kitchen. *The first day of summer with my family,* he says to himself. *Wait 'til we tell her that her mother is pregnant.*

HIS RUSTY GOLD CAMRY can't take it. She slams on the brakes so hard that the car feels like an airplane shuddering at its seams as it lands.

"You got to just ease into it, Nicole," he says. "Just ease into it. Don't hit the brake all at once unless you have to—like if someone stops right in front of you."

She slowly lets her foot off the brake and begins to drive in a big circle around the empty parking lot.

"Okay. Let's go out on the street."

He looks at her. She looks out the window at an old man walking a tiny dog. He imagines her looking at him instead, smiling, and saying thank you.

As she turns onto the street from the parking lot, he notices her forearms are shaking as they cling to the steering wheel.

"You got to relax, baby."

She hits the brake and turns sharply toward him.

"Don't tell me to relax."

He shakes his head and groans at her.

"Look at the road," he says.

Two cars pass, and she slowly releases the brake and pulls out. She does not pick up speed for a few minutes and then suddenly starts to go too fast.

"Slow down, Nicole. This is a residential area. You'll get me a big ticket here."

"Don't tell me to slow down!" she says.

The light 200 feet in front of them is turning red, and he knows she doesn't see it. As she looks out the side window at the car next to her, he reaches over for the wheel and jerks the car onto the shoulder. She grabs the wheel and pulls it back toward her at the same time. She finally slams on the brake, and they are both sitting there looking at each other with four hands on the wheel.

He tells her he is going to pay for her to take driving classes even though he can't afford to.

He lets go of the wheel and imagines what would be happening now if he had never become a ballplayer, he had never done drugs, he had never been caught, he had never been to jail, had raised her in a normal family. He imagines her next to him, looking up at him, and saying sweetly, "Thank you."

Instead, he feels himself about to say it to her. He is saying it to spite her, but he feels deeper down that he is saying it because he means it. He means to spite her and he wants to thank her, so why not kill two birds with one stone?

"*Gracias,* Nicole," he says. He manages to eliminate the sarcasm that part of him wanted to include in his tone. He says the two words quietly and plainly, and as he listens to them in his ear he knows he has said them with the right tone, said them with the perfect pace so that he means it, and makes her feel bad and might just make her say the two words back.

But she puts the car into park and opens the door and walks over to his side. She stands there staring at him. He sits there without opening the door for a minute. He decides that he really said thank you to himself. *Somebody needs to say it to me so it might as well be me since no one else will,* he thinks. *Lucia says it to me, but she is so far away it almost makes it hurt when she says it. Maybe the only daughters at this age who say it to their fathers live far away, anyway.*

A WOMAN WHOSE wandering son he befriended at the Royals ballgames offers Nicole a job as an intern in a law firm. She works afternoons—he drives her to work at noon then picks her up at the end of the day. In the car, he stops asking her how her day was because he has grown tired of grunts and three-word answers. There are two weeks until her test.

This morning before he takes her there, they have an appointment to straighten out Sara's papers at the immigration office in Kansas City. Sara wants to tell Nicole she is pregnant while they are all in the car so she can't run away.

"She's crazy enough that she'll just open the door and jump out," Willie says.

"No, Willie," Sara says. "She will get over it. You have to be more patient. We have to tell her."

As they walk into the immigration office, Willie drops his cell phone in front of the metal detector. The battery snaps off, and the parts careen toward opposite ends of the room. Nicole chuckles, and Willie stops and looks at her.

The security guard, a bald white guy with a big belly that sticks through the gaps in his shirt, looks at Willie and smiles kindly. Willie can tell he is a father. *That is the only way he would look at me like this,* he thinks.

The guard walks over and picks up the battery while Willie picks up the phone. Sara and Nicole put their bags on the conveyor when suddenly the guard leans his head back and laughs.

"Wait," he says.

Nicole looks up startled.

"You're Willie Aikens," he says.

Willie smiles and starts to wonder how much he will have to pay this guy for teaching his daughter a lesson.

The guard looks at Nicole.

"Your father was quite a ballplayer," he says to her. "You're probably too young to remember, but he had this town in the palm of his hand."

"I wasn't even born yet," she says and looks at the floor. "And I grew up in Mexico."

"Well then you really missed something," he says.

He hits a button that starts the belt, and he doesn't even look at the bags as they go through.

They each walk through the detector, and it beeps as Willie goes last.

"Go 'head, go 'head," the guard says as he waves him forward. "Willie Aikens isn't gonna blow this place up. Nice to see you, sir."

"Nice to see you," Willie says.

"I sure hope the Royals play someday like they did when you and George were around."

"Me, too," Willie says. "Me, too."

As they walk toward the clerk, Willie looks at Nicole. She looks even further away into the distance until they come to their place in line. Then she looks up at him.

"I never realized you were still famous," she says.

"Your father still gets recognized all over town," Sara says.

"That make you want to call him 'papa'?" Willie asks.

"Let's not start with that again," Nicole says. She shakes her head. "Please don't put any more pressure on me to call you 'dad.'"

He wants to cry for the first time since he got out. She is right. He wants to tell everyone she is a spoiled brat who has been given too much. He hears lots of parents saying this now. But he realizes she has been given nothing. He gave her diddly and now he would give her everything, but that is no way to be a parent. He realizes he may never be able to make it up to her because he is down 9–1 in the bottom of the ninth, and even if he hits a grand slam that still only makes it 9–5.

"WILLIE," Mark Liebl says.

Willie is waiting to board a connecting flight to New York via Chicago. Liebl is connecting through Chicago to Hawaii, where he now lives.

Willie knows it is him; his voice is the same—happy, welcoming, warm. They wrote a few times during Willie's stay in prison—nothing profound, but the old bond just was unbreakable despite just cause. They are short on words at first, then Liebl says they should try to sit together on the connecting flight. The passenger next to Willie obliges, and as they take off the both just start laughing.

"I don't know how the hell I did two and a half years and you did a decade and a half," Liebl says through his laughs. Willie keeps laughing, too.

"Sometimes, Mark, man, I wanted to find you and kill you," he says.

"I bet," Liebl says. He is a bartender at a hotel in Hawaii now, still hosting the party, albeit drug free.

"But then I realized how much money you saved me!" Willie says. "You probably gave me $200,000 worth of free cocaine, Mark! How did you keep doing that?"

They laugh some more. They talk about the Royals for a good bit, who is doing what. The plane starts to descend and their laughter is fading.

"Mark, man, I know people blame you for a lot of this, but I had a really fun time," Willie says. "You were a good guy. You love baseball man. We just loved to laugh, just like we are doing now."

"Except now you don't stutter anymore," Liebl says. "That used to add a lot to the party!"

They laugh again.

They don't talk as they exit, and they hug as they part ways. For a second Willie feels that old impulse to follow Mark Liebl, to go with him because wherever he leads they will arrive at a good time.

But then he catches himself. Liebl towers over everyone on the concourse, so Willie can see his head until he turns off in the distance. A lady bumps into Willie as he stands there.

"Excuse me," the lady says.

"Got that right," he says back.

He is sitting there on a rainy day at noon watching a DVRed episode of *Are You Smarter than a 5ᵗʰ Grader?* The Dallas Cowboys cheerleaders are the special guests. Sara and Nicole are upstairs. They segregate themselves more and more. They do girl things. He likes it; he dislikes it. It pleases him to see them together; it also makes him think they are plotting their getaway as soon as she finishes college.

The cheerleaders are wearing their outfits, and he recalls his stay at the Fort Worth Correctional Facility. Specifically, he recalls the girl there. Specifically, one cheerleader—bright blonde hair, bubble butt, Texas-wide smile—reminds him of the girl he had sex with behind the carts of plates in the kitchen at the Fort Worth Correctional Facility.

The question is, what is the most basic element of matter?

The blonde cheerleader rejects the help of an overweight boy who looks like Fat Albert.

"Tissue," the cheerleader answers.

Willie sits there shaking his head and studies the cheerleaders, and he knows Nicole knows that even though the cheerleader is stupid, he thinks she is sexy and he is looking at her there in her cheerleading outfit and she could answer every question wrong but he would still look. He feels like he is sneaking a peek at dirty magazines in Seneca as a boy. He taped this episode and hid it because he knew if he watched it with Nicole she would have looked at him and known that these used to be his type of girls. *And you fucked my mother just like you fucked all of them, but it so happened to turn out differently and here I am and you are no more my father than any other man who fucked those stupid cheerleaders. That is what she will say,* he thinks. But she will say it in Spanish, the language she elects when she says what she knows will hurt him.

Mickey sits on the gray shag carpet and looks at him. Mickey thinks the cheerleader isn't the brightest in the world, either.

Then Mickey jumps at the scream from upstairs. It is an animal cry, and Willie for a moment is more fascinated by Mickey's reaction to it than to its own significance as the voice of his daughter. Mickey stands up straight; his tail stands up straight; he looks at the ceiling, and he howls back.

Then Willie leans forward on the couch and puts his head down. *I knew Sara would tell her,* he says to himself. *I knew it. They talk. Girls talk.*

He rises and walks to the stairs. Mickey runs through his legs. He stops halfway down the stairwell and howls some more. He comes back up, walks into the family room, and begins to stoop.

Willie leaps toward him and kicks him in the tail. A tidbit of shit snaps out and falls on the floor, and Willie kicks Mickey into the brick base of the fireplace.

Nicole is screaming now.

He turns and heads up the stairs. His bedroom door is locked, but the screams are coming out from the gap between the door and the floor like bullets. He leans his shoulder into the door and pops the lock.

She sits up at a 90-degree angle with her legs outstretched. And it seems like all the tears instantly dry up and her eyes pierce him.

"You wanted somebody to take my place," she says. She says it quietly at first, like a doctor beginning to explain a diagnosis.

But then she sits even taller and screams it: "You wanted somebody to take my place!"

Willie looks at Sara.

"I thought you were going to wait," he says. "I thought we were going to tell her together."

"*Willie, es que yo no podia más, no podia,*" Sara says. I couldn't wait any longer.

He shakes his head and puts his hands in his pockets.

"Nicole, you are 21 years old, and this has nothing to do with you. Now get up and be an adult."

She stands and points her finger at him like she is going to knife him with it.

"Nicole, this has nothing…."

She moves closer to him, holding her finger a few inches from his heart.

"My mom has lupus, and she will have health problems!"

The tears start again. She drops her hand and crumples onto the floor in a ball.

Willie looks at Sara. She is crying, too. She looks afraid of him; she half-hides her head behind her shoulder.

"You know what you both are doing?" he asks. "That baby hears you. That baby knows. Your mama's lupus ain't hurtin' that baby. You are."

THEY REFUSE TO ATTEND his church. They say the service is too long; he thinks they think it is too black. And too long. They are right on that. *Too long for people who don't need a long service,* he thinks.

So he sits in their Catholic church near their house every Sunday before going to his service alone on the other side of town where the poor black people live. The priest says the first two words of the "Our Father," and the congregation picks up with "who art in heaven." Everyone is holding hands, Nicole in between Sara and Willie.

His hand could cover hers twice over. Tiny and soft, it more or less a fist but not clenched. He realizes he is holding her hand literally, holding her cupped hand. She is not squeezing back.

He bends his head down and looks sideways at how Sara and she are holding hands, their fingers woven together. They are holding hands so tightly he thinks he can see their pulse beating in their fingers.

"And forgive us our trespasses, as we forgive those who trespass against us."

He squeezes her hand tighter and says these words louder, so tight that she pulls it toward her and looks at him and so loud that she lifts her eyebrows at him.

As everyone says "Amen" and slowly drops hands, she and Sara keep their hands intertwined. She pulls hers away from him.

And so he decides to pray his own prayer like he did in prison. He closes his eyes tightly and stands there for a few seconds even after everyone else has sat down.

It is my duty to forgive her as much as hers to forgive me, he thinks. *I forgive you, my daughter, even though you won't forgive me. You are the one who is trespassing now. But I forgive you.*

SHE FAILED HER first driving test two weeks ago. She parked too close to the curb; she went through a stop sign; she forgot to put on the turn signal once. The instructor left her in the car crying—just walked away. She scowled at Willie and kept on walking past.

This morning he wakes her up. He feels a funny sense of determination. *I am going to do it anyway,* he says to himself. *Get her to pass this, do it for myself at least before she goes. Someday she will realize what I am doing for her.*

He opens her door without knocking. She is lying there with her eyes wide open, looking up at the ceiling. He tugs on her big toes sticking up through the sheets.

"Nicole, I am going to take you out to practice again before I drop you off for work," he says. "I think we should do the same course. Just do it over and over. I bet you they are going to take you on the same course as the first time. And even if they don't, the practice will help you."

She yawns and rubs her eyes.

"I don't want to," she says. She rolls onto her side.

"We have to," he says. "Come on. *Levántate.*"

THEY DO THE COURSE five times and then practice parallel parking five times more. She is nailing it by the end—back, turn, cut, straighten.

"You are going to pass with flying colors," he says to her.

"If they don't give me the same tester, I will," she says.

"Don't matter who it is," he says. "You can do this. You are a perfect driver. Now don't even think about who gives you the test. When I played baseball, if I thought about who was pitching all the time I'd never have hit a ball. You got to focus on you. Stay on you, and you'll do fine."

They pull up to the DMV and walk in. A different woman—gray hair and a paunch—walks out and smiles at Nicole. She smiles back. Willie smiles, too.

They leave him there, and he stands inside the glass doors, watching for the car to come back.

He feels like he did sometimes before a game. Not nervous, but different. More alert, sharper. His vision is different—he sees everything in front of him, each car moving and person walking and branch blowing in the breeze.

They pull up in front of the building and sit there. The teacher is waving her hands around, but she is facing Nicole and blocking her face. Then he sees Nicole's head moving and suddenly she pops up outside.

She looks right at him looking right at her. Her face is blank.

He opens the door and walks out toward the car. The tester opens her door but stays seated there filling out papers.

Then Nicole smiles.

"I passed!" she shouts. She raises her hand in the air.

He keeps walking toward her.

"Come here and give me a big hug, Nicole!"

She wraps her arms around him, and he covers her up with his body like he did her little hand in church.

And as he holds her he thinks, *This is what it is like. This is what it is like. Keep forgiving me. Please keep doing it.*

As THEY DRIVE HOME, he keeps looking at her. He wants to look at her for hours just like he looks at photos of Lucia winning her beauty pageant for hours on the Internet. He remembers parents at the Little League games and high school games changing their expressions when they watched their own kids. They grew entranced; they glowed. He remembers wishing Cille did that.

She keeps switching the radio station from pop station to pop station. Willie switches it back to the news, then turns it off.

"Why do you keep looking at me?" she asks.

"Because that is what a father does when he is proud of his daughter," he says.

She laughs.

"You know, I never knew my father at all," he says to her.

She looks out the window.

"At least you have the opportunity to know me," he says. "You don't really care about me, I know that, Nicole. But I am going to do what I can to support you and after that, it is up to you. This will be our last week together, so we can at least try to get along for one week. I have enjoyed my time with you, even though I know you haven't. But one day you will regret this. I know it."

She looks straight ahead as they come up to the condo.

"Just take care of my mom when I am gone," she says. "Okay?"

THIS IS MY REAL World Series moment, he thinks as he sits at the long table in front of the House of Representatives Subcommittee on Crime, Terrorism, and Homeland Security. Alongside him are lawyers and scientists testifying for the reform of the crack sentencing regimen. He is the case study, but he is also the star of the show.

Congressman Robert Scott, a Democrat from Virginia, began by saying what Willie learned in the prison library in Atlanta many years ago:

> Turning to today's hearing, it appears that many Members of Congress, as well as the general public, agree that the current disparity in crack and powder cocaine penalties makes no sense, is unfair and not justified, and it should be fixed. However, there is not yet a consensus on how to do it.
>
> After extensive study on the issue over the last 20 years, there appears to be no convincing scientific, medical, or public policy rationale to justify the current or any other disparity in penalties for the two forms of cocaine.
>
> Scientific and medical research has found that crack and powder cocaine have essentially the same pharmacological and physiological effects on a person.
>
> The indicated method of how powder cocaine becomes crack cocaine is to cook the powder with the water and baking soda until it hardens into a rocklike formation. This diluted and cheaper form of powder cocaine is then generally ingested by users through smoking a pipe.
>
> No other illegal drug has a severe penalty differential based on the different formations of the drug, and certainly not for a lesser amount of the illegal substance, nor is the method of the ingestion of cocaine or any other drug a justification for a different penalty, whether it is smoked, snorted, injected, or otherwise consumed.
>
> Moreover, neither violence nor any other associated history of use between the two forms of the drug seem to justify penalties.
>
> The Sentencing Commission reports that 97 percent of crack offenders do not use weapons, compared to 99 percent of powder transactions do not use weapons.
>
> Such a small difference in the use of weapons in crack and powder could be adjusted by sentences based on the particular case, not whether crack or powder was used in the crime.
>
> The original basis for the penalty differential was certainly not based on science, evidence, or history, but on media hysteria and political bidding based on who could be the toughest on the crack epidemic then believed to be sweeping America.

While there are no real differences between crack and powder cocaine, the distinction between the penalties of the two drugs have very severe consequences.

More than 80 percent of the people convicted in federal court for crack offenses are African Americans. They are serving extremely long sentences, while people who have committed more serious drug offenses or more violent crimes serve significantly shorter sentences.

Many people in African American communities have lost confidence in our criminal justice system because of unfair policies such as the federal crack cocaine laws.

Soon after, it is Willie's turn. He puts on his spectacles to read, and the place listens transfixed, as if Vin Scully were reading a bedtime story. Representative Charlie Rangel stops coughing and clamoring for attention. Al Sharpton is standing on the side of the room, and he probably realizes he can't get the attention he craves, either. A bespectacled gentleman, and a baseball star at that, is testifying.

Willie reads what he has written without a single stutter:

The story I am going to tell you today began when I was drafted by the California Angels after my first year in college. I played three years in the minor league system before I was promoted to the major leagues. I had my first taste of the big show in 1977. I also had my first taste of powder cocaine that same year.

This is my first encounter with drugs. I was traded to the Kansas City Royals in 1979 and played in the World Series in 1980, where I hit two home runs in Game 1 and Game 4 of the series, a record that still stands.

But I was also using drugs on a regular basis, as were many other major league baseball players at that time. In 1983 I was convicted on misdemeanor drug charges along with three other Royals players, and we were sentenced to three months in prison. We were the first active major leaguers to see jail time for drugs.

After that I was traded to the Toronto Blue Jays, and my baseball career went downhill. I ended up playing in Mexico for the next six years, where I started back using drugs regularly. I retired from baseball in 1990 and returned to Kansas City, where I became a recluse in my own home, going out mainly to buy cocaine.

I had started smoking cocaine in Mexico, so I knew all the ins and outs of preparing the drug. I went through two bank accounts of over $300,000 and didn't think twice about what I was doing. I was living a destructive lifestyle and was enjoying every bit of it.

Finally, in 1994 all of this came to a stop. One day out of nowhere a woman arrived at my house in a car, looking for someone to get her drugs. It turned out that she was an undercover officer for the Kansas City Police Department, which had started the investigation on me because of anonymous telephone calls.

Over the next several weeks, she accompanied me to my supplier's house to purchase powder cocaine, and each time she asked me to cook it into rock cocaine or crack, which I did. Four purchases of crack cocaine put me in the mandatory minimum 10-year guideline. The Kansas City police turned my case over to the federal authorities for prosecution to make sure I got the longest sentence possible.

I took my case to trial and lost. I received a sentence of 20 years and 8 months, the highest sentence that the jurors could give me under the sentencing guidelines. A similar amount of powder cocaine would have resulted in a sentence on drug charges of, at most, 27 months.

During my 14 years in prison, I rededicated my life to Jesus Christ. I came to realize that being taken off the streets at that time saved my life. It didn't take 14 years to change me, but it did take being incarcerated to leave that lifestyle behind.

While I was in prison, I completed three different drug rehabilitation programs, which helped me realize that I have an addiction problem. I came in contact with so many other people that had the same problem I had.

I also came in contact with a lot of people that had life sentences because they were convicted of selling crack cocaine. Many of them were first-time offenders with no criminal record and had no violence in their case. My case is very sad, but theirs were sadder. These people were never going home.

After I spent 14 years of my life in prison, Congress finally allowed the Sentencing Commission to reduce the crack cocaine guidelines. I benefited from this change in law, and the courts gave me almost five years off my sentence. I got out of prison last June. My original release date was 2012.

Since my release from prison, I have developed a relationship with my daughters, who were small children when I went to prison. I have found a job working construction in Kansas City, and I am in the process of getting back into professional baseball.

I have been clean and sober for 15 years, and I have a strong spiritual foundation. I am writing a book. I am doing speaking engagements in and around the Kansas City area about the dangers of drugs and alcohol. God has truly blessed my life.

In closing, I would like to add that I didn't come to Washington, D.C., to testify for myself. I came for all the people I left behind in prison. I made a promise to those people that if God allowed me to leave prison before them, then I would do everything in my power to help them. That is the main reason why I am sitting in this chair today.

We have so many sad cases of drug addicts being locked up, and the key is then thrown away. We have so many families that are suffering right now because a son, a father, a mother, a brother, or a sister will never come home from prison.

Look at me and look at the progress that I have made in my life, because I was given another chance to live my life as a free man. I believe many more people would do the same thing, if they are given a chance.

I am praying that this will be the last time this Subcommittee will meet regarding these unfair laws. These mandatory minimum laws and the crack versus powder cocaine disparity need to be eliminated. Cocaine is cocaine, regardless of the form it comes in.

Thank you for hearing me.

A few congressmen ask questions, and Willie feels himself answering, feels his stutter-free speech, relishes it.

Patti Baum, one of his most loyal letter writers during the prison years, is there in the audience beaming, and afterwards, Willie ignores a few autograph seekers and the handshakes of several new fans and walks right up to her.

"You were the star," Patti says.

Willie smiles sheepishly.

"Was, wasn't I?" he says back.

London, he thinks. *England. London, England. My daughter. London, England. My half-breed but more-black-than-Mexican daughter in London, England.*

The flight leaves at 2:00 PM for New York. He wakes up at 5:30 and lies there looking at Sara curled up in a ball. *Fourteen years in prison and two and a half months as her real father,* he thinks as he looks at the alarm clock glowing green next to his head.

He sees himself in his cell; he sees himself this summer anguishing over Nicole's gestures, looks, funny noises. He connects the two images with a line.

Suffer I must, suffer I can. That worked in prison. Inside these walls the suffering stings, man. Way more. There you just numb yourself. Here, with her, you can't get numb. You can numb your heart, but then she will sting you in your soul.

He staggers his first two steps out of bed.

He knows the sound of the shower will wake them up, and he wants them both to wake up early to prolong the day. He turns the faucet, and the pipes sound like airplane engines. When he comes out of the shower, he stands still and listens for movement. He hears them talking in Nicole's room. Mission accomplished.

And then he feels like he is going to cry. He hasn't cried since he was a child, but he can't even remember why that might have been. He just supposes he cried once or twice when he fell on gravel or when he got beat up. Then he remembers crying that time they kept intentionally walking him in a ballgame. This memory distracts him from crying; he cringes for a second at the sight of himself bawling at a ballgame; he finishes toweling dry and no longer feels the onset of the crying.

Sara comes back into their room.

"*Como estas?*" she asks.

"*Bien,*" he grunts.

"*Pues yo no estoy bien,*" she says.

"Me neither," he says as he ties his sneakers. "I feel like an old man. I feel like I got whacked by a two-by-four right on the inside of my gut."

Sara smiles and puts her hand on his neck. She slowly rubs it back and forth. He has never enjoyed being touched by her so much as right here, right now, as daylight slowly turns the blinds from gray to white. He closes his eyes and lets her keep rubbing.

"These suitcases weigh more than a bag of bats," he says as he smiles at her. They are at the curbside check-in.

"You're a big ballplayer, papa, you can lift it," Nicole says. She smiles back.

He nearly drops the bag back into the trunk. *She just said it,* he realizes. *She just used the word.* He wants to stop and point it out. Sara is still in the car so she did not hear. He wants to go tell her.

But he does not even look at Nicole. He decides to treat this whole thing as a non-event. He decides to lift up the bag and act as if this were something usual. *Don't show her what it meant to me,* he thinks.

And then he wonders if she really said it. *Did I imagine it? Did I finally hear what I wanted to hear, or did I put the word in her mouth?*

He looks at her as he carries the bag past her to a cart. Her face is expressionless. *She may not have said anything at all,* he thinks.

"Did you say something?" he asks.

She looks at him puzzled.

"What?" she asks.

He shakes his head, and they follow him as he pushes the cart with one hand and carries her carry-on bag with the other.

She sticks her ticket in her purse, and as they walk he thinks it is sticking out too far.

"Nicole, that ticket cost a lot of money," he says. "Can you zip it up?"

She rolls her eyes but complies.

"*Tenemos dos horas todavia,*" he says. "Let's sit here and have a drink."

They sit at a table in a coffee shop and don't even order. He watches a woman run over the foot of another woman with her suitcase.

"Nicole, the most important thing is to be careful," Willie says.

A film of tears coats Sara's eyeballs, but the tears never form. And he thinks of her again as he has been doing since she told him she was pregnant. He never thought of her this way, but it is happening all the time now. *Where would she have ended up if she hadn't met me? If her mother hadn't thought I had money? If they had never visited me?*

And then, *Why? It has to be more than the money now because she knows I have none. Why?*

Sitting here, not talking to each other. Nicole and Sara sick to their stomachs 'cause they are leaving each other. Me sick to my stomach because I screwed up so much. I guess this is what it is. What everyone else does and feels.

Sara looks at her tiny silver watch first, then Nicole looks at her bigger one, then Willie takes out his phone and looks at the time.

"*Bueno, tienes que ir,*" he says.

They are both crying now, and he feels it, too. *This shit is contagious,* he thinks. *Never cried once when they left after visiting me in prison. I'm getting soft out here.*

They get up, and he nearly tips the chair over as he pushes it back. He can feel the outline of his stomach inside his belly. He puts his arm around Sara as they walk toward the gate. She looks up at him with surprise, tenses up, then he feels her shoulders relax.

They get to the security line. Sara and Nicole hug each other and talk about Skype for the 200th time in two days.

Then they let go. Nicole doesn't turn to him. She stays sideways. But she turns her head. And he walks up to her and hugs her. Her arms tighten around him. He feels her hands meet in bottom of his back and grip each other. He smells the shampoo she uses in her hair. It smells like her pillow and like the cushion on the sofa in the spot she always sits to watch television. He kisses the top of her head. He sees her walking into the visitation room at Atlanta the first time they came.

"I'll take good care of Mickey for you," he says. He doesn't know where that one came from. *What the hell am I saying*, he says to himself. But she laughs. And he forgives himself his stupid line immediately.

"*Te quiero hija*," he says. "*Mi hija*."

She smiles, and he feels her hands let go of each other.

He lets go, too, but as she walks away he can still feel her imprint in his body. He and Sara stand there together as she passes through security, and the whole 10 minutes he feels her exact outline in every inch of where her body pushed into his.

He stops the car on the shoulder and sits there for a second before turning off the engine.

"*Que estas haciendo?*" Sara asks.

"I want to watch the plane," he says. "What company was it?"

"Delta," she says.

He gets out of the car and walks into the field next to the road. He sits down, and Sara opens the door and smiles at him.

"Willie, I told you to be patient with her heart, and you are now," she says as she sits down beside him.

"I have a blanket in the trunk," he says.

He gets up and opens the trunk and grabs a red and blue blanket. He puts half of it under Sara as she lifts her bottom up off the ground with her arms and legs extended. He flops the other half down and sits beside her again.

The planes are all over the place, and he can only make out the ones that turn and fly in front of them. Others just keep going straight out the way they are taking off.

"Which direction is east?" he asks

"*No se, Willie,*" Sara says. "*Creo que esta en esa dirección.*"

She points in the direction that the planes are banking. He looks far into that direction and shakes his head.

"No," he says. "It is that way. The planes that just keep going."

He looks at his watch.

"*Es la hora,*" he says.

A big white plane lifts into their line of vision and then keeps heading straight up. There are no clouds. He squints as it disappears into the sky. He sees it again glimmering for a second after he stops seeing it. Then he cannot see it anymore.

"I tried to count how many airplanes I took in my career," he says.

He looks at her. She is crying and smiling slightly, too.

"I figured about 2,000 flights," he says. "Never had one bad one. A few bumps but never anything real bad."

He looks at the tears curling into her lips as she smiles.

"And here I am praying she don't crash," he says.

Sara laughs out loud.

"Don't make no sense, do it?" he says.

He chuckles. Then he smiles at her and does not look up at the sky again.

As THEY DRIVE to the courthouse, she is silent. He asks her why.

"*Tenemos que casarnos en una iglesia,*" she says. We have to get married in a church.

He ignores her. He doesn't know why. But he does. He wants to get married quickly so he can make love to her in peace, and this is the quickest way and they will do the church thing later.

As he is parking he struggles. His hip hurts and he shouldn't be driving, and he is parallel parking on the street to save the money even though it is only $1 an hour in the lot.

He quits. The Camry is 2 feet from the curb, but he doesn't care and it hurts too much.

As he turns off the car he turns to her, and she looks afraid.

"Why didn't you come?" he asks. "Why did you stop in Jacksonville? You didn't even come there, did you? You just took the money or your mother did, and you never even got on the plane."

She can't understand three quarters of the words he is saying, but she knows what he is talking about, and she cries three words into it. And she cries as they walk into the courthouse, he limping with his hip and she limping with her lupus which is acting up these weeks far more than she tells him. They limp along together toward the Justice of the Peace's office, and they don't look at each other.

But when he says, "You may kiss the bride," he does, and he knows and she knows, too. They know that for the first time together that each of them is doing the right thing, be it out of need or want or both.

THE ROOFTOP TERRACE LOOKS out over all the monuments and looks down right at the White House. The Capitol gleams in the fall sun.

A big man who calls himself Piggy is telling everyone his incarceration story—how the feds considered him public enemy No. 1 in the crack wars and would move him clear across the country to a different prison each time there was an incident at the prison that housed him.

He speaks with the glee of a certain celebrity accorded him at this gathering, and he compares his time with Willie's time as if they were counting home runs or RBIs.

They are here to celebrate the reduction in crack cocaine/cocaine sentencing from a ratio of 100:1 to 18:1. They toast on the rooftop—some with cider and others champagne—and a few of the instrumental players deflect credit for the reform onto each other, and each then says the fight has just begun because 1:1 is the goal.

They raise a toast, and everyone moves downstairs for the speeches. Margaret Love, a D.C. attorney who worked doggedly on Willie's pardon efforts, whisks in. Looking befuddled and piercing, waifish and ruthless all at once, she darts toward Willie and hugs him.

In the elevator she lets everyone know she was late because she was busy trying to get someone else out of prison.

There are shrimp and perfect plates of vegetables, cheese, and cold cuts on a table next to a full bar in the meeting room downstairs.

Then the speeches. Willie goes first because he has to get the last flight back to Kansas City to take Sara to the immigration office first thing in the morning. Margaret Love introduces him.

"Willie was my favorite client of all time," she says. "And not only because he was a legend, a baseball legend."

At that word Willie raises his eyes. His eyes are squinting and they betray what he is really thinking as he listens.

Legend, he repeats to himself. *I ain't no baseball legend. Maybe a cocaine legend. A cocaine legend is the only kind of legend I am.*

As he stands he nods to Margaret Love and then says exactly what he knows many people don't want to hear.

"I deserved time," he says. "I needed it. I got too much time, we all know that. But without the prison getting me off the streets, I wouldn't be here today."

Buzz kill. He didn't intend it. In fact, he feels at home here with this group committed to reducing the sentencing inequality that he sees as counterproductive to the reform of lost souls like him who need drugs in the first place.

But hell, you can't be selling drugs and not expect to serve time, he thinks. He doesn't say this. He calibrates his words after the controversial opener. He thanks the right people and says he will do whatever he can to help those families in attendance whose children are still behind bars.

But his austerity, his forceful sobriety, changes the tone of the gathering.

He finishes by thanking Jehovah, and a woman hands him a plaque that she reads out loud for the audience to hear.

From out of nowhere Margaret Love bolts into the gap between Willie and the woman holding the plaque. A few cameras flash. Willie keeps looking at the plaque the whole time. He smiles slightly.

Cocaine legend, he says to himself again as the people clap with the zeal reserved only for a celebrity.

NERVE. THAT'S WHAT GRACIE says he has, looking at a waitress like that in front of Sara. They are in a Mexican restaurant in the fall of 2010, and a Mexican waitress who looks like a waitress he used to date in Mexico gives him that signal only an available waitress can give.

And Gracie notices. She has been waiting patiently for Willie to call, and she cried tears of joy at the news of Sara's pregnancy.

But she turns all schoolteacher on him in a split second.

"You have a lot of nerve, Willie," she says.

She says it in English, and Sara doesn't even catch whiff of it because Gracie says it in the middle of a conversation about the best Mexican restaurant in Kansas City, but Willie hears her loud and clear and turns his head away because he is blushing and doesn't want Sara to see even see that.

This is the first time he has seen Gracie since he first saw her in Leavenworth. He realizes she cared for him like his doctor cares for him, from a distance and coolly. She still cares for him professionally.

"You've got a lot of nerve to look at her like that, Willie, after how she has stood by you," Gracie says. She huffs and anger comes over her face. "You've got a lot of nerve."

In fact it is a slip up, a silly departure from a growing sense of devotion and respect that he feels for Sara. He sat there remembering the time he was talking with her on Skype one night from Arizona. The Royals sent him down to their instructional camp to give hitting advice to some of their minor leaguers. The Royals have the best group of hitting talent in the minor leagues, and they turned the tables on him. He always hoped for a job talking about the disaster of his life, making a living, however modest, from his errors and corrections. But they saw something in him—George Brett saw it first, and then general manager Dayton Moore and his front office eventually agreed. People could connect with Willie. Young people took to him. And he knew baseball, he knew hitting even though his approach was funky and his years away from the game meant he had not kept up with the latest technical advances.

He described his day teaching, there were long pauses as there usually were when they spoke, and she seemed distracted by Mickey chewing on the leg of the computer table.

They said, "*Te quiero,*" as they began to hang up, but she didn't hang up properly. She was no computer whiz, and he hung on for a moment to watch her. And then he saw it. Her shrine was right next to the computer, and she made the sign of the cross, closed her eyes tightly, held her hands together in front of her chest, and prayed. She prayed that he would get the job from the Royals, she prayed that Mickey would learn to settle down, she prayed that Nicole would forgive Willie and love him like he loved her, she prayed that God would bless them in holy matrimony and bless them with a child so they could get a second chance and do it right this time.

He was amazed. It wasn't just that she needed him. She more than needed him. She loved him. She finished and stood up and, since her lupus acted up when she felt stress, she limped out of the room.

He clicked off his Skype and closed his computer without turning it off and sat there. And then he prayed, too. Not for his stuff, but for her—her lupus, her English, the dog she had to put down back in Mexico when she decided to stay with him, even for her mother Silvia. It was 9:00. The next day he had to tell his story to the young minor leaguers before their workout. He lay in bed rehearsing his speech, but he adjusted the ending. He added Sara to it, added their story and how it takes nerve to resist all the stuff fame and baseball throw at you; it takes nerve to commit; it takes nerve to keep your focus on what really matters in life.

He wants to tell Gracie this story to show her his love is real. But he decides not to. She has made her point. She wants actions, not words. That's Gracie. Words were all they had when all they could do was write letters. But now the proof is in the pudding. Gracie is that kind of lady.

THE DAY HIS BABY daughter, not son, is born, he is not stuttering because he cannot speak. He sits in the delivery room holding Sara's hand, and when the time comes he watches this baby come into the world like God himself is coming out of his wife to bless him one more resounding time.

They had decided to call her Sarah with an *h*. And as the doctor hands her to him to hold, he feels for the first time that he can forgive himself.

But he catches himself quickly. *All this thought about me*, he thinks. *I got a wife and baby girl here to think about. Enough about me.*

He gives Sarah back to Sara and watches them look at each other.

A FEW MONTHS LATER Dayton Moore calls Willie to tell him the Royals are going to hire him as a minor league hitting instructor. He is sitting in the den—the once-named Captain's Room where he estimates he snorted and smoked enough cocaine over those self-indulgent years to fill the whole room floor to ceiling. He gets up and walks up the same steps he used to jog to work off some of the coke so he could do more coke. Sara is sitting by the fireplace, and Mickey is at her feet.

"*Me ofrecieron el puesto*," he says. They offered me the job.

She has a boil on her right eye. The baby is resting its head on her hip like a cat does. She has to turn her head to see him with her left eye because her right eye won't open.

"*Lo vas a hacer bien*," she says. He expects her to cry or at least shed a tear or two.

But that is all she says—you are going to do it well.

Then she holds her hand to her head and closes her left eye.

"*Es peor tu dolor de cabeza?*" Willie asks. Is your headache worse?

She shakes her head up and down. She refused to go to a doctor yesterday; he leaves for the Royals Fantasy Camp tomorrow. He'll be humoring middle-aged men like himself, thick around the middle, men who once played baseball as kids but only dreamed of playing in the major leagues. *This will be our life*, he thinks, since he will have to travel so much as a roving coach. *Worry, so much worry, her with the baby and me alone, her with her mother and her mother badmouthing me for being away so much.* But he can't pass up the Fantasy Camp. Nevertheless he offers to stay home one more time.

"*Vete Willie, lo hemos hablado,*" she said. Go, Willie, we have already talked about this. Then she says, "You owe this to your teammates to go be with them. You owe it to all them like George and Hal who stood by you."

And he keeps seeing Pat Gillick's kind face. He found out recently that Gillick has become his godfather, recommending him to the Royals, calling old contacts in baseball to talk Willie up, testifying as to Willie's character. *Pat always knew I had it in me*, he thinks. *Character, but how the heck did Pat know I had it in me?*

AT THE BAR that night in Surprise, Arizona, George is drinking and Willie is listening along with the rest of the ex-players and Royals Fantasy Camp attendees. And the more George drinks, the more everyone listens. George was always a gabber, and Willie realizes tonight that he gabs most, always gabbed most, when Willie is around. I may not always have brought out the best for him on the field, Willie thinks, but I sure bring out the best in him when it comes time to joke around.

Then George starts in on his favorite story, the one Willie hears just about every other time they get together. They're together in the outfield during spring training in 1981, the season after George nearly hit .400 and during which Willie, not George, made the record books at the end. Willie jogging past George in that delicious sunlight, asking the Royals' star how many women he has slept with. George blushing. Willie stopping in mid-stride, turning for all to see, stuttering out the claim that he had slept with 401. And George and the whole Royals team doubling over, some guys falling on the grass they are laughing so hard.

The rapt bar, now stocked with locals and staff, roars. This time, Willie blushes. George hits him on the back and throws his head back laughing. He imitates Willie's stutter, and everyone laughs even more.

Then George stops stuttering and stops laughing altogether. He even stops smiling. Then for all the world to hear, he says it was an honor to have Willie as a teammate. Says he loved playing with Willie and considers him a brother.

George is getting all emotional, just like during his Hall of Fame speech, Willie thinks. But this time it's all over me.

"I consider it an honor to call Willie Mays Aikens my friend," George says, putting his arm around Willie's shoulder.

And for the first time Willie realizes that maybe he didn't let George down. Maybe, by coming back, by cleaning things up now, he actually did the job George always wanted him to do.

THEY RIDE TOGETHER on the bus each day, and even though they all look older they still act as young as they used to when they traveled on buses and airplanes 30 years ago. George still teases him; Hal still wisecracks and grumbles; some guys still fart on purpose—he won't name who.

This is the third day, and Willie is already the big hit with the campers— stockbrokers and lawyers and doctors and businessmen who pay to spend a week in a simulated baseball camp with their Royals heroes.

He is out on the field teaching a chubby investment adviser how to stay back on his back leg even though the guy will never get it. But Dina Wathan, John's daughter and a Royals employee, walks up and stands beside them, and Willie can feel the worry even though he hasn't even looked straight at her.

He stops and she motions to him to come closer.

He thinks. *The baby.*

She puts her hand on his shoulder.

"Willie, Sara fell and she is in the hospital," she says. "It sounds like she is hurt badly. We are arranging a flight for you right now back to Kansas City."

FRIENDS PICK HIM UP at the airport that night and all he can notice is the cold and the wind and all he can think about is that other flight when he arrived so late from Atlanta that he almost missed his deadline at the halfway house.

No one speaks, and they drop him off at the hospital entrance. He walks to the ICU, and as he walks in the door he can see her at the end of the row of rooms enclosed in glass. Tubes are sticking in her mouth and nose, and her eyes are shut so tightly that it looks like it would take a crowbar to pry them open. As he walks up to her, he can see that her right side is twisted and limp.

A nurse is wiping her forehead and tells him as soon as she realizes who he is that she likely had a brain aneurysm.

He stands at the foot of her bed for an hour. His hip hurts, but he cannot budge. The machine is pushing air in and out of her lungs, and he notices his breathing replicates hers after a while.

He stands there for another hour and doesn't make eye contact with anyone as they come and go.

He is watching himself in the mirror out of the corner of one eye. As he watches her breathing, he is taking estimation of himself. And he states to himself firmly, *Every catastrophe has brought me more grace, and tonight the grace is coming down in buckets.*

EARLY THE NEXT MORNING he goes home and stands above the baby and tells her what happened to her mother. Sara's mother has arrived from Mexico, but she is asleep. Willie tells the baby that everything will be okay. Then he blows up the air mattress and sleeps on the floor beside the baby's bed.

The next day he calls Nicole's school and asks them to have someone there with her when he tells her the news. He buys a plane ticket for her that night. She does not speak on the phone, and in the car on the way to the hospital all he can wonder is how this girl, this girl I created, must look at me and hate me for the life I have led her into.

As they enter the hospital room, she wobbles. He catches her.

"*Esta muy enferma, pero siempre hay esperanza,*" he says to Nicole. She is very sick, but there is always hope.

The Royals' GM Dayton Moore is again arranging for her to be transported to the top neurological center in Missouri. Even the Royals doctors are involved. They are going to do a clinical trial procedure on her—insert a catheter into the blood clot on her brain and drain the blood. It should work, he tells Nicole. I have already had friends tell me stories about people who recover from this. They can even walk again.

He keeps sneaking looks at Nicole as they sit there, and he realizes he can't even imagine how she sees her life. *You dare mention Job in the same breath as yourself? Think about this creature you helped create. This poor girl. You ain't been through the half of it compared to her.*

That night he calls George. And George can't even talk. He makes George cry like he used to make Gentleman Pat Gillick cry whenever he messed up and broke Pat's heart.

Then, minutes after hanging up with George, Gentleman Pat himself calls. *Don't even think about crying, Pat,* Willie thinks. *I ain't gonna even let you this time. This time it wasn't me, it was life, and we ain't gonna cry over that.*

TODAY IS SARA'S BIRTHDAY. He goes to the flower shop while Nicole is taking a shower and spends 10 minutes trying to choose the right bouquet. His phone rings and he takes it out of his pocket to read a text from George: "Hang in there, Mick." The texts from the guys are piling up; he can't bear to answer them they mean so much to him. He knows that is odd, but they mean so much to him that they hurt.

The girl working at the store keeps asking him if the one he is looking at is the right one. He thinks she thinks he is going to try to rob her.

He picks a huge one, the most expensive one, and she stands up straight behind the counter and wraps her arms behind her back.

"These are for my wife," he says as he puts them on the counter. "It is her birthday."

The girl smiles and takes his credit card.

"Do they remind you of her?" she asks.

He smiles.

"No," he says.

Her head snaps up at his answer.

"No," he says again. "She is tiny and very sick. They are big and healthy. But she is strong, too, and they look strong. Like they will last for a while in the hospital room."

She smiles as he signs.

"They are very fresh," she says. "I just prepared them early this morning."

NICOLE WALKS IN ahead of him, and he peeks over her shoulder to see if Sara is—please, God—awake. But she isn't. They drained most of the blood on her brain yesterday, though some still trickles out of the tube stuck in her head.

Nicole is rubbing her arm as he walks up on the other side of the bed and holds the flowers in front of her. *They smell so strong that they could be turned into moonshine,* he thinks.

Their smell fills the space, and for a second he thinks he sees Sara's nose twitch. He looks at Nicole and tears are dropping off her cheeks onto her mother's arms.

He starts to cry, too. His tears water the flowers. And then Sara opens her eyes. She blinks and blinks and then finally manages to keep them open. She stares at him. He keeps crying, but the cause of the tears adjusts itself in a split second from grief to disbelief to joy. She lifts up her arm to wipe them from his face.

And he feels like the hand of God has touched his face. Sara closes her eyes again; Nicole's face is stuck between a smile and a gasp. He can't help but keep seeing himself in the mirror out of the corner of his eye every time he is in the room. And this time he stands and takes accounting of himself there in the mirror. And a word comes across his brain, dangles there, and then his brain and the word agree that it needs to be pronounced.

"Amen," he says softly to himself there in the mirror. The word surprises him. Nicole looks up. Then he sees her body relax. They look straight at each other. She stands taller and nods slightly, as if to say she is willing and ready to serve as the stand-in mother of this baby he created with her mother to try to make up for all they had lost out on because of him.

He blinks and looks away first. He tightens his jaw, looks himself dead in the eyes in the mirror, and says it one more time, "Amen."

Epilogue

October 2011

He likes this kid from Texas, Patrick Leonard, for one reason—the velocity of his bat. It is detectable to Willie. The time it takes for the kid's bat to move from its cocked position above his shoulder through the zone to meet the incoming, spinning target is that barely detectable thing that Willie loves.

Well, there's one more reason. Patrick Leonard also is struggling like Willie did at his age. The curveball, Willie told him, is like the flu—no one found a cure for it yet.

So this October morning in the endless Arizona sun, they start with flips, then do some work on the tee, and now Willie is standing behind the side mound repeatedly dropping balls into the fastball machine, studying Patrick to see when his brain gets accustomed to fastballs so he can slip a ball into the curveball machine and shock him out of his complacency. A few days before, Willie learned he had been given a new contract and expanded duties as a hitting instructor within the Royals' organization.

Dayton Moore, the general manager of the Royals, is wandering around this morning. He gives Willie a hug, asks about Sara's progress, for about the fourth time extends his condolences for Cille's passing, and uses his eyes the same way Gentleman Pat Gillick always did—first probing to assess Willie, then softening slightly as if having reassured himself of Willie's steadfastness, and then abruptly locking in more firmly as if to demand more of the same behavior in the future.

That morning Willie called Sara as soon as he woke up, as he always does when he travels as one of the Royals' roving minor league hitting instructors. He noticed she didn't slur her words as much as the day before, and she even managed to lift her right arm a little bit as she spoke in front of the computer screen. She is a third of the way back, and even though the doctors are now telling him that is as far back as she will come, he leaves that third-of-the-way synopsis as the answer to

Moore and anyone else who asks. He might add occasionally, "I know a little bit about long ways back, man."

He doesn't get into the details with Moore—he has learned to contain the chat to the business at hand, even though Moore is one of those rare birds who cares about both the business of baseball and the harder business of life after the day's business is done. But he does indulge for one moment when Moore asks him about his daughters.

"Lucia is in acting school in Mexico City," Willie says, beaming. "And Nicole, she's back at school now. But boy you should have seen how she took care of her mother and her baby sister, Sarita. Just something beautiful, man. Took to changin' her diapers and everything!"

Then they talk about this Texas kid, Patrick Leonard, and how Willie has a plan to make sure Leonard doesn't make the same mistakes Willie did as a young player. They don't speak metaphorically, don't even acknowledge its potential in this conversation. They talk about bat speed and curveballs and adjustments just like guys on Willie's road crew used to talk about concrete mixes and plumb lines and levels.

From the side mounds, Willie can see Moore making the rounds of the coaches and players, and Willie tries to look extra sharp for him.

He picks up a handful of balls and moves to the machines.

"All these pitchers are throwing harder than ever," he says to Leonard. "And that's hard enough on a hitter today. But their velocity makes their curveball and changeup even more effective. So you're getting smacked upside both sides of the head."

This kid Leonard looks frustrated, and steps back from the plate. And Willie laughs.

"Okay, let's go," Willie says. "We're gonna master the damn curveball, cause that's what they're gonna throw a kid like you. They'll keep throwing it and throwing it until you get it or they break your spirit."

Leonard smiles slightly, steps back into the box, and looks out as Willie lifts up the first ball. Willie fakes to drop it into the fastball machine, then quickly drops it into the curveball bin and watches as it launches toward the plate and then plummets in midflight. Leonard slows his bat and lowers its plane as he brings it in front of his body. Willie turns as the ball arcs out to shallow left field where no one would have ever been able to catch the thing.

Acknowledgments

The author wishes to thank sweet Virginia and Dr. J; Ankie Barnes, Tom Dann, Debbie Fine, Michael MacDonald, Meghan Riordan, Kent Kildahl, Paul Hardart, and Jim and Karen Shepard; and Ken Bean, Mark Mirsky, Eric Schmitt, Mark Taylor, Clara Park, and Doc Fitz. And Ali.

To Tom Bast at Triumph Books, *mil gracias, amigo*; to Richard Rosen at ESPN, *mil y mil mas, amigote*. Also, thanks to Steve Wulf for his conviction, and Noah Amstadter for his keen eyes. And to Derrick Donovan and Eric Winkler from the *Kansas City Star*.

Special thanks to The National for the use of "Terrible Love," and for their music; also to Tony Hoagland and Stephen Dunn, for their music, too.

And to Willie Mays Aikens and Sara, for many things, not least your hospitality.

Index